THOMAS AQUINAS AND GABRIEL BIEL

THOMAS AQUINAS AND GABRIEL BIEL

Interpretations of St. Thomas Aquinas in German Nominalism on the Eve of the Reformation

John L. Farthing

Duke Monographs in Medieval and Renaissance Studies 9

Duke University Press Durham and London 1988

Printed in the United States of America
on acid-free paper ∞

Library of Congress Cataloging-in-Publication Data
Farthing, John L., 1947–
Thomas Aquinas and Gabriel Biel.
(Duke monographs in medieval and Renaissance studies; no. 9)
Bibliography: p.
Includes index.
1. Thomas, Aquinas, Saint, 1225?–1274—Influence.
2. Biel, Gabriel, d. 1495—Views on doctrines of
Saint Thomas Aquinas. 3. Nominalism—History.
4. Philosophy, Medieval—History. 5. Catholic Church—
Doctrines—History. I. Title. II. Series.
B765.T54F36 1988 230′.2′0922 87-27431
ISBN 0-8223-0806-1

FOR HILDA

sine qua non

CONTENTS

PREFACE

There are at least three reasons for paying close attention to the role of Gabriel Biel as an interpreter of the religious thought of St. Thomas Aquinas. First, because Biel's procedure is notoriously eclectic (rather than original or innovative), we cannot fully understand what Biel is trying to do theologically until we assess his use of the resources available to him in the medieval traditions with which he was in dialogue. There is considerable evidence for the view that St. Thomas is one of the more important of these medieval sources of Biel's thought. A study of Biel's use of Thomistic materials, therefore, should help to clarify the significance of Biel's own theological enterprise. Secondly, the importance of St. Thomas's theology in the history of religious ideas in the West includes not only what Thomas himself thought and said on various issues but also the ways in which his work was received, revised, and interpreted by those who took his work seriously. In view of Biel's influential role in certain theological circles on the eve of the Reformation, the image of St. Thomas in the *Expositio* and *Collectorium* sheds light on one important phase in the history of the interpretation of St. Thomas's thought. Thirdly, students of Luther's early development will be interested in assessing the place of Thomism in the intellectual milieu within which Luther's theological formation took place. Since the young Luther read Biel's *Expositio* and *Collectorium* carefully and with considerable enthusiasm, one might hope to find that an analysis of the Thomistic materials in these texts would shed some light on Luther's indirect exposure to St. Thomas's theology.

Although the present study is directly responsive to the first and second of these concerns, no claim is made with respect to the third. The following chapters describe the shape of St. Thomas's theology as refracted through the prism of Biel's interpretation; they show what can be seen by looking at St. Thomas through the eyes of one prominent late medieval nominalist theologian. The direct or indirect relevance of these conclusions for a more thorough understanding of Luther's development, however, cannot be determined apart from a careful analysis of evidence from the writings of Luther himself.[1] Here my intention is to outline an important part of the basis for an evaluation of Luther's relation to St. Thomas as an underground source of his own thought. To trace the boundaries of Luther's indebtedness to St. Thomas—and to assess the uses to which he put whatever knowledge of Thomism he may have had (from whatever sources)—are important issues for further research.

Special thanks are due to several teachers, colleagues, and friends, without whose encouragement, support, and criticism this book could not have been written. At several critical junctures, the assistance of Professor David C. Steinmetz and Professor Edward P. Mahoney of Duke University has proven invaluable. Professor Walter Moore of Florida State University provided a thoughtful and encouraging evaluation of the principal themes of this book at a critical point in the process of revising the manuscript for publication. Professor Denis R. Janz of Loyola University in New Orleans read the manuscript and offered an incisive and very helpful critique. To my friend, Tom Phillips, who helped in the preparation of the footnotes, and to my wife, Hilda Mann Farthing, who typed and proofread the manuscript in its earliest form, it would be impossible to overstate my love and gratitude.

ONE

THOMAS AQUINAS AND THE *VIA MODERNA*

Contemporary research has brought a great deal of energy and insight to bear on the attempt to make sense of Martin Luther's career in its late medieval setting. For a number of very good reasons, this enterprise has focused largely on the nominalist context of Luther's struggles and discoveries. In 1906 Heinrich Hermelink called attention to the need for a close study of the Occamist milieu in which Luther received his theological education at the University of Erfurt. Hermelink argued that a final evaluation of Luther's distinctive position in the religious history of the sixteenth century cannot be made apart from a detailed account of the impact of Occamism (as mediated by Gabriel Biel and Jodocus Trutvetter) upon his theological formation.[1] Over the course of the last four decades, Hermelink's program was still being pursued by such figures as Bengt Hägglund, Paul Vignaux, Irwin Iserloh, Steven E. Ozment, William J. Courtenay, and Heiko A. Oberman.[2] In the context of a revised view of nominalism, Luther's debt to Staupitz has recently been reexamined by David C. Steinmetz.[3] Along a number of lines, then, the nominalist setting of Luther's thought has been subjected to close and often illuminating scrutiny.

Meanwhile, especially among Roman Catholic interpreters of Luther, there have been numerous attempts to assess the relation between Luther's theology and non-Occamist traditions, especially the late medieval school of thought that found its inspiration in the theological vision of St. Thomas Aquinas. Almost simultaneous with Hermelink's call for an examination of Luther's sources in the *via moderna,* Heinrich Denifle's *Luther und Luthertum in der ersten Entwickelung* focused attention on the quality of the young Luther's appropriation of the larger medieval heritage, with special concern for his relation to the theology of St. Thomas. Denifle's critique of Luther's theological education posed the question in sharp, polemical terms. In view of Denifle's Dominican loyalties, it is not surprising to find that he is most severe in reproaching Luther for what he regards as an unforgivable ignorance of St. Thomas's teachings. In Denifle's view, it is primarily this lack of grounding in the sound, Catholic theology of St. Thomas that accounts for Luther's fall into schism and heresy: Luther was, theologically, semiliterate at best, "*ein Halbwisser,*" trained only in the decadent nominalism of Gabriel Biel, woefully ignorant of the richness and depth of Thomism.[4]

In 1939, Joseph Lortz's *Die Reformation in Deutschland* revised Denifle's interpretation at several points. In contrast to the polemical harshness that scarred Denifle's work, Lortz's approach is marked by a generous, ecumenical spirit: rather than ridiculing or demonizing Luther, Lortz freely acknowledges that Luther was a religious genius, a profound thinker, a substantial scholar whose gifts might have been fruitfully invested in the struggle for reform within the Church. Yet on the question of Luther's familiarity with St. Thomas's thought, Lortz in the end reaffirms Denifle's view that Luther was ignorant of scholasticism in its highest form.[5] In 1970, Otto Pesch expressed an overwhelming consensus among students of Luther's theology when he claimed that "Thomas Aquinas is not to be counted among the sources of Luther's thought, not even as an underground source."[6]

More recently, Denis R. Janz reopened the question of Luther's relation to the Thomist tradition by examining the interpretation of St. Thomas's perspective that Luther encountered in his confrontation with late medieval Thomism. Janz's approach is helpful in steering the conversation away from both the harshness of Denifle's polemic, on the one hand, and the ahistorical, speculative quality of Lortz's hypothesis, on the other. Janz notes that Denifle's critique of Luther's theological literacy fails to take account of the presence of Thomists on the faculty both at the University of Erfurt (where Luther received his early training in theology) and at the University of Wittenberg (where Luther began his own teaching career in 1508).[7] At the other extreme, Lortz, for all his ecumenism and generosity toward Luther, approaches the Luther-Aquinas question in an ahistorical way. Lortz's suggestion that Luther's ignorance of Thomism caused him to become a Protestant remains hopelessly speculative. Recent discussions of possible points of contact between Luther's perspective and that of St. Thomas have tended to be abstract and speculative rather than concrete and historical. Both Lortz and Pesch, for instance, studiously avoid asking the questions that are, from an historical point of view, decisive. Was Luther himself ever involved in a serious study of St. Thomas's theology? Did Luther know what he was rejecting when he dismissed Thomism as just another part of what he regarded as an anemic, decadent scholasticism? As Janz puts it, "Was Luther's confrontation with late medieval Thomism in fact a confrontation with Thomas himself?"[8] In order to shed light on these crucial questions, Janz examines the interpretations of St. Thomas's perspective by a number of representatives of late medieval Thomism, on the assumption that Luther's encounters with such Thomists provided his best opportunity to come to a knowledge of what Thomism is all about. Historically this strategy is far more promising than the approach of either Denifle, on the one hand, or Lortz and Pesch, on the other: the connections between Luther and the Thomists are considerably more accessible to the historian than are those between Luther and St. Thomas himself.

Janz's reference to the vitality of Thomist perspectives at Erfurt and Wittenberg is suggestive. Although the orientation of the theological faculty at the University of Erfurt was largely toward the "modern way" (*via moderna*) represented by Occam and his followers, it would be misleading to assume (as do both Denifle and Lortz) that the climate of thought at Erfurt was uniformly hostile to the Thomist point of view. In his *Zur Geschichte der Stadt und der Universität Erfurt am Ausgang des Mittelalters* (1919), Friedrich Benary demonstrated conclusively that the intellectual atmosphere at the University of Erfurt was anything but homogeneous. Benary was able to show that the distinction between the two *viae* was far from absolute; the theological faculty at the University of Erfurt included several scholars who devoted themselves to the work of devising a synthesis between the two major orientations (the "ancient way" of the Thomists and Scotists and the "modern way" of the Occamists).[9] And in 1927 Gerhard Ritter found considerable evidence that by the mid-fifteenth century Thomas's authority was "almost canonical" at the University of Erfurt.[10] Such findings raise the question of St. Thomas's standing within late medieval schools of thought other than Thomism itself. We must seriously consider the possibility that a source of indirect access to Thomist perspectives might be found not only in the Thomist school as such but also in the theological writings of certain Occamists, such as the texts that were in use at the University of Erfurt on the eve of the Reformation. Among these must be numbered two massive works by Gabriel Biel, the *Epithoma pariter et collectorium circa quattuor sententiarum libros* and the *Sacri canonis missae expositio.*

In view of the importance of Biel's role in transmitting the heritage of medieval scholasticism not only to Luther[11] but also to a number of influential figures in Luther's theological milieu,[12] it is interesting to note that most of Janz's references to Biel are designed to show the relation of Biel's own position to that of Luther. Only rarely—and briefly—does Janz discuss Biel's role as an interpreter of the medieval tradition in general and of St. Thomas's theology in particular. Apparently the only aspect of Biel's interpretation of St. Thomas that Janz finds relevant to his argument in *Luther and Late Medieval Thomism* is Biel's error in citing Thomas's authority in support of a semi-Pelagian doctrine of sin and grace. Anthropology and soteriology, to be sure, lie at the heart of the crisis from which Luther's reformation was born, but there is vastly more to Thomism than a view of humanity and a doctrine of grace. By the same token, these were not the only topics that Luther found it necessary to reexamine in the course of his career as a theologian/reformer. Certain questions of sacramental theology and social ethics, for instance, were also crucial in the development of Luther's perspective. In dealing with the question of Luther's relation to the Thomist tradition, therefore, it makes sense to begin with the problem of sin and grace, but it does not make sense for the inquiry to end there. A wide range of issues beyond those having to do with questions about human nature and justification must be examined in order to provide a comprehensive view of the place of St. Thomas's thought in Luther's intellectual milieu. What we need to assess is the importance of Thomism in the work of those with whom Luther was in dialogue during the years of his early theological development. What we need is a history of the interpretation of St. Thomas on the eve of the Reformation.

Here we can hope to provide no more than one significant chapter in such a history. Since Luther's earliest theological formation took place in an Occamist setting, it seems appropriate to focus on the interpretation and evaluation of St. Thomas's theology not only within Thomism per se but also in the *via moderna.* An obvious first step is to take a close look at the treatment of St. Thomas in the Occamist literature in use at the University of Erfurt during the first decade of the sixteenth century. Luther's encounter with the Thomists, after all, took place in a polemical, adversarial context, which is hardly the best setting in which one might come to appreciate the subtleties of a theological system as complex as Thomism.[13] By contrast, even though Luther finally repudiated the kind of scholastic theology he had studied at Erfurt, it is clear that his early studies in Biel's *Expositio* and *Collectorium* were serious and empathic. And St. Thomas, it turns out, is a major source for Biel's project. Like St. Thomas himself, Biel is a mediating figure who seeks, wherever possible, to synthesize positions that are apparently—but only apparently—irreconcilable. While Biel is himself an Occamist without apology, his Occamism never causes him to treat St. Thomas with contempt or to become closed to Thomistic perspectives. On the contrary, Biel makes it clear that he is eager to make common cause with St. Thomas wherever possible.

In 1972, when Wilhelm Ernst made an exhaustive inventory of the ancient and medieval authorities cited in the *Collectorium,* he found that only three—Augustine, Occam, and Scotus—are quoted more frequently than is Aquinas.[14] In view of Augustine's unique prestige in virtually all the schools of theology in the late medieval period, it is not at all surprising to find that Biel invokes Augustine's authority more often than that of any other extrabiblical source. That William of Occam should rank next to Augustine in frequency of citations is, again, what one would have anticipated, given Biel's protestations of loyalty to the *venerabilis inceptor.* What is more remarkable is the observation that two voices from the *via antiqua*—Scotus and Aquinas—rank third and fourth in frequency of citations in the *Collectorium.* While a merely statistical accounting proves nothing about the quality and function of the materials cited, this pattern of citations is compatible with the view that Biel is essentially a voice of moderation, a mediator, who seeks to synthesize what he regards as the best elements of the two *viae.* The presentation of St. Thomas's theology in Biel's *Expositio* and *Collectorium* is far more detailed and sympathetic than one might expect to find in the work of an Occamist partisan. If it makes sense to complement Janz's study of the interpretation of St. Thomas in late medieval Thomism with a similar study of the place of St. Thomas's theology in fifteenth-century nominalism, it seems appropriate to focus the inquiry on a figure such as Biel; for there was hardly an Occamist author more important to Luther's theological formation—or more serious about taking Thomas's thought into account—than was Gabriel Biel.

What is the image of St. Thomas in late medieval nominalism (as summarized in Biel's *Expositio* and *Collectorium*)? How often, and how completely, does Biel quote from the works of St. Thomas? On what topics? How reliable is Biel as an interpreter of Thomas's theology? How sympathetic is he to Thomas's basic concerns? How much could a bright, earnest student learn about Thomism just by a close reading of Biel's major theological writings? Answers to these and related questions will emerge from a close examination of the 421 *loci* in which Biel alludes to positions advocated by St. Thomas.

Although this inquiry was originally inspired by an interest in the Luther-Aquinas question, it should be emphasized from the outset that we will not attempt here to define Luther's relation to Aquinas or even to assess the scope of Luther's knowledge of Thomism and its influence on his development as a theologian. This is not a study of Luther's theology; it is strictly an analysis of Biel's interpretation of St. Thomas's theology. Any attempt to draw a close connection between Biel's image of Aquinas and the degree of Luther's familiarity with Thomism would be suggestive at best and hopelessly speculative at worst. When Joseph Lortz, for instance, argues that Luther fell into heresy and schism because he was untrained in Thomist theology, he clearly takes a major step beyond the realm of what can be affirmed on the basis of strictly scientific-historical research. When Lortz argues that Luther would not have become a Protestant if he had studied at the feet of a Cajetan or a Capreolus, he is indulging in a contrary-to-fact conclusion, which as such is intrinsically unverifiable. In point of historical fact, Luther did not study under a self-avowed Thomist; the historian should admit, in all candor, that one simply has no way of knowing, historically, what might have happened if Luther had received a different education from the one he did in fact receive at Erfurt. But what the historian can hope to establish is an outline of the materials from St. Thomas's theology that were accessible in the young Luther's milieu. We should be able to establish the boundaries of what Luther could have learned about Thomism from a body of literature that he read with great enthusiasm at a time when his own theology was in the process of formation. Given the state of the evidence available to us, however, we are simply not in a position to say what Luther did in fact learn about St. Thomas's theology in this indirect way; nor can we know with certainty how much attention Luther paid to secondhand summaries of the views of such figures as Aquinas. What we can hope to show is the quality of Biel's appropriation of Thomistic materials in his attempt to forge a synthesis of the *via antiqua* and *via moderna.* We will not ask, "What did Luther learn about Thomism in his encounter with Biel, and what impact did such an exposure to Thomist ideas have on his development?" We will ask, rather, "What is the shape of St. Thomas's theology when it is refracted through the prism of Biel's interpretation? What do you see when you look at St. Thomas through the eyes of a prominent spokesman for fifteenth-century Occamism?

While such an inquiry is only indirectly relevant to an analysis of Luther's development as a theologian, it should at least help us to gain a more balanced view of the nominalist setting in which Luther pursued his earliest theological studies.[15] Gabriel Biel was an influential proponent of Occamism in the generation preceding the rise of the Protestant Reformation; his writings were widely read during the early decades of the sixteenth century, and his influence was felt at the Council of Trent.[16] Thus the question of Biel's relation to Aquinas is a matter of considerable interest in its own right. In view of Biel's highly eclectic approach, his use of classical and traditional materials is an important part of his own project; an analysis of Biel's ways of exploiting the resources offered by the medieval tradition, therefore, is crucial to a thorough assessment of Biel's work as a theologian. This study of Biel's role as an interpreter of Aquinas is undertaken, then, not primarily for the sake of a more thorough understanding of Luther's transition from monk to reformer: it is a step, rather, toward a more exact view of the genius of late medieval nominalism.

It is also a chapter in the history of the interpretation of St. Thomas, a step toward the comprehensive assessment of St. Thomas's fate at the hands of his interpreters. The significance of Thomistic thought in German theological circles on the eve of the Reformation extends far beyond the school of self-avowed Thomists. A full appraisal of the importance of Thomism as one element in the intellectual matrix of sixteenth-century religion must also include an inventory of the ways in which Thomistic perspectives were treated in the curriculum of a non-Thomist university (such as the University of Erfurt) and in the theology of a moderate, synthesizing nominalist (such as Gabriel Biel).

TWO

GOD AND CREATURES

The waning influence of Thomism in late medieval theology is sharply focused in the nominalist doctrine of God. Drawing on both biblical and traditional resources, an increasing number of voices were raised in rejection of Thomas's vision of God as primarily intellect.[1] Within the boundaries set by the doctrine of divine simplicity, nominalist voluntarism had the effect of reformulating the relation between divine will and intellect in order to safeguard the freedom and omnipotence of God. Ultimately, of course, the irreducible simplicity of the divine being means that there is really no priority or posteriority in God. Will and intellect are distinct logically but not ontologically; indeed, "will" and "intellect" are but two of the ways in which it is proper to name God's essence when it is considered from different points of view. Thomists also affirm God's simplicity, but critics could find evidence suggesting that an excessive Thomist emphasis on the divine intellect betrays a tendency—in effect, if not in principle—to compromise the simplicity of the divine essence.

Nominalist discourse about God is marked by an emphasis on God's will rather than on his intellect. The doctrine of divine simplicity, of course, implies that will is not prior to intellect in God as he is in himself (*ad intra*): it is appropriate to speak of a priority of will to intellect in God only insofar as he is in relation to what is external to his own being (*ad extra*) as Creator, Lawgiver, Judge, and Redeemer. In this dimension his will is prior to his intellect, although strictly speaking such a statement reflects our own ways of knowing and talking about God in relation to creatures rather than the divine essence as it is per se. In itself, after all, the divine essence is eternally ineffable and incomprehensible. But what comes to expression in nominalist theology is a sense that the freedom—hence the graciousness—of God's saving work in history can be affirmed only in terms of a voluntarist conception of deity. God's liberality cannot be fully acknowledged without first emphasizing the radical contingency of everything external to God, including the orders of nature and morality. The nominalists, therefore, tend to stress that in his dealings with creatures God is subject to no norm external to his own will. Apart from the law of noncontradiction and the reality of God himself, what is true and just must be defined with reference to the content of the divine will. It is not God as intellect who affirms truth as it is in itself; it is, rather, God as will whose utterly unconditioned decisions and choices from an infinite spectrum of possibilities are in the most radical sense constitutive of whatever truth there may be. Justice is not an external norm to which God is somehow accountable. Justice receives its very definition from God's concrete acts of willing; it is not the norm but the product of the divine will. Otherwise God's freedom—hence his liberality and graciousness—would be only partial.[2] In contrast to the ontological cast of Thomist language about God (as "the pure act of being"), such nominalists as Gabriel Biel found in this kind of voluntarism a basis on which to make sense of a more biblical conceptuality in which event, deed, decision, and promise are the principal categories. Without exactly deontologizing the Christian doctrine of God, nominalist theology involves an attempt to recover the historical emphasis of a conception of deity whose roots are ultimately Hebraic.

The basic cosmological analogue to this shift in emphasis is an uncompromising insistence on the contingency of anything that is not divine. One important consequence of this emphasis is its implicit denial that there is any possibility of gaining information about God from the way things are. They could have been otherwise, after all. God's own character is not revealed in the created order, since the divine nature is equally transcendent of (and thus equally compatible with) any of the possibilities that were excluded when God freely chose to create *this* world. Natural theology, therefore, is not merely inadequate or partial; it is in principle absurd. We must begin to learn who God is by looking at what he has revealed about himself in history. The cosmos may not be regarded as an image—however partial or faint—of the divine essence. The nature of creatures, which are by definition finite and contingent, can tell us nothing positive about the nature of One who is both infinite and necessary.

On both counts a powerful argument can be offered to show that in some respects what is under attack here is but a caricature of Thomas's doctrine.[3] Thomas, for instance, is as emphatic as any nominalist in affirming God's freedom from any kind of external impingement. Thomas's God, after all, is the unconditioned act of pure self-existence. In no respect at all is he passive.[4] If he acts in conformity to law, it is to a law of which he is himself the author.[5] If Thomas's doctrine of divine transcendence prompts him to speak of God as the pure act of being, it is surely a superficial reading to find in such language an insensitivity to God's immanence in nature and history.[6] Although Thomas's teaching that the divine essence is itself the prime exemplar of the whole cosmos provides grounds for positing a certain continuity between creation and Creator, still the scope of any natural theology will be brutally circumscribed by the qualifications attached to the Thomist doctrine of analogy. In the end the natural theologian's propositions about God are all reducible, on Thomist principles, to the single affirmation, "God is."[7] Even that is but to affirm a truth whose full meaning is eternally hidden from any finite intellect. Thomas knows that, in contrast to everything created, God's being is undivided;[8] indeed, the simplicity of the divine essence is what accounts, in large part, for the inadequacy of any language (derived, as it must be, from our experience of composite realities) to express the "what" of God's perfect being. And no one, finally, knows better than Thomas the utter contingency of the created order and the infinite ontological distance separating the Creator from even the most exalted of his creatures.[9]

Yet it must be admitted that Thomas gives God's intellect a certain logical priority over the divine will. "Will follows upon intellect,"[10] he argues, not vice versa. "It is impossible for God to will anything but what his wisdom approves."[11] Ontologically, to be sure, Thomas's doctrine of divine simplicity[12] ensures that such language should be understood as referring not to real distinctions in the Godhead but to the distinct ways in which the simple essence of God may be considered.[13] Yet there can be no doubt about where Thomas looks for the key to whatever knowledge of God's inner life[14] and outer operation[15] we may attain in this life. It is God's intellect that determines what is good (i.e., the divine essence as its own end and other things insofar as they are ordained to that end). "Then" it is God's will that ratifies the decision of his own intellect. According to Thomas, moreover, ideas that serve as the pattern of God's creative work are in the divine essence; indeed, God's essence is itself the archetype of the cosmos as a whole. Thus creatures do in some sense "participate" in the same perfections that exist "preeminently" in God.[16] So in spite of Thomas's frequent caveats concerning God's simplicity and the inevitable inadequacy of our language about him, his notion of the correspondence between creaturely perfections and the divine essence can easily be misunderstood as the basis for a too ambitious program of natural theology. Again, the Hellenic metaphysical language and presuppositions underlying Thomas's definition of God as the pure act of being lend themselves to caricature. How can the pure act of being involve himself in human history? How can the pure act of being love—or be loved? How can he be incarnate? There are, indeed, good Thomist solutions to such questions, but a non-Thomist may be forgiven for seeking a more Hebraic-biblical alternative to what can be viewed, with some cogency, as an excessively Greek-ontological conception of deity.

At several points, then, the ways of talking about God and creation that are typical of late medieval nominalism stand in more or less self-conscious opposition to the Thomist doctrine of God. It should come as no surprise, then, that Gabriel Biel tends to cite Thomas less frequently—and less favorably—here than elsewhere. Of the 421 references to Thomas in Biel's *Collectorium* and *Expositio,* only 34 involve the doctrines of God and creation. Of these, seven are summaries of various aspects of Thomas's teaching about angels and thus only indirectly related to the doctrine of God. Biel's accuracy in stating Thomas's opinion is less impressive here than at other points. He is also more likely to treat Thomas's views in a perfunctory manner: rather than spelling out Thomas's argument in detail, Biel is prone to make mere bibliographical references or simply to note that Thomas's opinion is discussed—and, more often than not, refuted—by Occam. Finally, it is significant that Biel is considerably more likely to reach a negative verdict on Thomas's value as a theological resource in connection with the doctrines of God and creation than in most other contexts. (The sole exception is anthropology.)

The Thomistic materials that Biel cites in discussing the doctrines of God and cosmos fall into four principal divisions: God in himself, God in relation to creatures, cosmology, and angelology.

GOD

Biel's response to Thomas is sometimes—though by no means always—conditioned by his prior commitment to an Occamist point of view. He notes, for instance, Thomas's distinction between "one" as convertible with "being" and "one" as "the principle of number." Thomas's claim, according to Biel, is that when God is called "one," the term is used only in the former sense; otherwise such language would speak of God in terms appropriate to composite beings, in effect quantifying the divine essence.[17] Although Biel's reference to the *prima secundae* is misleading, his citation is virtually a verbatim rendering of Thomas's opinion as expressed in the *prima pars* of the *Summa theologiae* (q. 11 a. 3 ad 2). But Biel presents

Thomas's opinion strictly as the object of Occam's critique. What he emphasizes is not Thomas's opinion (though he cites it with great fidelity) but rather the fact that Occam finds Thomas's opinion unacceptable. In view of Occam's massive authority for Biel's project, the effect of such a presentation is to associate Biel with Occam's verdict, although Biel does not linger on that point.

Strictly speaking, Biel is on solid ground in his account of the way in which Thomas reconciles the plurality of persons with the simplicity of the divine essence. According to Biel, Thomas believes that a purely logical distinction (*distinctio rationis*) between person, essence, and relation will permit us to affirm both the undividedness of God's essence and the plurality of the divine persons.[18] Biel makes it clear that he is working with a secondhand description of Thomas's perspective: the opinion "is said to be St. Thomas's." Biel claims to be following Occam here, but in fact Occam merely ascribes this view to "certain ones" (*quidam*) without mentioning Thomas in particular.[19] How Biel comes to identify this opinion as Thomas's is not immediately clear. The language Thomas employs in his defense of divine simplicity, however, is entirely compatible with Biel's characterization. If the terms *suppositum* and *persona* are understood as synonymous,[20] one might guess that Biel is following Thomas's dictum that "God's essence and *suppositum* are the same in reality but differ conceptually (*in ratione*), as do the divine attributes."[21] (Here the context makes it clear that Thomas is using the terms *suppositum* and *persona* interchangeably.)[22]

A critic might fault Biel's summary for obscuring Thomas's parallel claim that while the distinction between essence and person is only formal, the distinctions among divine persons are altogether real. But Biel's claim is quite specific. In citing Thomas he does not intend to address the question of the logical status of the personal distinctions within the Godhead or to suggest that Thomas adopts a Sabellian solution to that problem (by denying that such distinctions are real). He reports only that Thomas reconciles the unity of essence with the plurality of persons by means of a formal (logical) distinction between essence and person. In that claim he cannot be accused of misrepresenting Thomas's position. (The notion of a logical distinction between relation, on the one hand, and essence and person, on the other, enters into Thomas's discussion of the basis on which a real plurality of divine persons can be affirmed. Such a notion is reflected, however summarily, in Biel's report of Thomas's way of treating the prior question of the compatibility of essential simplicity and personal distinction.)[23]

Elsewhere Biel reports—correctly—that Thomas posits a purely logical distinction between origin and relation in the Godhead. Thomas claims, according to Biel, that "the persons are constituted and distinguished not by origins but by relations, considered not as relations but as characteristics peculiar" to the several persons.[24] Something of Thomas's subtlety is lost in Biel's rendition, since Thomas's formula is more complex than Biel suggests. According to Thomas it is not a question of either/or, because the persons are properly distinguished in both ways (by origin and relation). Yet Thomas does insist that they are distinguished "first and chiefly" by relation; this priority is what Biel extends to the point of exclusiveness. Thomas's language does lend itself to Biel's interpretation, for Thomas speaks of "the origin, which is not distinctive and constitutive of the hypostasis."[25] (In this context Thomas uses the terms "person" and "hypostasis" interchangeably; Biel opts for "person.") By understanding relation in the sense of personal peculiarity, Biel is following Thomas's usage in which *relatio* and *proprietas* are clearly used (in Trinitarian discussions, at least) as synonyms. Biel is not overstepping the evidence when he reports that Thomas associates *relatio* (or *proprietas*) with *hypostasis* in such a way as to view the former as the principal basis of personal distinction within the deity. What he suggests in passing—but does not emphasize, as does Thomas—is that, since the distinction between relation and origin is conceptual but not real, it is strictly from the human point of view (as Thomas puts it, *secundum modum significandi* or *secundum modum intelligendi*) that relation rather than origin is said to be the basis of personal distinction.

Biel is quite accurate in his references to Thomas's doctrine of the Holy Spirit. In the course of explicating some of the issues involved in the ancient dispute over the *Filioque*, Biel finds Thomas's comments worth citing. In particular, he asks whether Father and Son may be called "two spiratings" or "two spirators" of the Holy Spirit. Before giving his own solution Biel offers a very precise account of Thomas's opinion: "Because 'spirating' is an adjective but 'spirator' a substantive, we may say that Father and Son are two spiratings (because of the plurality of the subjects [*supposita*]), but not two spirators (because of the one spiration). For adjectival terms are numbered according to their subjects, but substantive terms derive their number from themselves according to the form signified."[26] So if Hilary says that "the Holy Spirit is from the Father and the Son as authors," the substantive (authors) must be understood in an adjectival sense.[27] Thus Biel includes Thomas among those who hold that Father and Son may properly be called "one spirator of the Holy Spirit." Here Biel's inference is grounded in Thomas's statement that Father and Son are the same spirating principle (since "principle" does not imply a determinate *suppositum* but stands indistinctly for the two persons at the same time).[28]

A comparison with Biel's statement of his own opinion indicates that he is at one with Thomas in holding that Father and Son are "one spirator" and "one spirating principle" of the Holy Spirit.[29] But like Occam,[30] Biel is not at all satisfied with Thomas's argument. He insists—along with Occam—that the term *spirans* may be predicated not just of persons as such but of "anything that spirates."[31] In this broader sense, of which Thomas does not take account, we may say that Father and Son are one spirating. But neither Occam nor Biel will involve himself in heresy by simply denying Thomas's conclusion that Father and Son are one spirating principle of the Holy Spirit.

A similar pattern may be noted in Biel's treatment of Thomas's position concerning the authority of the *Filioque* in the Nicene Creed.[32] Like Thomas, Biel asserts that the Spirit proceeds from the Father and the Son. Thomas, he reports, tries to demonstrate this truth by means of rational arguments. Thus Biel provides a brief but not uninformative glance at Thomas's characteristic ways of using reason theologically. Biel does not go into the particulars of Thomas's proof, however. Apparently he shares Occam's view that such arguments are fruitless (and therefore hardly worth repeating). But at least he does make it clear that Thomas is no fideist.

In other contexts, Biel frequently voices his displeasure with Thomas's attempt to prove affirmations that, in Biel's view, must be made strictly on the basis of the Scripture's pronouncement or the Church's determination. But while Biel ordinarily shows little sympathy for Thomas's positive use of reason (to establish what is to be believed), he often associates himself with Thomas's negative use of reason (to refute those who deny certain elements of the Church's faith). For instance, Biel follows Thomas both in formulating an objection posed by the *Filioque*'s opponents and in responding to it.[33] This relatively late addition to the Creed became necessary, according to both Biel and Thomas, when the opposing error became a serious threat to the peace and unity of the Church. Here the context of Biel's citation leaves no room for doubt concerning his intention to associate himself with Thomas's argument, for Thomas's opinion is cited as part of Biel's response to an objection raised against the orthodox view of the *Filioque*.

Typically Biel condemns Thomas's use of reason only when he suspects that its effect is to erect a separate rational source from which those propositions to be affirmed by all Christians (*credenda*) may be derived. But over and over again, when Thomas reasons about matters concerning which neither Scripture nor the Church has spoken decisively, Biel is eager to use Thomas's arguments in responding to concerns (*dubia*) of his own. Thomas argues, for instance, that since the forms of dove and fire were assumed by the Spirit for no other purpose than to signify certain things, we need not suppose that they were retained any longer than was necessary for achieving that purpose. At this point Biel ratifies Thomas's opinion and the argument by which it is supported.[34]

Some of the main outlines of Thomas's doctrine of God's knowledge are accurately reported, but Biel's summaries are at once incomplete and unsympathetic. Thomas's opinions are given only in very general terms, since Biel finds in them little of value. Biel makes it clear, for instance, that Thomas agrees with Biel's thesis that "God knows all things other than himself clearly and distinctly."[35] But Biel is convinced that the only basis for such a conclusion is the Church's faith. He reports (and refutes) Thomas's claim that it is also a matter of rational proof. For the most part, Biel does not discuss the content of Thomas's arguments, merely noting that Thomas's estimation of the religious value of reason is far higher than his own. In a negative way, he does intimate one basis of Thomas's proof when, "contrary to what Thomas says," he denies that a being's power of knowing is in direct proportion to its immateriality.[36] And even though Thomas's doctrine of divine ideas is unacceptable to Biel, he correctly cites Thomas's argument to the efffect that of those things that are possible but at no time actual there are no divine ideas in the fullest signification of the term. Of such "possibles," according to Thomas, there are ideas only in the imperfect sense; ideas of things that are possible but never actual exist as objects of God's intellect but not of his creative will. "Idea" in its complete meaning includes the notion of "exemplar" (the pattern according to which something is made); "possibles"—which, by definition, are producible but never produced—have no exemplars, hence no ideas in the strictest sense.[37] Following Occam and d'Ailly, Biel rejects Thomas's argument, but he reports it faithfully, almost verbatim.

It is undeniable, however, that Thomas's doctrine of God's knowledge, focused in his doctrine of divine ideas, is far richer and deeper than Biel's brief citation would suggest.[38] It functions for Thomas as a link between Creator and creation, thus providing some limited basis for theological reflection apart from faith in what is communicated through the Church's tradition or through Scripture. Perhaps it was for this reason that Biel saw fit to report it only partially and with explicit warnings about its erroneous assumptions. But one can hardly fail to be impressed by the careful, precise way in which Biel characterizes Thomas's opinions even when he believes that Thomas is hopelessly mistaken.

GOD AND CREATION

Biel's reference to one aspect of Thomas's doctrine of divine ideas raises the question of the ways in which God and created beings are related.[39] Biel takes note of Thomas's claim that while some concepts are properly common to God and creatures, none constitutes a genus within which God is included.[40] Biel agrees that there are such concepts but insists, against Thomas, that there is a sense in which it is proper to say that God is in a genus, insofar as certain genus terms, either adjectival or substantive, are properly predicable of him. God's actual *being,* to be sure, is included in no genus; genus, Biel insists, is a device for categorizing terms, not beings.[41]

From a Thomist point of view, what is missing from Biel's discussion is Thomas's doctrine of analogy: Biel phrases the question in such a way as to trivialize it. Thomas's concern is to show that radical transcendence means that no concept will be univocally common to God and any creature, while his equally radical immanence means that it is possible to speak informatively (not just equivocally) about God. It is the doctrine of analogous predication that allows Thomas to reconcile those two fundamental affirmations.[42] Terms and their referents—in this case, "God" and God—cannot be so glibly dissociated without introducing needless complications into a task that is already difficult enough. A categorization of terms is arbitrary and nonsensical unless it reflects some commonality in their respective referents. Language does not, of course, deal immediately with things. On Thomas's principles, one may grant Biel's premise that a concept or genus is a classification of names but still insist that such a classification must be made on the basis of commonalities perceived in the distinctive properties of certain things. Hence, when we ask whether God is contained under any genus, the issue is whether any of his perfections can serve as a genus in this sense: is there a perfection that God shares univocally with any creature or by reference to which his essence can be defined circumscriptively? On both counts Thomas's response is clear and negative. Language—including genus—is a human artifice, hence finite, hence inadequate to characterize One who is infinite in being. Yet human language about God need not be absolutely uninformative, since some perfections are proper to God and creatures analogically. This whole complex of issues is simply bypassed in Biel's perfunctory rejection of Thomas's claim that God is contained in no genus.

Biel acknowledges Thomas's teaching that God acts freely and contingently with respect to everything external to himself.[43] In view of the voluntarist tendencies in the Occamist doctrine of God, it should come as no surprise to find that Biel wants to associate himself with Thomas's opinion at this point. But in view of the Occamist critique of the religious competence of human reason, it is equally predictable that Biel will have nothing to do with the rational process by which Thomas arrives at this conclusion. Biel's only mistake in reporting Thomas's opinion is his substitution of the phrase, "necessity of the creature," for Thomas's phrase, "necessity of nature." In this context, the contrast between *natura* and *creatura* corresponds to the distinction between God's being (*ad intra*) and his doing (*ad extra*). Thomas is arguing (in the *De potentia Dei*) that God is free from any kind of internal necessity in determining his external actions (*opera ad extra*). Biel obscures this emphasis when he assimilates "nature" to "creature." Thomas is talking about the uncreated nature of God himself, whereas Biel shifts the focus to the created natures of things. Yet while misunderstanding (or ignoring) the point Thomas wants to make in the text cited, Biel attributes to him a view that Thomas does, in fact, hold. No less than Biel, Thomas knows that God is dependent upon no creature in his actions *ad extra.*[44] Perhaps it was for this reason that Biel felt free to do some violence to Thomas's language, since the effect was to express what Thomas clearly intends in other contexts. It is, of course, somewhat less radical to say that God acts from no external necessity than to say that his actions *ad extra* bear no necessary relation to his own inner being and character. Biel opts for the less radical formulation in view of the consideration (which always hovers over his reflection on God's freedom and causality) that not even the omnipotent God is free to act in a way that is truly—not just apparently—irrational by violating the law of noncontradiction. That is why his omnipotence is always a matter of his ability to make actual what is already logically possible. Not even God can create absurdities. For all his insistence on God's freedom from any sort of ethical, cosmological, or soteriological necessity, Biel—no less than Thomas[45]—understands that although God needs no external act in order to establish his own inner perfection, still his utterly contingent works are subject to the laws of his own wisdom (which includes the law of noncontradiction). Thus Biel follows Scotus (and a larger tradition reaching back to Hugh of St. Victor) in defining omnipotence with reference to what is already logically possible. In the strictly theological sense, the notion of omnipotence extends precisely to what is neither necessary nor absurd.[46] This minimal inner necessity—of which Thomas also is aware—may be what prompts Biel to soften Thomas's "necessity of nature" to "necessity of the creature." It is already clear that Thomas would find nothing offensive in the language that Biel thus places on his lips. It should be equally clear that the concern motivating Biel's interpolation is shared by Thomas, who realizes that even God "cannot make the number four greater than it is."[47]

Given the fact that God has freely established the present created order, Biel notes Thomas's teaching that God as the cause of all created being is present to all things by his essence. Biel puts Thomas in the position of inferring, from the fact that God is in all things by his power, that he is essentially ubiquitous.[48] In his dissent, Biel attacks the premise that Thomas borrowed from Aristotle, who says that the mover and the moved must be somehow together. Neither for natural agents nor for one who acts by his intellect and will, Biel argues, is this universally the case. Therefore Thomas's inference is invalid.[49]

It should be noted that here again Biel is exercising a certain degree of editorial freedom in paraphrasing Thomas. In the text cited Thomas does not explicitly draw the inference that Biel attributes to him. In Biel's rendering, Thomas teaches that (a) God is in all things by his power, such that (b) he is the immediate cause of all things; hence, (c) he is everywhere by his essence. When we take account of the fact that Thomas uses the expressions "to be everywhere" and "to be in all things" as equivalent, it is clear that all three of these propositions are affirmed in the *locus* that Biel has in mind (*S.T.* I q. 8 a. 3). At first glance, however, the "hence" may seem problematical—and it is precisely the inference that Biel attributes to Thomas. But in fact it is as their cause of being (*causa essendi*) that Thomas's God is in all things by his essence. Biel cannot be faulted for understanding "cause of being" as connoting God's creative power. Thomas does speak of God as present in all things "by his power" (*per potentiam*). Further, in positing God's presence in all things "by his essence" (*per essentiam*), Thomas's intention is to refute the emanation cosmology that holds that God is not the *immediate* cause of all things. Clearly the connection that Biel draws is implicit in Thomas's argument. Since Thomas's God is present to all things as the cause of their being, he is in them by his power; since Thomas's claim that God is in all things by his essence is directed against the thesis that not everything is the immediate effect of God's exercising his creative power, Biel infers that in Thomas's view God's presence to all things by his power implies that he is omnipresent by his essence (as the cause of being).

Admittedly, Biel does not define his terms with Thomas's care and precision or in the context of Thomas's concerns. In speaking of God's presence in all creatures "by his power," Thomas wants to refute the Manichees' denial of God's immanence in the material world, while his thesis concerning God's omnipresence "by his essence" is directed, as we have noted, against all forms of emanationism (as in Neoplatonism). More generally, however, his intention in both cases is to affirm that God as Creator is omnipresent. While Biel's interpretation is not a mere report of what Thomas says, it is certainly a fair extrapolation from Thomas's ways of using the phrases "by his essence" and "by his power." The inference that he attributes to Thomas is entirely compatible with the thrust of Thomas's logic. For God to be present to all things by his power is, according to Thomas, for all things to be subject to his creative power; but to be in all things by his essence is precisely to be present to them as the cause of their being. Thomas correlates God's presence "by his essence" with his presence to creatures "as the cause of their being"; Biel rightly associates "as the cause of their being" with "by his power" of creating.

Biel goes on to note Thomas's teaching that to be present everywhere is proper only to God.[50] Biel agrees with Thomas's conclusion, adding only the caveat that it is within the scope of God's freedom and omnipotence to share his creative power (hence his omnipresence) with a creature. Biel's qualification echos the nominalist concern to safeguard God's freedom by pointing to his absolute power to do otherwise than he has in fact elected to do. That God *could* communicate his ubiquity to a creature, however, remains for Biel a purely hypothetical possibility. His language leaves no doubt about his own belief that Thomas is right—though for the wrong reasons—in reserving omnipresence to God alone.[51]

When Biel poses the question of God's ability to create sheer potentiality—purely formless matter—he takes note of Thomas's opinion and some of the arguments underlying it.[52] Thomas, he reports, denies that prime matter in this most radical sense could actually exist, since to exist is precisely to be in act by means of some form. Therefore, "if matter were without form it would be in act without act," which is patently absurd. In addition, matter and form are less separable than an accident and the subject in which it inheres; since the latter are inseparable, so are the former. So far so good. But now Biel ascribes to Thomas another syllogism in support of this conclusion: to be deprived of all forms is to be the subject of all privations, some of which are mutually incompatible. This rather too clever argument—which, with slight modifications, could be used to show that matter is eternal[53]—is not found in the text cited by Biel (nor, to the best of my knowledge, anywhere else in Thomas's works). But at least Biel has correctly identified Thomas's position and two of the proofs by which he seeks to defend it.

Biel proceeds, however, to challenge a number of Thomas's assumptions. Here again his basic complaint is that Thomas's solution compromises the principle that God is absolutely free to actualize any logical possibility whatsoever.[54] Thus Biel's assault on Thomas's reasoning aims at showing that no absurdity is involved in the notion of the existence of sheer formless matter. He argues, for instance, that to be in act is not always through a form; prime matter could be in act not through some form but through its own essence. "If we understand 'act' in this way, the act is not distinguished from the existing thing; neither is 'to be' (or existence) distinguished from the existing thing."[55] Biel seems unaware of the fact that his contrast between essence and form makes no sense at all within Thomas's framework. Needless to say, any self-respecting Thomist would find such language highly offensive. Prime matter could exist by its own essence? Prime matter could be its own existence? Such can be predicated, on Thomist principles, only of pure actuality, that is, of God, who is at the opposite pole ontologically from prime matter. But Biel is so eager to safeguard divine omnipotence that he rushes headlong into what can only be regarded as a careless, hastily contrived argument, without pausing to consider even the broad outlines of the obvious Thomist rebuttal. Such evidence strongly suggests that Biel is reading Thomas out of context—unempathically—however accurate, technically speaking, his summary may be in other respects. When he attributes to Thomas the unlikely argument that prime matter could not exist because it would be the subject of mutually incompatible privations, Biel confirms our suspicion that he is having difficulty following the logic of Thomas's position or seeing its function within his cosmology as a whole.

COSMOLOGY

One of the most recurrent of the ways in which Biel uses materials borrowed from St. Thomas is seen when he appeals to Thomas for help in defining basic terms or concepts that will then enter into Biel's own discussion of the question at hand. Typically, this will involve no account of Thomas's own position. An example of this kind of appeal to Thomas is found in Biel's attempt to define the term "heaven."[56] Here Biel follows Thomas in distinguishing among three senses in which the term may be used. Properly (as in Genesis 1), "heaven" denotes the elevated body surrounding the earth, which is actually or potentially luminous. Improperly, "heaven" may be predicated of anything that shares some property of heaven in this stricter sense (e.g., air or fire). Metaphorically, the term may be used in reference to any incorporeal being who exhibits spiritual analogues to the rarity, elevation, and light of heaven properly so called. (The best candidate for such metaphorical predication, according to Thomas, is obviously the Trinity itself.) This summary is scrupulous in its fidelity to Thomas's exposition of the term. By citing Thomas's definition in a preliminary note, Biel clearly intends to affirm the value of Thomas's presentation and to presuppose it as part of the basis of his own commentary.

At other points Biel is only partly in agreement with the opinions that he attributes to Thomas. He correctly includes Thomas, for instance, among those who affirm the materiality of the heavens. He notes—also correctly—Thomas's insistence that celestial matter differs in species and in concept or definition (*sit alterius rationis*) from the matter found in earthly elements.[57] In support of this latter view, according to Biel, Thomas argues that celestial matter is in potency to the form that it actually has and to no other: it is subject to no privation and thus tends toward no form other than its own. The heavens, therefore, are material without being corruptible, since a thing is corrupted (changed) only when its matter "seeks" (*appetit*) a form different from that which it already possesses. In lower bodies, matter tends toward different forms, either more or less perfect than its own. That is what it means to say that these lower bodies are subject to privation. This "desire" for change is natural to the inferior creature and cannot, therefore, be frustrated forever. Hence every inferior body will eventually achieve a form different from the one that it already has, and this will entail the corruption not only of its form but of the composite as a whole.

Here Biel is closely following Thomas's treatment of this question in the *Sentences* commentary and in the *Summa theologiae.* Biel agrees with Thomas's opinion that the heavens are material but rejects his claim that celestial matter is radically different in kind from that found in the earthly elements.[58] He goes out of his way to refute Thomas's arguments in detail.[59] Yet he shows himself to be a conscientious interpreter of Thomas even in areas in which his own dissent from Thomas's position is quite emphatic.

In other references to Thomas in cosmological contexts, Biel clearly regards Thomas as a valuable resource for his own project. He uses Thomas as a source for his account of Origen's spiritual interpretation of "the waters above the firmament" (Genesis 1.6).[60] He follows Thomas in reporting the opinion of some philosophers who contended that the motion of a uniform heaven above the firmament is required in order to account for the continuance of generation (through the regular motion of heavenly bodies).[61] In neither of these cases, however, does Biel give any information about Thomas's own cosmology. Instead he turns to Thomas, as to a theological encyclopedia, for information about definitions and alternative formulations that must be considered in the prolegomena to the forthcoming discussion.

While Biel values Thomas for the help he offers in this kind of preparatory, ground-clearing exercise, he is less sympathetic to the positions that he reports as Thomas's own. For instance, in discussing various interpretations of the essence (*quidditas*) of light, Biel correctly summarizes Thomas's opinion and the argument underlying it.[62] Thomas, he notes, regards light as an accidental form inhering in a body. Here Biel infers Thomas's position from a careful reading of two denials that Thomas makes explicitly. Thomas denies that light is either a body or the substantial form of a body. Biel concludes, correctly, that Thomas views light as an accidental form or quality inhering in a body, not making it to be a body but causing it to be luminous. Thomas refers to light as "an active quality."[63] In view of his denial of the claim that light is a substantial form, Biel correctly interprets "active quality" as the "accidental form" of a body. Biel, however, rejects Thomas's opinion in favor of the view that light is the substantial form of certain bodies.[64]

We may conclude by reiterating that very little information about Thomas's own cosmology is reported by Biel, and even this is usually presented in contrast to what he regards as more satisfying alternatives. Since Biel seems generally hostile to Thomas's cosmology, it is not surprising to find that he refers to it but sparingly. Indeed, he is favorable to Thomas primarily in his capacity as an aid in preliminary terminological analysis or as a source-book for information about opinions other than his own.

ANGELS

Biel is somewhat more favorable to Thomas in his discussion of the number, species, and condition of angels. Only with respect to the question of species is he clearly hostile to Thomas's position.

By noting Thomas's criticism of Origen's angelology, Biel correctly invokes Thomas's authority in behalf of the view that angels are by nature incorporeal and immaterial.[65] Biel goes on to argue (as does Thomas)[66] that while they are themselves incorporeal, angels are nevertheless capable of assuming bodies. Although he does not explicitly attribute this conclusion to Thomas, Biel does suggest Thomas's view, to some extent, by associating himself with Thomas's explanation of what it means for a spiritual being to assume a body.[67]

Twice in his discussion of angelic species, Biel reports, and rejects, Thomas's opinion. He correctly observes that it is inimical to Thomas's thesis to hold that "all angels of the same order are in the same species."[68] After referring to Thomas's discussion of various ways of solving the problem, Biel summarizes Thomas's solution: "He holds that it is impossible for two angels to be of the same species because, according to him, things which agree in species but differ in number agree formally but differ materially. Angels do not have matter; therefore" they cannot differ in number without also differing in species.[69] Biel's own view is couched in terms that reveal his cautious, moderate approach in using traditional materials. Only when a "willful questioner" (*improbus exactor*) demands a decision between Bonaventure's doctrine and Thomas's does Biel reject Thomas's opinion as improbable and unfounded. But he does so with some reluctance. He seems a bit uneasy about having to dismiss Thomas's view that each angel is in a species of his own.[70]

Biel agrees with Thomas that the number of the angelic host is very large, although he insists that Thomas errs in attempting to prove this conclusion by rational means. Yet he cites Thomas's argument extensively and almost verbatim. Then he refutes Thomas's argument with a careful counterargument of his own, whose conclusion shows that his disagreement with Thomas concerns not angels but theological method: "Hence the question is to be answered by saying that the multitude of the angels is very great, although its number is hidden from us. Each part of this conclusion is proved by the authority of Scripture."[71]

Biel associates himself with Thomas's view that an angel's cognition is strictly intellective and independent of the sensory apparatus inhering in any body assumed by him.[72] Biel concludes that cognitive acts that seem to arise in an angel through sense-experience are actually independent of the body and would have been possible even if the body had not been assumed. Biel does not claim that Thomas ever expresses this conclusion in so many words, but he does note that it is in harmony with the thrust of Thomas's arguments concerning the angels' knowledge (*est de intentione . . . Thomae*).

Finally, Biel's reference to Thomas's position regarding the status of angels in relation to justifying grace provides a good example of the cautious, moderate way in which he seeks to find a place for Thomas's insights within his own system. However profound his debt to Occam, Biel's instinct is that of a synthesist. Noting that Thomas is a participant in the debate over whether angels are created in a state of justifying grace, Biel summarizes the opposing opinions[73] and then tries to show how either may be affirmed without verging on heresy. The term "grace," he explains, may be understood in three different senses. At the most general level, it means anything added to a creature beyond his purely natural endowment. More strictly, it means what is added to the natural faculty of free choice in order to dispose it toward moral rectitude. Most properly of all, the term denotes "that which is added to the virtues, completing and elevating them and making them acceptable to God."[74] Depending on the sense in which the term is used, either Thomas's opinion or that of his critics may be correct. Biel believes that the arguments posed by each party to the dispute can be shown to be inconclusive.[75] If neither of the opposing opinions is irrefutable, neither is to be excluded as heretical. Each is permissible at the level of opinion, neither at the level of dogma.

CONCLUSIONS

One who knows Thomas only through Biel will receive a partial (and largely unfavorable) image of Thomas's doctrines of God and creatures. The glaring lacunae in Biel's presentation of Thomas's teaching involve God as the pure act of being, divine simplicity, exemplarism, the doctrine of participation, and above all analogous predication. Biel's portrayal does provide some insight into Thomas's characteristic ways of doing theology, especially with regard to the role of reason. But it is clear that Thomas's views on the place of reason in theological research are not argued fully or convincingly in Biel's account, and they are presented in a uniformly unfavorable light. Even when he agrees with Thomas's opinion, Biel is usually suspicious of his arguments; he wants to replace Thomas's appeal to reason with a greater reliance on the voice of Scripture and the Church. This pattern will become even more distinct in subsequent chapters.

Thomas's profound sense of the continuity between Creator and creation is to a great extent lost in Biel's report. In his discussion of prime matter, it becomes clear that Biel's fundamental complaint involves his fear that Thomas is prone to compromise the omnipotence and freedom of God. The nominalist emphasis upon God's "absolute power" to do anything that is not logically absurd generates much of Biel's dissatisfaction with Thomas's doctrine of God.

Yet we have had occasion to note that even when disagreeing

with Thomas, Biel is usually quite careful in characterizing his positions on various issues. Sometimes he reads Thomas superficially, but in no case does Biel ascribe to Thomas opinions that Thomas explicitly denies; only twice are Biel's summaries in any significant respect misleading.[76] We should be cautioned against a perfunctory assumption that Biel distorts Thomas's opinion whenever he finds it to be in basic conflict with his own.

THREE

CHRIST AND MARY

CHRISTOLOGY

The elements of Thomas's Christology[1] that find a place in Biel's system lean heavily toward affirming the true humanity of the incarnate Christ and expounding the dynamics of his saving work. Thomas's doctrines of the divinity of the preexistent Christ (and thus of his duality of natures after the incarnation) are not altogether missing, but Biel finds Thomas most helpful in explicating the function or office of the incarnate Christ. Within this area of emphasis, Biel is only rarely hostile or inaccurate in his discussion of Thomas's Christology.

Divinity and Humanity

Biel turns to Thomas for a summary of orthodox Christology as it emerged in the struggle against fourth- and fifth-century heresies.[2] This body of affirmations is presented as the lowest common denominator of all orthodox Christologies, however divergent they may be in other respects. So here Biel reports not what is distinctive to Thomas but what Thomas shares with all orthodox theologians, who concur in four fundamental affirmations by which the heresies of Eutyches, Nestorius, the Manichees, and Origen are excluded. A close analysis will show that Biel is successful in expressing the four propositions as formulated by Thomas, but he is confused about identities of the heretics against whom the first two are directed. The four dicta embraced by all who adhere to Catholic truth are (a) that in Christ there is but one person—the divine person of the Word; (b) that in Christ there are two natures (divine and human) and three substances (deity, soul, body); (c) that the human nature of Christ consists of a body and a soul, which were assumed by him; and (d) that Christ's human nature preexisted the union of the divine and human natures, but the flesh and soul assumed by him did not. Biel's only mistake is to suggest that (a) is directed against Eutyches and (b) against Nestorius; this reverses an identification made correctly by Thomas. But Biel is correct in stating that, according to Thomas, (c) is directed against the Manichees (who deny the reality of Christ's body) and (d) against Origen's teaching concerning the preexistence of souls. Since (b) commits Thomas to the doctrine of diphysitism, Biel's reference to Thomas's interpretation of Isidore's dictum (about the sharp distinction between who Christ is in relation to the Father and who he is in relation to the Virgin) has the effect of confirming the already clear impression that Thomas is no monophysite. Thomas is represented as interpreting Isidore's language as a way of affirming the doctrine of Christ's two natures.[3] The only respect in which Biel's report could be considered misleading is that, in the text that Biel claims to be following, Thomas does not invoke this interpretation as if it were his own. Instead he simply lists it as one possible way in which the words of Isidore may be understood as consistent with Christ's personal unity. But it turns out that Thomas's teaching in the *Summa theologiae* follows the line of approach with which Biel associates him here.[4] The thrust of Biel's citation, therefore, is first to associate Thomas with Biel's rejection of the claim that Christ is in any sense two and then to show how Thomas refutes an objection based on language employed in Isidore's *De Trinitate.* (Christ is not two natures; Christ is one who has two natures.) In both respects Biel's appeal to Thomas is fully justified.

Posing the question of Jesus' Sonship in relation to the Holy Spirit, Biel turns again to materials drawn from the Christology outlined in Book III of Thomas's commentary on the *Sentences.*[5] Christ is not the son of the Spirit because the actions by which the Spirit effected Jesus' conception did not involve the use of semen as something arising from within himself (as in paternity); the Spirit acted, rather, as an artisan who works in material external to himself. Thus from the standpoint of his humanity—in his flesh and body—Jesus was the product but not the Son of the Holy Spirit. Here Biel faithfully reports and affirms both Thomas's opinion and the argument undergirding it.

In addition to his allusions to Thomas's doctrine of the two natures in Christ, Biel discusses Thomas's understanding of the relation between Father and Son in terms of the communicability of the Father's generative power.[6] He correctly portrays Thomas as denying that the Son could generate another Son, but Thomas's argument is not identical to the one that Biel attributes to him. According to Biel, Thomas's denial of any active generative power to the Son is simply grounded in his claim that there cannot be several sons in the Godhead. Actually Thomas's argument is a bit more complex than Biel suggests. To possess a power without using it, Aquinas suggests, would be envious (*invidus*), which is repugnant to the Son. Since he *does not* in fact generate, then, it follows that he *cannot.* "And thus," according to Thomas, "there cannot be more than one Son in the Godhead."[7] Biel reports this conclusion but omits the premises of Thomas's argument. It is not difficult to surmise why he sees fit to make that omission; to say that the Son cannot have a power that he does not exercise seems to undermine the entire nominalist program by calling into question the notion that God, by his absolute power, could actualize an infinite number of possibilities, which, by his ordained power, he chooses to leave unrealized. Thomas, of course, does not intend to reject that claim, because he knows that God's creative power (*ad extra*) is not exhausted by the created order as it actually exists.[8] But in the immediate context his language is susceptible to the accusation that it unduly circumscribes the power of God. Following Occam, Biel grants Thomas's conclusion, but will have nothing to do with his arguments. He agrees that the active generative power of the Father is not communicated to the Son, but he regards Thomas's arguments as inconclusive: only on the authority of Scripture can such a conclusion be established.[9] Yet it is noteworthy that Biel avails himself of Thomas's analysis of the threefold sense of the term "generating" (active, passive, impersonal).[10] Here as elsewhere Biel turns to Thomas for preliminary terminological analysis, and he ends by accepting Thomas's conclusion even while rejecting the attempt to demonstrate it rationally. As is often the case, Biel's dispute with Thomas is basically over the question of methodology.

Incarnation and Redemption

Biel's attitude toward the materials that he borrows from Thomas becomes overwhelmingly positive when he turns to a consideration of the earthly career and saving work of Jesus. For instance, he takes his cue from Thomas in assessing both the fittingness and the necessity of the incarnation. Without going into great detail, Biel correctly associates Thomas with Bonaventure's claim that the incarnation exhibits a certain correspondence to several of the divine perfections.[11] Clearly Biel thinks that Thomas has something of value to say, since he refers his reader to Thomas for further information on the question.

Then Biel sides with Thomas in his treatment of the dispute over whether the incarnation would have occurred if Adam had not fallen into sin.[12] Thomas's caution is reflected in Biel's report. The question is held to be unanswerable with certainty; patristic authorities can be cited in support of each of the opposing solutions. But Thomas is inclined to the view that the incarnation would not have occurred if man had not sinned, and his arguments prove to be quite congenial to Biel. Things that depend solely on God's will must remain hidden from us unless they are made known in Scripture. Now the biblical witness consistently locates the reason for the necessity of the incarnation in the sin of Adam. This should not be understood as a limitation of God's power, however; he could have been incarnate apart from human sin, but in fact his will, as revealed in Scripture, was to effect the incarnation only in view of

Adam's fall. Here Thomas emphasizes God's will and power, along with the priority of Scriptural authority, in ways that Biel must have found compelling. He associates himself with Thomas's opinion and refutes each of the arguments for the opposing view (held by Scotus and Alexander of Hales.)[13]

The only point at which Biel explicitly rejects Thomas's solution to a problem relating to the character of Christ's humanity involves the question of divine knowledge in the human soul of Christ.[14] Biel's dissatisfaction with Thomas's doctrine of divine ideas spills over into his discussion of Christ's knowledge.[15] He cites Thomas's opinion extensively, beginning with the distinction between the Word's knowledge of vision and his knowledge of simple intelligence. By his knowledge of vision the Word knows all things that exist (whether in past, present, or future) external to himself. These he knows distinctly, according to Thomas, by means of the idea proper to each. But those things that are possible but at no time actual cannot be known distinctly, since they are indistinctly one in God's power. Furthermore, there are no ideas (in the strictest sense) corresponding to things that are merely possible; hence the Word does not know them through ideas (and thus distinctly), as is the case in his knowledge of existents. He knows them only in knowing the full scope of his own power, and this is called his knowledge of simple intelligence.

Now any created intellect—including that of the incarnate Christ—is by definition finite. Therefore it will be unable to know the infinity of possibilities that God could actualize. The number of things that God does in fact create, however, is finite. Thus it is not absurd to suppose that a created intellect could come to know them all. It will know them in direct proportion to its intimacy with the eternal Word, by whom they are known perfectly in a knowledge of vision. Of all creatures, the human soul of Christ most perfectly apprehended the Word; in knowing the Word, Christ's human soul came to a knowledge of all things that actually were, are, or shall be. For a perfect knowledge of any cause entails knowing all of its effects, just as one more perfectly understands a principle insofar as one comes to know more of its implications. For a human soul, to know the Word perfectly is to know what the word knows (i.e., all existents); yet this is not to comprehend the Word, since it is to know what he knows not infinitely (by a knowledge of simple intelligence) but finitely (by a knowledge of vision).

Thomas does deny, as Biel implies, that the inability to comprehend the Word is grounded in the finitude of Christ's soul. In his commentary on the third book of the *Sentences,* Thomas leaves open the possibility that the finite soul of Christ *could* know the infinity of possible beings, though in a finite way. This, he argues, is not to suggest that the soul of Christ could comprehend the Word, since the notion of comprehension involves not only the fullness of the object known but also an infinite clarity that characterizes the mode of knowing.[16] But in the third part of the *Summa theologiae,* we can detect at least a slight shift in Thomas's emphasis. Without bothering to ask whether it would be *possible* for the human soul of Christ to know all possibles (evenly dimly), Thomas clearly claims that he does not in fact have such knowledge.[17] In both cases Thomas denies that the soul of Christ could comprehend the Verbum; in neither does he unequivocally affirm that Christ could know all of the possibles that the Word knows with a knowledge of simple intelligence. (And in the *Summa theologiae,* Thomas does make the denial that Biel attributes to him.) To this point, then, Biel has represented Thomas fairly. He glosses over Thomas's distinction (in the *Sentences* commentary) between knowing all that the Word knows (obscurely) and comprehending the Word (by knowing all things that the Word knows in the infinite way in which the Word knows them, i.e., to the full extent of their knowability). But in the *Summa theologiae* Thomas abandons this view and proceeds just as Biel's summary suggests: "Some of the things known by the Word exist only in the divine power, and in this respect the soul of Christ does not know all things in the Word. For this would be to comprehend all things that God can do, which would be to comprehend the divine power, and consequently the divine essence."[18] One notes that Thomas speaks of comprehending the divine essence, while Biel expresses Thomas's concern in terms of comprehending the Word. Granted that "Word" and "divine essence" are not synonymous terms for Thomas, it is not difficult to see that to comprehend either is to comprehend both. To comprehend something, in Thomas's usage, is to know all there is to know about it. Only if the Word were less than fully divine could one who comprehends the Word fail to comprehend the divine essence. It is clear, then, that Biel follows Thomas's argument in the *Summa theologiae* very closely. He claims to be aware of Thomas's earlier discussion in the *Sentences* commentary, although he makes no reference to the slight shift in Thomas's way of viewing the possibility that Christ's soul could know all of the possibles known by the Word (in view of the axiom that the infinite cannot be comprehended by the finite). The development of Thomas's thought at this point is interesting but not decisive for Biel's purposes.

For a number of reasons, Biel rejects Thomas's solution to this problem. (1) Biel denies that to know all that the Word knows is to comprehend the Word. He does not support his critique with the sort of argument available to him in Thomas's *Sentences* commentary; he merely asserts that the soul not only of Christ but also of any saint in heaven can see an infinity of things known by the Word, yet without comprehending him.[19] (2) He rejects the analogy that Thomas bases on the claim that in knowing more conclusions from a principle (or more effects of a cause) one comes to a more perfect knowledge of the principle (or cause) itself. No perfection, Biel argues, flows to the cause from its effects or to the principle from its implications; knowledge of the former, therefore, cannot be dependent on knowledge of the latter for its degree of perfection. One who knows a cause more fully will know more of its effects, but we may not say conversely (with Thomas) that to know all of its effects is to know the cause perfectly.[20] (3) Biel is unhappy with Thomas's distinction between the Word's knowledge of vision and his knowledge of simple intelligence. The Word, he insists, sees the possibles with the same degree of clarity (*aeque clare*) and distinctness (*ita distincte*) that characterizes his knowledge of actual existents.[21] For the same reasons that lead Biel to affirm (with Thomas) that the Word has a distinct knowledge of future contingencies, he goes on to claim (against Thomas) that the Word sees those things that are merely possible with the same infinite degree of distinctness. Here again Biel finds in Thomas's doctrine of divine ideas—especially his distinction between ideas as exemplars of existents and quasi-ideas as principles of the intelligibility of what is merely possible—a source of error and confusion. This distinction in Thomas's doctrine of divine ideas finds expression in his correlative distinction between the two kinds of knowledge in the Word. Biel will have nothing to do with either of these distinctions; he suspects that, in effect, they force us to define God's intellect (essence) in terms of what is external to himself. "For the divine intellect receives nothing from things, but his essence is the knowledge of all things."[22] There are two sorts of things—the possibles and the actuals. To import this division into God's intellect, however, would be to compromise the simplicity and impassivity of the divine essence. Just as the Word does not have to wait for a future event to pass from possibility to actuality before he can know it clearly (*clare*) and distinctly (*distincte*), neither is he dependent on the ideas of actual beings for a distinct knowledge of them.[23] (4) Finally, Biel notes, the souls of Christ and the blessed can know, in the Word, that he is able to actualize any possibility that he does not in fact actualize; hence we cannot say that the culmination of their knowledge of the Word is restricted to a sharing in his knowledge of vision, that is, his knowledge of things that are at some time actual.[24]

On both logical and theological grounds, then, Biel advises his reader to take Thomas's doctrine of Christ's knowledge with more than a grain of salt. This negative verdict proves to be an exception to Biel's generally sympathetic treatment of the Christological materials that he borrows from Thomas. He concurs with Thomas in viewing Christ as the fulfillment of the Old Testament promise, the light whose coming fully dispels the Mosaic shadow.[25] He appropriates Thomas's distinction among three kinds of powers (in terms of authority, excellency, and ministry) and proceeds to apply that distinction to Christ in a way that conforms closely to Thomas's usage.[26] But it is above all in portraying the humanity of Christ's psychology and in explaining the mode of his redemptive work that Biel displays both a keen appreciation of Thomas's insights and a remarkable degree of competence as an interpreter of Thomas. First of all, Biel finds in Thomas a way of showing how Christ's human will was uniquely conformed to the divine will (in the act of willing even if not in the thing willed). When Christ willed that the cup of suffering be removed, his act of willing was willed by God and pleasing to him, even though the thing that Christ thus willed was itself contrary to the divine will.[27] For in keeping with his saving purpose, which required the assumption of a genuine and total humanity, God willed that Christ's sensuality as well as his rationality should do and endure what was natural to it. To will the avoidance of pain and death is natural to human sensuality. Accordingly, even though it was not in harmony with God's will that the cup should pass from Christ, God did will that Christ's sensuality should show itself to be fully human by willing to be spared the cup of pain and death.

Similarly, Biel finds in Thomas a compelling account of the equilibrium of sense and reason that is seen uniquely in Christ. He follows Thomas in explaining how the human soul experiences the rebellion of sensuality against reason, first in the contrast between what sense desires and what reason approves, secondly in the rashness with which sensuality seeks to avoid the governance of the reason, and finally in the distraction of reason by the allurements of sensuality. The second and third kinds of rebellion could not have occurred in Christ, since there was in his sensitive appetite no inclination that was contrary to the dictates of his rational will. In Christ "a motion of sensuality never took place except insofar as it was preordained by his reason. And thus, even though the will of his reason did not will the same thing toward which his sensuality tended, still it willed that his sensuality should tend toward it."[28] Thus even as Christ's reason never interfered with the natural workings of his sensual nature, neither did his sensuality struggle against the dictates of reason. Such was the harmony of Christ's will with God's—and of his sensuality and rationality with each other. In this context Biel borrows from Thomas language depicting the ways in which Christ's humanity recapitulated Adam's original integrity and thus stood in sharp contrast to the disorder of powers that all other human beings experience as a consequence of sin.

Far more typical is Biel's use of Thomas as a resource for sharpening our sense of the respects in which Jesus shared the weakness and ambiguity of *our* humanity. (Already it is clear that Biel sanctions Thomas's emphasis on the naturalness of Christ's sensual nature.) It is above all in connection with the Passion that Biel turns to Thomas for an analysis of Christ's utterly human uncertainty, sorrow, and pain. He concurs with Thomas in holding that the Passion was the most fitting of all possible ways in which man's redemption could have been effected.[29] Significantly omitted from Biel's allusion to Thomas are the reasons by which Thomas establishes this conclusion. Thomas implies that God chose this way *because* it was the most fitting. Biel ignores his arguments and reverses the logical sequence: the supreme fittingness of this particular mode of redemption is seen precisely in the fact that it is the one which was ordained in accordance with God's infinite wisdom.[30] (*Iustum est quia Deus vult!*)

Christ's prayer in the garden illustrates for Thomas (and for Biel) the true humanity of the Savior.[31] To pray is appropriate to Christ if—and only if—he is fully human. Prayer is an act of the reason, but Christ's prayer shows how his reason pleads the case of his sensuality. This would be inappropriate—a kind of weakness or failure—only if his humanity were altogether other than our own. Biel approvingly cites Thomas's comment to the effect that a major purpose of Christ's prayer was to reveal his solidarity with us and his kindness toward us. One who shares our humanity so fully can be expected to show mercy. At the same time, Christ's ordeal in the garden—and the conditional terms in which he prayed for the cup of suffering to be taken away—give us an example of obedience and of reliance upon God as the Source of whatever meaning or value human life may have.

The Gospels' description of the Savior's travail in Gethsemane poses the question of his apparent uncertainty about the Father's will. His prayer for the passing of the cup seems to suggest that he is unclear about whether to proceed toward Calvary. Such ambiguity is almost reassuring to one who seeks evidence of Christ's true humanity, but it also raises questions about how this uncertainty can be reconciled with his divinity. At this point Biel grounds his discussion in Thomas's analysis of the term doubt (*dubitatio*).[32] Strictly speaking, doubt is the intellect's movement toward contradictory propositions, together with a reluctance to choose either to the exclusion of the other. In this sense, Christ was not subject to uncertainty, since there was no defect in his knowledge. But there is an improper usage in which the term *dubitatio* takes on the psychological connotation of apprehensiveness or anxiety. Here what it suggests is not a lack of knowledge but a lack of courage. And because Christ's sensuality retained an all-too-human dread of injury and pain, there was indeed a certain trepidation in him. According to his reason, Christ knew that divine assistance was near at hand, but this could not be perceived by his sensual nature. Christ's humanity expressed itself in shrinking from the pain that lay before him, and this is what was misunderstood as uncertainty in the strict sense.

Nowhere does Christ reveal his humanity more fully than in the pain that he suffered. Biel correctly associates Thomas with the opinion of Scotus, Bonaventure, and Alexander of Hales, who hold that "the will of Christ, in itself and as conjoined to the senses, grieved over the same things that occasioned grief in the sensitive power."[33] Here we note the cautious, minimal character of Biel's allusion to Thomas. His claim is not that Thomas draws this inference explicitly but that it is one that is consistent with Thomas's Christology and congenial to what he means to affirm about Christ's will.[34] Biel's point is that Christ's suffering was entirely real, because it took place in the fully human will of sensuality assumed by him. The unity of Christ's person ensures that his human will is not insulated from the sorrow arising from what is suffered by his senses. While Thomas does not in so many words commit himself to this position, Biel is taking no liberties with Thomas's language when he suggests that Thomas would probably have no qualms about affirming it. Thomas too emphasizes the duality of wills in Christ,[35] the depth and reality of his pain and sorrow,[36] and the voluntariness with which he assumed human passibility.[37] Biel infers, therefore, that Thomas would tend to agree that the will of Christ that was conjoined to his sensuality suffered over the same things that caused pain in his sensual nature. The caution that we have noted in his reference to Thomas suggests that Biel has read him very closely and wants to characterize a tendency in Thomas's Christology without going so far as to imply that Thomas makes Biel's point expressly.

Biel associates himself with Thomas's statement that Christ's pain was the greatest of all pains that can be experienced in this life: the magnitude of Christ's pain arises from all four genera of causes, and in respect to each of them his pain was the greatest possible to any *viator.*[38] The efficient cause of his pain embraced every condition to which one can be subject in this life. The material cause of his pain was, objectively, the sin of mankind in general and of the Jews in particular; subjectively, it was the totality of his human body and mind. On both counts, the material cause of his pain was total and incapable of being exceeded. The formal cause included the comprehensiveness of his rejection, which was as total as any experienced in this life. And the final cause of his pain—the end for whose sake he suffered—was the salvation of the whole human race. Although a slight pain suffered by a divine person would have been sufficient, Christ assumed the maximal pain in order to redeem the human race not by sheer power but also according to justice, that is, in his human capacity. As a man, he could redeem the greatest sin—the sin of the whole race—only by bearing the greatest pain. (For both Biel and Thomas, the only exception to this conclusion is the pain endured by souls in hell or purgatory. For even as the glory of heaven exceeds any good experienced in the present life, so does the pain of separated souls exceed any evil suffered here below.)[39]

In discussing the descent into hell, Biel borrows from Thomas a fourfold topography.[40] At the deepest level lies the abode of the damned, characterized by a lack of grace, a lack of the divine vision, and sensible penalties. At the next level is the *limbus* of infants who die without receiving baptism, who experience the privation of grace and of the vision of God but no sensible penalties. Above this lies purgatory, where souls are subject to sensible penalties and a lack of the vision, but not to a lack of grace. Finally, there is the abode of the Old Testament patriarchs, who are being purged by a privation of the vision but who are not deprived of grace or subject to sensible penalties. Biel joins Thomas in holding that Christ descended only to this fourth and highest infernus.

The saving acts of Christ impinge upon the human situation through the application of his merit. Biel endorses Thomas's view that Christ did not merit union with God for himself, since he merits for himself only what he lacks, and union with God—by virtue of the perfect union of humanity and divinity in his person—he has never lacked. "The union which is in the person, which is final and most complete, presupposes every other kind of union with God. Hence from the very fact that the soul of Christ was united to God in the person, the union of fruition was owed to him, and that not through some operation."[41] What is naturally due to Christ cannot be merited by any act on his part. But Biel, like Thomas, knows that Christ's passion would be pointless if it merited nothing at all. In order to show how we may speak of Christ's merit, Biel follows Thomas's analysis of the three ways in which something is said to be merited.[42] First of all, merit may mean that something that was not due to the agent is made a debt to him as a reward for his actions. (Thus the first act of charity after the infusion of justifying grace makes eternal life something owed to a believer.) Secondly, a meritorious act may make what is already owed even more of a debt (as when charity is increased through an act of merit). Thirdly, a meritorious act may make what is due in one way to be due in another way. (Thus eternal life, which is already owed to a person by virtue of the habit of grace infused through pedobaptism, comes to be owed to him through an act proceeding from charity when he reaches the age of discretion.) In the first sense of the term, Christ merited his own glorified body, the impassibility of his human soul and, for us, eternal life. These were lacking until merited by Christ in the first instant of his conception. In the second sense, Christ could not merit because it was impossible for grace to be increased in his soul: in the first instant the soul of Christ received all the grace it was capable of receiving. But in the third sense, all of Christ's acts after the first instant of his conception were meritorious, since they all proceeded from charity. At this point Biel's radical emphasis on charity as the root of merit causes him to take one step beyond Thomas: in this third sense, he insists, Christ may be said to have merited the beatific vision. What was already owed to him only by virtue of his natural union with God now is owed to him, in addition, as a consequence of the merit of his passion. But this application of Thomas's "third way" of meriting to the question of what Christ merited for himself is entirely consistent with Thomas's intention. After all, Thomas shares Biel's commitment to the view that charity is the principle of merit, and Biel has already made it clear that, according to Thomas, Christ did not merit union with God in the first and most proper sense of the term. But after citing Thomas, Biel goes on to speak in a way that would probably make Thomas a bit uneasy. An act of charity, in Biel's view, simply must be rewarded, and Biel is not sure that a glorified body and an impassible soul are sufficient reward for the infinite merit of Christ's passion. He argues, therefore, that while Christ did not merit the union of fruition—that was already owed to him, as Biel's citation of Thomas's opinion has already made clear—he did merit its continuation. Such a view is not really plausible unless one is prepared to grant—heretically—that Christ's natural union with God was contingent, mutable, or temporal. But in any case this part of Biel's conclusion is not included in what he lays at the feet of St. Thomas.

MARIOLOGY

In relation to their teachings concerning the Blessed Virgin, the contrast between Biel and Thomas is well known.[43] In particular, Biel is less cautious than Thomas in his attitude toward the doctrine of the immaculate conception; he is less concerned about the absence of clear biblical sanction, finding in the Church's tradition sufficient basis for the doctrine. This opposition is reflected in the sparse and frequently hostile references to Thomas's teaching in Biel's discussion of questions concerning Mary's sinlessness.

Biel reports (and endorses) Thomas's interpretation of the sense in which Mary is properly called the mother of the God-Man; Sonship is the eternal hypostasis of the Word, who was born of the Virgin as a man.[44] Here Biel's precision leaves something to be desired. Thomas's claim is not that Sonship *is* the hypostasis but that it is especially related to (*respicit*) the hypostasis. (The hypostasis *is* not Sonship but the Son.) And Thomas more clearly distinguishes between Christ's temporal generation, in which he is born of the Virgin, and his eternal generation, in which he is not. Something of Thomas's clarity is lost in Biel's report. Yet the basic thrust of his characterization is fair to Thomas's intention. Biel has Thomas teaching that "according to that eternal hypostasis he was temporally born as a man in the world; that is, this eternal hypostasis became a man."[45] In another context Thomas does grant that God (Biel's "eternal hypostasis") is a man, that is, the incarnate Christ.[46] So far as Mary is concerned, Biel rightly enlists Thomas in support of his claim that she is the true mother of the eternal hypostasis (the Son) in his temporal generation.

It is in connection with the question of Mary's sinlessness that Biel is most prone to distort or reject Thomas's opinion. He is correct in noting Thomas's agreement with Bernard's conclusion that Mary was sanctified in the womb of her mother. He misrepresents Thomas, however, by suggesting that Thomas sanctions Biel's own view that Mary was never infected by original sin at all.[47] The argument that Biel seems to attribute to Thomas is as follows. The authority of the Church sanctions celebrating the feast of the Virgin's conception, and this would be inappropriate if her conception were not holy. But if holy, then it was unstained by sin and thus without the taint of original sin. In point of fact, Thomas specifically refutes this argument by saying that the Church of Rome merely tolerates the feast of Mary's conception. The most that Thomas is willing to affirm is that Mary was sanctified in the womb. He pointedly denies that the Church's authority can be invoked to show that her intrauterine sanctification preceded her animation. At some point between animation and birth—while still in the womb—Mary was sanctified. Prior to that point, however, she was subject to original sin along with all other mortals except Jesus.[48]

Biel's carelessness here is especially puzzling, because he goes on to excuse Thomas, so far as possible, for denying the doctrine of the immaculate conception.[49] (The Church had not yet decided the issue in Thomas's day; he spoke moderately, not with an excess of pride or obstinance that would have marked him as an heretic.) Elsewhere Biel outlines in detail the sharp disagreement between Scotus and Thomas on this question.[50] Although he ends up in Scotus's camp, he carefully summarizes the basic tendencies of Thomas's way of understanding Mary's sinlessness. One is left with a sense that perhaps Biel's intention in the previous text (concerning the proof from the Church's celebration of the feast of the conception) was no more than to acknowledge that Thomas takes note of this argument, which in fact he does. Biel makes no attempt to minimize the extent to which his own opinion may be challenged on the basis of Thomas's authority.

Despite his critique of Thomas's doctrine of Mary's sinlessness, Biel is not insensitive to the value of Thomas's Mariology in other respects. Nowhere is this more striking than in Biel's discussion of the "tinder of sin" (*fomes peccati*) in relation to the twofold sanctification and the assumption of the Virgin.[51] Biel adheres closely to the logic of Thomas's discussion in his commentary on Book III of Lombard's *Sentences.* Thomas speaks of Mary's sanctification in her mother's womb, at the moment of Jesus' conception, and at the moment of her entrance into the beatific vision of God in eternity. In the first of these sanctifications, the essence of the *fomes* remained in Mary, but it was so restrained that it neither inclined her toward sin nor held her back from doing good. This is presented as an instance of Aristotle's principle that a habit of the soul may be restrained in such a way that it cannot be expressed in the act proper to it (as when a man's knowledge is restrained by drunkenness).[52] But in her second sanctification, the very essence of the *fomes* was eradicated.

Thomas, Biel observes, argues that in this second sanctification Mary's soul was cleansed from evil and inclined toward the good only to the extent of the highest perfection that is possible under the conditions of temporality. In her glorious assumption, however, Mary was sanctified in a manner appropriate to a heavenly perfection. The essence of the tendency toward sin was removed in her second sanctification, but certain penalties of sin, such as mortality, remained. She was liberated from even these in the glory of her assumption. Thus in the first sanctification grace was bestowed in order to incline Mary's will toward the good; it was not sufficient, however, to render her will indefectible in its choice of the good. In the second sanctification, grace was added in such abundance as to perfect her will so that it could no longer be deflected away from the good. In this way the defect in her will was healed, but the nature of her faculty of free choice remained intact. But in the third exaltation, the assumption into glory, Mary's soul was so radically united to God that she now shares in his perfect immutability.

CONCLUSIONS

In relation to Christ, Thomas is most helpful to Biel in explicating the genuineness of the humanity assumed in the incarnation. The focus of the Christological materials that Biel appropriates from Thomas is the saving work of Christ, in which his true humanity is revealed in the depth of his solitude, pain, and death. In this connection, Biel is a conscientious interpreter of Thomas. Here, moreover, he evinces a keen sensitivity to the positive value of Thomas's thought.

In relation to Mary, Biel alludes to Thomas a bit less carefully, somewhat less favorably, and much less frequently. Primarily it is the dogma of the immaculate conception that marks the dividing of the ways for Biel and Thomas. In view of this fundamental cleavage, it is not surprising to find Thomas is not a major source for Biel's Mariology. But we have had occasion to note the gentle, friendly way in which Biel excuses what he regards as an unfortunate error on Thomas's part. Even in dissenting from Thomas's opinion, Biel treats Thomas himself with real respect and cordiality. Thomas's authority may not be decisive in every instance, but at the very least it is to be considered with great seriousness and humility.

FOUR

THE HUMAN CONDITION

The semi-Pelagian optimism that finds expression in Biel's understanding of man's moral and religious powers contrasts sharply with St. Thomas's Augustinian realism.[1] Here lies, at least in part, the basis for the incompleteness and the frequently unsympathetic tone characterizing Biel's citations of Thomas in connection with the doctrine of man. For Thomas and Biel alike, the quest for an understanding of human nature represents a prolegomenon to soteriology. At stake is not just man in himself but man in relation to the Source and End of his existence, from whom he has fallen away, in returning to whom he may yet be saved. Thus it is clear that Biel's unwillingness to enter more fully into the dynamism of Thomas's theological anthropology foreshadows a certain insensitivity in his treatment of Thomas's doctrine of justification.[2]

NATURE, SIN, AND MORTALITY

One cannot fully understand who man is without considering the ideal from which he has fallen. For now man exists as sinner, and the depth and impact of his sin cannot be gauged apart from a sense of the contrast between Adam's original integrity and the desperate predicament in which all his descendants find themselves. But a careful reading of Biel's academic works will offer only limited insight into Thomas's image of Adam's status before the lapse into sin.

The major distortion to be noted in Biel's presentation of Thomas's anthropology concerns the question of the location of the image of God in man.[3] Thomas teaches that the image is primarily in the soul's acts and only virtually in its powers. Biel mistakenly represents Thomas as claiming precisely the opposite, that is, "that the image of God consists in the powers, not in the acts, of the soul." By thus misrepresenting Thomas's opinion, Biel suggests that he is in conflict with Thomas at this point. Actually they both agree that the acts (of willing and of understanding, in particular) fulfill or perfect the powers that in themselves—unactualized—do not constitute the image of God.

In connection with questions of sexuality and procreation, Biel appropriates Thomas's image of the hypothetical condition in which man would now find himself if Adam had not fallen (*si homo stetisset*). In such a state of innocence, the two genders would have remained in perfect equilibrium numerically.[4] Biel follows Bonaventure in an argument designed to establish this conclusion. The end of sexual differentiation is procreation. In view of the monogamous nature of the sexual bond as ordained by God, the perfection of the prefallen condition would include a stable balance of the sexes, so that neither celibacy nor polygamy would be necessary for anyone. Otherwise, either procreation or monogamy would be unattainable for some, which would be unnatural or immoral, and in either case repugnant to the primordial perfection. After outlining this conclusion and the argument on which it is founded, Biel suggests that Thomas agrees with himself and Bonaventure at this point. Thomas does agree with Biel's conclusion, and Thomas's argument reflects the emphasis on procreation (as the end of sexuality) that is decisive for Biel's solution to the question. In the text cited, Thomas does not raise the matter of monogamy, but Biel is justified in assuming that Thomas is no polygamist. Thomas's argument contains elements that Biel overlooks, but in general Biel's report does no violence to Thomas's handling of the issues at hand. And Biel's citation of Bonaventure and Thomas is the core of his own response to the question.

Then Biel proceeds to ratify Thomas's contention that sexual union in a state of innocence would have been accompanied by sensible delight (*delectatio*).[5] In contrast to what happens to sexuality in our fallen condition, however, this delight would not have been filthy or unbridled but, on the contrary, pure and utterly subject to the rule of reason. (Thus what is sinful about the sexuality of fallen man is not coitus itself or even the accompanying delight but rather the inordinate and irrational way in which such pleasure comes to be enjoyed for its own sake.)

This contrast between primal integrity and present perversion raises the question of original sin. First Biel summarizes the three dominant medieval schools of thought concerning the essence of original sin. Whereas Lombard defines original sin as concupiscence and Anselm defines it as the privation of an original justice that man ought to have, Biel correctly notes Thomas's attempt to synthesize these two extremes.[6] According to Thomas, Biel reports, the formal element in original sin is the privation of which Anselm speaks, while the material aspect of original sin is the inordinate desire for created things (concupiscence). Thus original sin involves both a privation of original justice and an imbalance in the disposition of the soul's faculties. Hence it is not a mere privation but rather a perverse habit of the soul, which is neither infused nor acquired but inborn through the corrupt origin of each person (in the sexual act, which is always characterized by inordinate delight).

Biel's summary is a fair rendition of Thomas's teaching. Denifle was wrong, then, when he claimed that Luther could not have known about Thomas's way of regarding concupiscence as the material element in original sin.[7] Although his own moderate instinct inclines him toward Thomas's *via media,* in the end Biel seems unwilling to exclude any of the alternatives before him. Any of them may be affirmed without risk of heresy. None may be proved or disproved conclusively.[8] Thomas's opinion, he admits, "seems easier to maintain . . . because it is a medium between the other two; as such it easily takes account of the authorities cited in favor of each of them, because in a sense it embraces them both."[9] But the objection that Biel does not think Thomas can refute is raised by those who believe that original sin cannot be adequately defined without reference to the "tinder of sin" (*fomes peccati*). Thomas's "material" element is concupiscence, but he does not specify that concupiscence is itself what weighs down the soul and inclines it toward sin. Biel believes that it is equally plausible to view this *fomes* as integral to the essence of original sin or to view it merely as something that is always conjoined to original sin. "For each view is held by holy men and renowned teachers. Neither has been excluded by the Church."[10] For this reason Biel shows great caution in handling the question. In the end of his own view seems to veer toward Anselm's privation theory, but he proves so moderate—or perhaps we should say eclectic—that his own opinion remains somewhat indistinct.[11] Here as elsewhere Biel wants to be, like Thomas, a synthesist.

The consequence of sin (original or actual) is death. Yet mortality is somehow related to our finitude as well as to our sin. Accordingly, in the context of a discussion of Christ's passion, Biel turns to Thomas for an analysis of the sense in which it is necessary for man to die.[12] To some extent the necessity of dying arises from the nature of man as a composite, an unstable mixture of antithetical elements seeking eventually to escape from one another. In the end this uneasy equilibrium proves untenable, and at that point the composite is dissolved in death. But before falling into sin, Adam received from God the gift of stability by which this natural entropy was held in abeyance. "For through this gift every corruption, and thus death, could be avoided. But because of sin man lost that gift, and thus human nature is left . . . in the condition which is proper to it by the nature of its own principles."[13] After Adam's fall, therefore, the necessity of dying is in man as a result of sin, whose effect, in part, is to remove the stabilizing gift by which dissolution of the human composite should have been prevented.

STRUCTURES OF THE SOUL

Biel notes that in Thomas's view there can be no plurality of substantial forms in a composite being (such as man).[14] Although he surveys a wide spectrum of alternative ways of resolving the question, he ends up in Thomas's corner, primarily because of the argument from simplicity. A plurality is not to be posited unless reason, experience, or authority requires it. And Biel does not believe that any of these provides compelling grounds for concluding that there are multiple substantial forms in man.[15]

In his analysis of the relations among the powers, acts, and essence of the soul, Biel cites Thomas's opinion extensively and faithfully.[16] A power is accidental, flowing from the soul's essence and mediating between its essence and its acts. Intellectual powers (memory, understanding, and will) are intrinsic to the soul. Because they flow from the soul's essence, they are never separated from it, even in death. Yet as accidents, these powers are to be distinguished from the soul per se; as the immediate principles of diverse acts, they are likewise distinct from each other. Biel cites Thomas's arguments in some detail, along with several arguments in favor of the contrary view that the soul's powers constitute its essence. Then almost instinctively he sets out to show that there is a sense in which each of these apparently contradictory opinions is tenable. Basically, he suggests, the problem is verbal, not substantive. The fact that the soul is the subject of various acts gives rise to various terms, which either may denote the soul absolutely (without connoting anything distinct from itself) or else may connote some operation in addition to the soul as such.[17] Thus "essence" refers to the soul denotatively, "intellect" connotatively. The term "power," furthermore, is used in two distinct senses.[18] At one level the word is used, in a broad sense, to express everything that is implied in the term; more narrowly, it refers only to some concrete referent of the term (i.e., that in which a certain potency is subjected). In the broader sense "intellect," for instance, connotes both the substance of the soul that is able to understand and its act of understanding. In this sense the powers are distinct from one another and from the soul itself, for the soul (understood connotatively) is an aggregate of its powers: parts are distinct both from each other and from the whole. In this sense Thomas's conclusion may be affirmed.[19] But "intellect" may be understood more narrowly as denoting precisely that which understands. When we speak of the higher powers of the soul in this sense, Biel suggests, Scotus is correct in denying that the powers are distinguishable from each other or from the soul itself.[20] That which understands or wills or remembers is precisely the soul itself (understood denotatively), which may be designated in different ways when it is considered under various rubrics. Thus Biel thinks it is possible to reconcile positions that initially seem antithetical through a close analysis of the different senses in which certain critical terms may properly be used.

At several other points, Biel invokes Thomas's authority in charting the topography of the soul. Thomas's exegesis of Aristotle's definition of delight[21] is recorded (and affirmed). The wholistic tendency of Thomas's anthropology—which we have already encountered in connection with the question of the singleness of substantial form—reappears in relation to the distinction between the soul's higher and lower powers.[22] Thomas's analysis of the relation between the irascible and concupiscible appetites is treated carefully and in detail,[23] even though Biel finds it defective in some respects.[24] Thomas holds that these two kinds of appetites are to be distinguished by reference to their respective objects. While the concupiscible seeks the good of delight, the irascible seeks the good of vindication, which is defined as "a difficult good" (*bonum arduum*), since it is provoked by what is experienced as hurtful and is expressed actively, not passively. Biel grants that the irascible seeks an object that cannot be obtained without difficulty, but he argues that this cannot be the basis on which it is distinguished from the concupiscible, which, after all, seeks a good exceeding its natural capacity (i.e., the highest good), a good that can be achieved, if at all, only with great difficulty. (The moral rigorism that marks Biel's understanding of man's religious situation finds an echo here.)

Finally, Biel refers to Thomas in connection with the distinction between conscience and synderesis.[25] Synderesis is the innate habit of the knowledge of first practical principles. Conscience, on the other hand, is the act by which such knowledge is applied to specific cases (*agenda*). Conscience bears witness against sinful acts or omissions, incites the soul to virtuous behavior, and accuses or applauds it for doing right or wrong.[26]

KNOWING AND WILLING

Conspicuously sparse and unsympathetic are Biel's references to Thomas's theory of knowledge. The immediate object of Biel's attack is Thomas's view of the role of phantasms, ideas, and abstractions in our knowledge of the material world. Thomas teaches that the human intellect cannot know individual material things directly, but only through the medium of sensible species; the principle of singularity in a material entity is its matter, which the intellect cannot grasp immediately. Biel disagrees with Thomas, and his account of Thomas's argument leaves something to be desired by way of clarity.[27] Part of Thomas's argument against any direct knowledge of singulars is that the soul's higher powers can do what the lower powers do but in a more eminent way: what the senses know materially and concretely the intellect knows immaterially and abstractly. Biel acknowledges the larger principle with which Thomas is working, but he fails to note the way in which it is applied to the case at hand.[28] And he clearly feels that Thomas's argument is defective. Here again the role of the abstractive process in Thomas's epistemology is rejected by Biel, and he alludes to it only in a general and somewhat confusing manner. Biel is equally hostile (and even more perfunctory) in his treatment of Thomas's comments concerning the adequate object of the human intellect.[29] In this connection Biel provides no indication of Thomas's own position; he merely notes that Thomas's opinion—whatever it is—has been refuted by Occam.

Another instance of this way of dealing with Thomas is seen in Biel's statement that Occam sides with Scotus against Thomas with respect to the will's enjoyment of its final end.[30] But an important example of Thomas's style of reflection is found in Biel's summary of the way in which Thomas characterizes the will in relation to the intellect.[31] Biel uses Thomas as a guide to the interpretation of Aristotle's distinction between what is rational intrinsically or essentially, such as the intellect, and what is rational only in a secondary sense ("by participation"), such as the will. Thus it is possible for something to be irrational by its own nature (*secundum se*) and yet rational in a derivative way, inasmuch as it is submissive to the dictates of reason. Biel associates himself with Thomas in claiming that when Aristotle speaks of "the irrational part" of the soul, he means that not only the irascible and concupiscible appetitive powers but appetite as such is capable of being rational only by participation.

CONCLUSIONS

Several generalizations are in order. First of all, more than in other areas, Biel tends to be hostile in his evaluation of Thomas's position on questions of psychology and epistemology. To the extent that the controversy between Occamism and Thomism is rooted in divergent understandings of the processes of human knowledge, Biel's lack of appreciation for Thomas in such contexts is just what we might expect. (The role of ideas in Thomas's psychology—like the place of divine ideas in his doctrine of God—is a large part of what Biel finds offensive.) Perhaps for this reason, secondly, Biel's references to Thomas's doctrine of human nature are relatively few and partial.

Yet, in the third place, when Biel does see fit to summarize Thomas's opinion, he shows considerable competence as a Thomas-interpreter. Only once—with regard to the locus of the *imago Dei* in the soul—does he completely misrepresent Thomas's opinion. And in this case, at least, it is not a disagreement with Thomas that motivates the distortion. In other words, Biel does not falsify Thomas's opinion in order to claim his authority for some position to which Thomas is actually antagonistic. For it turns out that Thomas is actually more congenial to Biel's interpretation than Biel himself suspects; the conflict that Biel thinks he sees is largely the product of his own misreading of Thomas.

Finally, the lack of a thorough account of Thomas's epistemology means that Biel's superficial treatment of the roles of faith and reason in Thomas's methodology is not corrected by a thorough analysis of the function (and limits) of reason in the dynamics of knowing. One who knows Thomas only as he is refracted through Biel will have a very shallow understanding of Thomas's way of conceiving the competence of the human intellect.

FIVE

ETHICS

In Biel's academic works, nearly a third of all citations of Thomas Aquinas occur in the context of discussions concerning the rights and wrongs of human behavior.[1] The sheer mass of this material will not be fully reflected in the length of this chapter. The ethical issues concerning which Biel is in dialogue with Thomas are not all equally significant or interesting. In some cases, moreover, Thomas's opinion on a particular issue is summarized more than once.

The distinction between personal and social ethics is not absolute, of course. Yet it seems appropriate to consider, first, Biel's appropriation of Thomas's ethics in connection with issues involving the individual agent as such, and then to ask about his use of Thomas's analysis of issues that speak more directly to the situations in which one finds oneself by virtue of belonging to the human community. In addition, Biel (like Thomas) raises a number of questions about the norms that should regulate the behavior of those discharging certain offices within the Church. This "practical theology" will be discussed here under the heading of "clerical ethics."

PERSONAL ETHICS

Virtues

We have already had occasion to note that Biel often finds great value in Thomas's analysis of basic terms and concepts. In his own ethical theory, Biel wants to inquire about the "parts" of a virtue, and he works back from Thomas's analysis of three kinds of wholes to a threefold sense of the term "part."[2] An integral whole is constituted by the parts of which it is composed; a universal whole is the concept (e.g., animal) that may be predicated of all members of a certain genus (e.g., man); a potential whole contains the perfection of certain things within itself immanently. Here Biel's one mistake is unfortunate—since it obscures the point of Thomas's characterization—yet understandable, paralleling the confusion often noted in the use of the adjectives "eminent" and "immanent" in English. Thomas says that a potential whole contains "virtually" what is actually in another; although virtually corresponds to the sense of *immanens,* Biel reverses the logic of the definition by claiming that for Thomas a potential part contains a certain perfection "eminently."

Correspondingly there are three kinds of parts. An integral part is to some extent constitutive of the whole. A subjective (universal) part is contained under a broader whole, as in the case of a species within a genus. A potential part shares, to some extent, the perfection or powers of the whole, but not to such a degree that it becomes a fit subject for whatever predications may be made of the whole. Thus an integral part of a virtue is one without which the virtue itself remains imperfect. A subjective part of a virtue may receive any predication that is properly made of the whole, as when a genus (e.g., prudence) is predicated of a species (e.g., economic prudence). A potential part of a virtue shares in some mode that is exhibited more perfectly in that virtue; thus the philosophical, dialectical, and rhetorical disciplines are potential parts of the virtue of prudence.

Elsewhere Biel notes that Thomas distinguishes between virtues and gifts of the Spirit, but he does not take account of Thomas's arguments or suggest what stake Thomas has in making such a distinction.[3]

Following Aristotle, Thomas claims that virtues reside in the irrational parts of the soul, which, nonetheless, submit to the reason and thus come to participate in it. Biel claims that in this context

Thomas is speaking of the sensitive appetite.[4] Actually, Thomas speaks somewhat more narrowly than does Biel. Thomas claims that virtues are subjected in the concupiscible and irascible powers. Yet Biel is on firm ground in speaking more generally, since Thomas holds, in the first part of the *Summa theologiae* (q. 81 a. 2 *corp.*) that the sensitive appetite consists in the irascible and concupiscible powers.

Biel reports that Thomas assigns a certain priority to prudence among the cardinal virtues, although he fails to take account of the reasons that lead Thomas to hold this view.[5] After noting Scotus's dissent (to the effect that a virtue that elicits acts according to the rule of prudence is more primary than prudence itself), Biel assumes the synthesizing posture that we have already noticed in numerous other contexts. There are two ways, he claims, in which one thing may be prior (*principalius*) to another—either as a *sine qua non* without which the other could not be what it is, or as an example of a higher perfection than that which is exhibited in the other. In the first sense, Biel concludes, Thomas is correct: prudence is prior to the other virtues inasmuch as any act that is not governed by the rule of prudence cannot be expressive of any other virtue. But in the second sense, Scotus is right: the virtues pertaining to the will possess an intrinsic nobility exceeding that of the intellectual virtues, since (1) the will is more perfectible than the intellect, (2) the dictates of reason aim at what is chosen by the upright will, and (3) what is prior in generation (the dictate of reason) is posterior in perfection (vis-à-vis the choice of will). Here Biel's voluntarism conditions his response to Thomas, but it is significant that he goes out of his way to make room for Thomas and Scotus to coexist within the boundaries of his own ethics.

Among the theological virtues, it is primarily love that Biel understands by light of Thomas's analysis. He follows Thomas very closely in distinguishing among four species of love.[6] In a broad sense, the words "love" (*amor*), "delight" (*dilectio*), "charity" (*caritas*), and "friendship" (*amicitia*) all refer to the same thing. Yet Biel joins Thomas in arguing that they are distinguishable, because friendship, according to Aristotle, is like a habit, while love and delight imply an act or a passion; charity may be taken in either sense. "Love" is a more general term than "delight" or "charity," which are kinds of love. "Delight" (*dilectio*) implies, in addition to love, a prior choice (*electio*); therefore it resides only in the will of the rational nature. Charity implies, in addition to love, a certain perfection of love, such that its object is deemed to be of great value (*carum/caritas*).

In this context love is considered quite generally as an activity of the soul. To speak of love as a theological virtue, however, is to pose the question of the interpretation of the Great Commandment.[7] We are enjoined to love God with the totality of heart, soul, mind, and strength. If some of these conditions are omitted in the various formulations of the commandment found in Scripture, that is because "heart," "mind," and "strength" may be understood as implying one another. (Here Biel's summary of Thomas's comment is somewhat loose. Thomas's analysis is actually a bit more complex than Biel suggests, but Biel attributes to him nothing that Thomas would not recognize as his own.)

Biel commends to his reader Thomas's discussion of the order of charity. When Biel asks whether one's close relatives or associates should be loved more than others who are, objectively, better than they, he follows Thomas's analysis quite closely.[8] The act of loving should be proportioned to both the lover and the beloved, lest it become, in either respect, inordinate. The first and highest object of human love is God, and other things are rightly loved in a manner that is appropriate to the greater or lesser moral distance between themselves and God. Charity, in loving God above all things, wills that his justice be preserved, as it is when those who are better receive a fuller share of beatitude. Thus the object of love is determined by reference to a comparison with the ultimate beloved—God. Yet the intensity of the loving act is properly gauged by a comparison not with God but with the one who loves. And thus one should love those who are nearer to him by wishing a lesser good for them more intensely than he wishes an even greater good for those who merit it by virtue of a greater nearness to the lovability of God himself.

The Christian is commanded to love his enemies.[9] But Biel adopts Thomas's view that in practice this requires only that the exterior signs of charity that are exhibited to all men generally (such as prayers for a whole community) should not be withheld from the enemy. For the exterior signs of love should be proportioned to the interior love from which they arise. An interior love of the enemy in general is absolutely required by God's command; thus the signs and effects of this general love must be extended to the enemy. But to offer the signs of love toward the enemy *as an individual* is required not absolutely but conditionally: we must be disposed to do so if a case of extreme urgency should arise.

God, neighbors, and even enemies are to be loved out of charity—God absolutely, neighbors and enemies according to their respective conditions. But what about demons? Biel responds by pointing to Thomas's distinction between the strict and broad senses of what it means to love someone out of charity.[10] Strictly speaking, it means to love him as a friend; and in this sense we cannot love demons, for they are not (and cannot be) fit to share with us in blessedness. (Biel fails to take note of the clincher in Thomas's argument: we cannot rightly will that demons receive beatitude, since this would violate the charity owed to God, by which we must affirm the dictates of his justice.) Except, indeed, for the human body, nothing that is irrational may be loved in this way. But in a broader sense, we love something out of charity whenever it is charity that prompts our delight in it; this is what happens when our delight in something arises from the prospect of using it for God's sake. In this sense any nature, including that of a demon, can be loved out of charity. (Underlying this argument, obviously, is Augustine's distinction between using, *uti*, and enjoying, *frui.*)

Norms

When Biel discusses the basis on which the moral value of an act is to be assessed, he frequently turns to St. Thomas for guidance. Here again Thomas provides the preliminary conceptual analysis that Biel appropriates as a prolegomenon to his own discussion.

Biel notes that, according to Thomas, human acts may be distinguished in the following way.[11] Some acts by their very nature always include something inordinate. Such acts—fornication, for instance, or theft—are intrinsically evil. Their agent, therefore, will always be implicated in some degree of guilt. Other acts are in themselves indifferent but become good or evil according to various circumstances under which they may be done. Yet a third kind of action is that which, in itself, is to some degree inordinate but may become permissible, or even virtuous, under certain circumstances. For instance, to kill or to persecute a person is in general inordinate, but to take a murderer's life or to flog a thief is not sinful but virtuous. The value of an act must be assessed both intrinsically and extrinsically.

A similar distinction is noted when Biel associates himself with Thomas's claim that the requirements of natural law are inelastic (prohibiting, for instance, only what is intrinsically evil) in contrast to the precepts of positive law (which sometimes prohibits what in itself is good or indifferent). Thus a certain flexibility is proper to our observance of positive law, for here the decisive consideration is not the deed itself but the lawmaker's intention.[12]

Biel claims to be following Thomas when he says that only a habit of the will is formally good. Other habits may be good materially; they exhibit only a derivative goodness dependent on the prior goodness of the will.[13] In the text cited, Thomas speaks not of habits but of acts: only an act of the will is formally good, but other acts may be materially good if they are suitable to the power by which they are effected. Biel appropriates Thomas's act-language as if it were habit-language. Biel asks how a habit can be good; Thomas states that certain habits are virtues, and defines a virtue as a good habit.[14] And Thomas concludes that a habit is a virtue if it perfects a power in some good act. Thus the goodness of a habit—its character as a virtue—is a function of the goodness of the acts that it empowers. So Biel draws a connection that is entirely consistent with Thomas's way of speaking when he reformulates Thomas's statement about habits as a statement about acts.

Some sense of the kinds of values that guide Thomas in dealing with moral questions is provided in Biel's observation that Thomas sanctions the deferral or omission of works that are in themselves good, if this is expressive of humility[15] or of the desire to avoid giving offense to a weaker brother.[16]

Sins

In an ethical system that is self-consciously theological in character, the violation of a moral norm that is rooted in divine and eternal law will be more than just wrong or immoral. It will also be an affront to the Source of law and justice; it will have to be considered under the rubric of sin.

Biel cites Thomas's analysis of some of the circumstances that predispose a person to sin. Sin is avoidable, after all.[17] No one sins in what he cannot avoid doing, unless this incapacity is itself voluntary on his part. Similarly, ignorance that is willed—either formally by desire or virtually by negligence—cannot serve to minimize the seriousness of one's misdeed.[18] Sin, like virtue, is voluntary, and an absolute, unavoidable ignorance about the nature or consequences of an act robs it of that voluntary character. But to will ignorance upon oneself is to transfer the voluntariness of such ignorance (hence its culpability) to the act that it preconditions.

Although each concrete act of sin is avoidable, man is always subject to temptation. Since to tempt is to put someone to the test in order to find out something about him,[19] it is properly predicated of God, as well as of man and the devil; less properly, the world and the flesh may be said to tempt a person, since they provide the immediate occasions of temptation.[20] Primarily, though, it is by the illusions and deceptions of the devil that one is led into sin.[21]

When tempted, one may sin not only by doing what is forbidden but also by omitting what is enjoined. Biel is only partially accurate in his references to Thomas's discussion of sins of omission.[22] He correctly notes, with Thomas, the opposing positions on whether some covert positive act is always involved in a sin of omission. Thomas, he reports, holds that "although in a sin of omission some positive act is frequently involved, still a positive act is not strictly necessary in order for there to be a sin of omission. For the act of not doing what is commanded is itself a sin of omission, apart from any positive act."[23] Biel's summary loses something of the complexity of Thomas's position on this question, for rather than excluding either of the opposing views (as Biel suggests), Thomas tries to show that each contains a measure of truth. If we look merely at the essence of any particular sin of omission, he argues, sometimes a positive interior act is involved (as when we will not to do what is obligatory), but sometimes it consists precisely in the negligence of not considering the obligation at all.[24] But if we look at the causes or occasions of the omission, it will always be seen to involve some positive act. A sin of omission occurs only when its cause is in our own power. When we decide what to do with what lies within our power, sin may arise from this movement of the will, which already entails at least an interior act. Thus Thomas answers the question "Is some positive act always involved in a sin of omission?" with a yes and a no. Biel focuses upon the no and identifies it as Thomas's solution to the problem. Then he affirms the view that he has attributed to Thomas: he grants that it is rare and unlikely for a sin of omission to be accompanied by no positive act, but he insists that it is not altogether impossible.[25] He does not respond to the other half of Thomas's answer.

Turning to sins of commission, Biel notes Thomas's definition of theft as the secret taking of what belongs to another.[26] Biel finds this formula too general (since it would apply equally well to simony or usury) and yet too narrow (since by common usage the term can suggest any kind of misappropriation, whether secret or not).[27] Yet Biel turns to Thomas's analysis of the distinction between theft (*furtum*) and robbery (*rapina*) and of the basis on which the relative gravity of different sins is to be assessed.[28] Theft and robbery are both mortally sinful, since they are, by definition, acts of injustice. Robbery, unlike theft, involves an element of violence and coercion. Generally speaking, therefore, robbery is the more serious offense, because it is more directly opposed to the will of the owner, who stands to suffer not only the loss of his property but also public humiliation and even physical injury. But the observed fact that men more readily experience shame over theft than over robbery should not be taken as evidence that theft is the more serious sin. For what is reflected here is a certain distortion in the sinner's perspective; he attaches excessive importance to the external strength that is manifested in an act of violence (though he pays little attention to the inner strength that is destroyed by sin). This distorted scheme of values fosters a greater sense of shame for what is actually the sin of lesser gravity.

In all these respects, Biel gives Thomas's analysis his unqualified endorsement. The same positive tone pervades Biel's rather full account of Thomas's treatment of the nature[29] and redemptive purpose[30] of excommunication; not surprisingly, Biel then follows Thomas's analysis of the scope and gravity of the sin of communicating with the excommunicated.[31]

Duties

At the opposite pole from sin is duty. St. Thomas becomes an important source for Biel's interpretation of the ways in which individuals are bound to give alms, observe the Church's fasts, and exercise fraternal correction. In these contexts his use of materials borrowed from Thomas is only rarely inaccurate or hostile.

Alms-giving. The obligation to give alms to those in need, Biel suggests, is not absolute. It is conditioned by both the donor's ability and the recipient's need. In each of these respects, Biel associates himself with Thomas's way of handling the problem. He affirms Thomas's observation that one is not required—except in cases of extreme necessity on the neighbor's part—to give alms of those things without which one's position in the community (*status*) cannot be sustained. But he goes on to qualify this maxim by noting Thomas's caveat to the effect that only extreme changes affect one's status.[32] Hence the maxim may not be used to justify stinginess. But to give alms of those things without which one's own life (or the lives of those committed to one's care) would be placed in jeopardy is neither commanded nor counseled.[33] Such extravagance, in fact, is contrary to the order of charity. The sole exception to this rule is that it is praiseworthy, though not obligatory, to make such a sacrifice for some important person whose death would endanger the public welfare.

On the part of the recipient, what activates the duty to give alms is extremity of need.[34] Rarely if ever can extreme necessity be recognized with absolute certainty until death is already imminent, but the obligation of alms-giving requires us to act prudently in light of probable signs that offer a moral (if not an absolute) certainty concerning the urgency of the neighbor's need. Even though the neighbor's condition has not yet deteriorated to the point of imminent death, such signs of distress will require that alms be given without further delay (which might result in the recipient's passing the point of being able to derive any benefit from them).

If mortal peril is not involved, the situation becomes more complex.[35] In such cases, it is a matter not of command but of counsel to give alms. Hence, while it is meritorious to give alms to those who are not in mortal danger, it is in no way culpable to forego such an act (provided that the omission is based on reason, not on malice or avarice). The precept, furthermore, does not cover every kind of necessity; it includes only those things without which the indigent person cannot survive but which no one else seems able and willing to provide.

Absolutely speaking, spiritual alms are preferable to corporeal alms.[36] Biel attributes to Thomas three reasons for holding this view: spiritual alms are more excellent because (1) what is given is nobler, (2) the soul, to which they are given, is nobler than the body, and (3) the result (*fructus*) is greater, since spiritual alms can have an impact upon the souls' eternal destiny. (In the text that Biel seems to be following, Thomas explicitly mentions only the first and third of these reasons, though the second is certainly not alien to his thought.) Yet in certain combinations of circumstances, this rule of thumb does not apply. One who is starving needs bread rather than a sermon. And from the donor's point of view, the giving of corporeal alms may have a spiritual effect. For when they are given out of charity, the donor merits an increase of grace and glory.

Finally, Biel invokes Thomas's authority on behalf of his thesis that the order of alms-giving should conform to the order of charity.[37] He joins Thomas in noting that it is difficult to determine precisely who has first claim upon our generosity, since individuals vary so widely in three critical respects: the recipient's present need, the donor's special obligation for previous acts of kindness on the recipient's part, and the integrity or merit of the needy person. These factors are often so complex and ambiguous that it is futile to try to measure them or to determine their relative weight in exact detail. General guidelines are the most that can be offered, and these must be applied according to the dictates of prudence and common sense. Generally speaking, need takes precedence over merit or special obligation, and the merit of the recipient is less important than the donor's prior indebtedness to him. Yet if need and special obligation are roughly equal, a good person is to be preferred over one who is evil (or less good).

Fasting. Biel appropriates Thomas's discussion of the negative purposes of fasting—to make satisfaction for sins and to restrain concupiscence, which might lead to further sins—but he omits the positive function mentioned by Thomas, which is to free the mind from distractions and thus to enable it to rise to a higher contemplation.[38] He notes, with Thomas, the mortal guilt involved in failing to observe the Church's fasts,[39] but he also follows Thomas in a number of reservations by which the force of such a view is somewhat mitigated. Minors, for instance, are excused from the obligation to fast.[40] A journey or some important official function that cannot reasonably be postponed may provide valid grounds for exemption from the fast.[41] Consumption of foods for medicinal purposes does not constitute a breaking of the fast.[42]

This series of reservations provides an opportunity for Biel to note several important tendencies in Thomas's way of handling ethics. In connection with his discussion of a nondeferrable journey as grounds for exemption from a fast, Biel associates himself with Thomas's observation that the precept (fasting) cannot be accorded an absolute precedence over the counsel (pilgrimage), since the intention of the one who gave the precept was not to exclude devout or necessary activities.[43]

In the same context Biel invokes the moderate, humane emphasis of Thomas's asceticism. What is absolutely necessary—that is, for the preservation of life itself—may not be withdrawn for the sake of fasting. What is only conditionally necessary—for the preservation of a certain robustness of the body—is twofold. At one level, such necessities are required in order to discharge one's office or position in society. These are not to be renounced, for this would be to sacrifice other binding obligations in the interest of keeping the fast. Likewise, any abstinence that keeps a person from doing useful works (even though he may not be strictly obligated to do them) is ill-advised, if not unlawful. But at another level, such necessities are required only in order to maintain an optimal disposition of the body. Of these it is lawful to partake but praiseworthy to abstain, for such abstinence aids in the spirit's conquest of the flesh and is not reckless: one's health is endangered more by the abundance than by the scarcity of such foods. But to abstain from those things that are not necessary in any of these ways is a matter of precept rather than of counsel.

Fraternal correction. Thomas's way of dealing with a number of moral problematics is reflected in Biel's lengthy discussion of the duty to admonish a brother who falls into sin. Biel agrees with Thomas that fraternal correction falls under a precept, not a counsel; therefore it is binding upon all Christians, though it may be especially incumbent upon priests and prelates.[44] Yet this does not mean that a monk is obliged to leave the cloister in order to seek out and admonish wrongdoers; a distinction must be drawn between specific and general obligations. When one owes a debt to some particular person, he must take the initiative in seeking him out. (For anyone who has a pastoral duty to look after the spiritual welfare of a fallen brother, correction is an obligation analogous to that imposed by a financial debt. Hence a priest must take the initiative in approaching wayward members of his flock.) But other benefits—where no such specific responsibility is in force—are owed to all of one's neighbors. Since no individual is capable of discharging this kind of obligation to all of mankind, it is enough to render the benefit to those who come seeking it. And this is what obtains in the case of the religious.[45] (Like Thomas, Biel grounds this discussion in Proverbs 24.15 and in proof-texts from Augustine's *On Christian Doctrine* and *On the Words of the Lord.*)

Fraternal correction is an act of charity, not of justice. Now the means must be ordered according to what the end requires. Thus charity dictates the end (the brother's reformation), and the whole process of fraternal correction is no more than a means to that end: it must be administered only when, and to the extent that, the sinner's restoration is likely to be effected.[46]

Thomas's sensitivity to the complexity of moral questions and his emphasis upon intention in resolving ambiguous cases find expression in Biel's discussion of the special problem that arises when the evangelical requirement of private admonition is ignored and the brother's sin is simply reported to a prelate.[47] Biel sides with Thomas's view that no general rule will cover all possible combinations of motives and circumstances, and he cites Thomas's rule of thumb with evident approval: it is one's intention that determines whether one who omits private admonition is guilty of mortal sin or of mere carelessness. One is obligated to deal with the delinquent in love (*ex caritate*), and this is done by seeking to bring about his improvement (or to prevent his future recidivism). If the prelate is discrete and responsible, and if it is reasonable to suppose that his admonition would be more conducive to the ends sought, one may mention the case to him without first approaching the brother privately. But if it seems likely that the brother's reputation would be needlessly endangered, or if there is no reason to suppose that he would fail to respond to a private warning, the ends must dictate the means: the evangelical order is then to be observed. What is decisive is the agent's intention, but one is also responsible for calculating the likely effects of one's actions.

A similar emphasis comes to expression when Biel adopts Thomas's threefold analysis of the moral implications of a failure to exercise fraternal correction.[48] It is meritorious to forego fraternal correction from a concern for the sinner's welfare; thus, for instance, correction may be postponed to a more suitable time and place. Sometimes the omission is an expression of fear or some other form of excessive self-concern, but not in such a callous way that the brother's welfare is consciously and intentionally subordinated to one's personal comfort or security. In this case, the omission of fraternal correction is a venial sin. But beyond a certain threshold of deliberate misvaluing, it becomes a mortal sin. Again the decisive factor is the agent's intention. A brother's claim upon our charity must be the basis of any attempt to reclaim him from the sin into which he has fallen. Fraternal love dictates the brother's welfare as the intended end; only that is nonnegotiable. But Biel's report mirrors Thomas's emphasis on our responsibility for the means employed in pursuit of a good end. He associates himself with Thomas's concern to avoid any injury to the sinner's reputation, if at all possible. Yet when all prudent attempts to save both his reputation and his soul prove unsuccessful, first things must come first. Charity demands that an attempt to improve a sinner's moral and religious condition cannot be held hostage to the desire to preserve his good name.[49]

SOCIAL ETHICS

In expounding his own social theory, Biel frequently appeals to St. Thomas for an understanding of the legitimate claims of state and law upon the individual conscience. In his analysis of the rights and duties of man-in-community, Biel finds in Thomas an important resource for his own discussion of the ethics of the marketplace and the courtroom. One other aspect of social ethics in which he is most likely to take Thomas as his guide involves the thorny medieval problems of simony and nepotism.

The *Res Publica*

Law and the commonwealth. Like Thomas, Biel appeals to Aristotle's understanding of the priority of the commonwealth over any private good.[50] According to Aristotle, the good of the individual is desirable, but the good of the race or of the community is "better and more divine." Biel turns to Thomas for an analysis of the way in which the common good is "more divine": it has a greater likeness to God, who is the universal good and the cause of all things that are called good. The reference to God as "the universal good" is Biel's explanatory gloss, but it is perfectly consistent with the thrust of Thomas's logic here and in other contexts.[51] Since the common good takes precedence over every private good, rulers are obliged to use their office in pursuit of the public interest rather than of personal gain. This obligation is integral to the very concept (*ratio*) of rulership. It is for this reason that certain revenues are assigned to rulers, out of which they may live comfortably without unjustly extorting a livelihood from their subjects.[52]

Man's life as a member of society is regulated by law. Human law directs him toward the preservation of the community as such, but divine law recalls him to the vision of a community "under God" (*sub Deo*). Biel appropriates Thomas's observation that two things are required at the level of human law in order that one may live well in a society: one must be positively related both to the ruler and to the other members of the community.[53] Taking his cue from Thomas's allusion to the role of divine law in a community under God, Biel interepprets the order of the Decalogue in Thomas's terms.[54] In a theonomous society (*de communitate fidelium sub Deo*) two things are required: first it is necessary that the faithful be in a proper relationship to God as the Lord not only of that community but even of all creation, and then it is necessary that they be in a proper relationship to one another as fellow subjects of the same Lord. That priority is reflected in the order of the first and second tables of the Decalogue.

Biel correctly notes that Thomas finds in Proverbs 8.15 warrant for claiming that positive human law, insofar as it is just, is derived from the eternal law and thus shares in its binding force. Hence the transgression of a just human law implicates the transgressor in mortal guilt.[55] (While Thomas merely notes that such a law is binding upon the conscience, Biel goes one step further in claiming the violation of a human precept derived from the eternal law will always involve mortal guilt. The only respect in which Thomas might qualify this conclusion would be to add some explicit reference to the intention and the premeditation with which the positive law is violated.)[56] If justice among men is discerned by reference to the eternal law from which positive law is derived, and from which it has its binding force, a law that is unjust is in reality no law at all.[57] (Biel follows Thomas—who follows Augustine—at this point.)

The binding force of human law, however, relates to the lawgiver's intention rather than to an overly literal interpretation of the words in which it is expressed.[58] One who, without reasonable cause or in contempt of the law, refuses to do what the law requires marks himself as a transgressor. But sometimes there are good grounds for believing that the lawgiver himself, in light of certain extraordinary circumstances, would not want to hold his subjects to the prescribed behavior, since in some unforeseen way it turns out to be inimical to the end he had in view when the law was framed. In such a case one may deviate from the letter of the law in order to help achieve that end; by so doing one does not become a transgressor of the statute.

Biel aligns himself with Thomas's dictum that all profits from games of chance are illegal, and in that context he provides some insight into Thomas's view of the relation between civil law and divine law.[59] By civil law, all such profits are prohibited. Civil law is not universally binding, however, and may be effectively repealed by a long-standing tradition of nonenforcement. If the law concerning games of chance has been repealed in this way, one may in good conscience retain such a profit unless it was acquired in such a way as to violate some prohibition in the divine law (by fraud, e.g., or by exploiting those, such as children, who lack the competence to dispose of property). But if the law has not been repealed in this way, profits from a game of chance must be restored to the person from whom they were taken or else given to the indigent. Biel agrees with Thomas that those who win in games of chance must make restitution of their profits if the civil law is still in effect. But then he goes one step beyond Thomas in denying that continued nonobservance constitutes an annulment of civil laws; even though nonobservance does not annul the law, however, one is not bound by the law to make restitution, unless the judge's verdict specifically includes such a provision as part of the punishment for gambling.[60]

The limits of authority. Like Thomas, Biel holds that justice is central to the common good that the ruler's office requires him to pursue.[61] If the prince uses his power for private gain rather than for the public good, he thereby becomes a robber. In human society the police power does not rest in the hands of private persons; when even the prince forcibly takes away what belongs to another, he is guilty of robbery unless his action qualifies as a legitimate exercise of public authority in pursuit of ends that are just. Biel correctly states that, in Thomas's opinion, public power is committed exclusively to the rulers so that justice may be advanced by force if necessary. The right to use force is solely the rulers' prerogative, but not even they are exempt from the norms of justice.

We have already seen how Biel invokes Thomas's authority in support of the claim that an unjust law is no law at all. In that context, Biel makes use of Thomas's analysis of three conditions that must be fulfilled in order for a law to be just.[62] A just law—or, rather, a genuine law, which by definition is just—must (1) aim at the common good, (2) not exceed the lawgiver's authority, and (3) impose any burdens that may be involved in a way that is commensurate with the end sought. Conversely, any positive "law" that is defective in any of these respects is unjust and thus ceases to have the binding force of law. It may therefore be disobeyed, unless disobedience seems likely to arouse some scandal or public disorder (Matthew 5.40–41). If a law is actually incompatible with obedience to God's commands, not only is it no longer binding, but we have a positive obligation to disobey it, for "we should obey God rather than men" (Acts 5.29). An unjust prince, who acts in defiance of law (or in pursuit of "laws" that are themselves unjust), forfeits any claim upon his subjects' obedience. Biel endorses Thomas's claim that citizens are not obligated to obey anyone except insofar as the order of justice requires it. A robber prince (or a usurper) is no longer a legitimate ruler: because he makes demands that are contrary to the order of justice, no one is obliged to obey him (unless, again, some intolerable scandal or danger is likely to result from disobedience).[63]

The interplay of authority and justice is sharply focused in the notion of a just war. Biel follows Thomas's analysis of the conditions that must be observed in order for a war to be just.[64] A war is just only insofar as it is waged (1) by a legitimate authority (2) in behalf of a just cause and (3) with the proper intention. Although the doctrine of the just war can provide a basis on which disobedience may be justified, Biel's emphasis is on Thomas's dictum that the first condition—a legitimate authority—takes the power of waging war out of private hands. The sword is committed exclusively to the ruler. The private citizen lacks the resources that must be marshalled in wartime, and in any case he is obliged to seek redress of grievances through the judgment of his superior. Just as it is lawful for rulers to defend the commonwealth against internal threats by punishing evildoers (Romans 13.4), so too it is lawful for them to defend it against external threats by means of the sword of war. But in both respects the guardianship of public affairs, and thus the use of coercive means to that end, belong strictly to the public authorities. Biel leaves no doubt about Thomas's view that it is just to withhold obedience from a prince who undertakes an unjust war.[65] But he gives no hint that under certain circumstances Thomas would be willing to sanction active rebellion (as opposed to passive disobedience) against an unjust prince.[66]

Commercial Ethics

Property rights. Moral problems involving the ownership and disposition of material goods provide Biel with several opportunities to claim continuity with the teaching of St. Thomas. He invokes Thomas's authority, for instance, in support of the view that a woman may possess property of her own that is not subject to her husband's control. She is free to dispose of such property as she sees fit; she may give alms of what is strictly hers alone without first seeking her husband's consent, and she need not make restitution to her husband if he should then pose some objection.[67] Thomas does insist that a woman should exercise such generosity in moderation, lest she impoverish her husband. Biel omits this caveat. Although in the text cited Thomas does not raise the question of restitution, Biel is careful to phrase his reference in sufficiently broad terms (*satis concordat sanctus Thomas*) to avoid placing strange words on Thomas's lips. Clearly, at any rate, he associates Thomas with a view that is implicit in Thomas's understanding of restitution as a means of repairing the effects of some injustice. In the case at hand, Thomas agrees that in disposing of what she owns apart from any relation to her husband (*bona sua propria*), a wife commits no offense against justice. Hence Biel infers—correctly—that it is at least implicit in Thomas's understanding of the issues at stake here that no restitution is obligatory in such a case.

Thomas's respect for the rights of private property is further reflected in Biel's discussion of the moral distinction between theft and the mere repossession of what is one's own.[68] To take back what is rightfully one's own is not to commit an act of theft, although some other kind of sin may be involved, depending on the way in which it is done. For instance, if it is possible for the rightful owner to regain his property through some judicial process, the plaintiff sins by taking the law into his own hands: no one may be a judge in his own case. But if such recourse is unavailable, one becomes guilty of no sin in reappropriating what is rightfully one's own. On the other hand, one who secretly repossesses what he has loaned to someone else sins in so doing, not by theft but by inconveniencing the borrower and by usurping the right of judgment in his own case. Under these circumstances he is obliged to compensate the borrower for the inconvenience caused him.

Finally, Biel considers Thomas a reliable guide in unraveling the moral issues involved in the disposition of property that has been lost by one and found by another.[69]

The just price. Biel's economic theory includes an emphatic defense of the medieval doctrine of the just price. In this connection he finds numerous occasions to align himself with Thomas's critique of exorbitant profits. He endorses, for instance, Thomas's thesis that anyone who knowingly defrauds his neighbor by more than half of the just price commits a grave sin and is obliged (by the heavenly tribunal, if not by the earthly) to make full restitution.[70] In this context, Biel follows Thomas in applying Aristotle's dictum that commerce is ordained for the mutual benefit of buyer and seller: what is established for the common advantage should impose no greater hardship upon one party than upon the other.[71] Therefore justice requires a certain equality of value between the things exchanged in commerce. Thus if the price exceeds the value of what it buys, or vice versa, the equality is destroyed and the whole transaction is rendered unjust. Accordingly, it is intrinsically unjust (and unlawful) to buy something for less or to sell it for more than it is worth.[72] Biel turns repeatedly to Thomas for guidance in assessing various conditions that enter into the computation of a just price.[73] He cites Thomas, for instance, in defense of the conclusion that one may not lawfully enter into a contract requiring compensation for any loss of future profits from an investment. The reason, which Biel borrows from Thomas, is fundamental to their common attack on all kinds of unjust prices, including usury: no one may sell what he does not yet have and may easily be prevented from having. What does not exist cannot be sold.[74] (Thus the critique of usury, to which we shall turn shortly, is to some extent an application of the doctrine of the just price.)

Biel follows Thomas, again, in arguing that if it is unjust to sell an object for more than it is worth, it is equally unlawful to conceal from the buyer critical defects that detract from its value.[75] If the defect is such as to cause danger of loss to the buyer, it must be brought to his attention. If the defect is not of this nature, it need not be revealed. Yet in this case the one offering an object for sale is obliged to reduce his price sufficiently to take account of the lower value of such defective merchandise. Otherwise he will be guilty of selling at an unjust price; he will be obliged, then, to make appropriate restitution to the buyer.

Usury. Biel and Thomas make common cause in their attack upon the fiscal basis of capitalist economics. In defining the sin of usury, Biel agrees with Thomas that not only money but anything that is measurable in monetary terms falls within the scope of the prohibition against usury. A lender who receives usury, either in money or in goods whose value can be expressed in terms of money, sins against the demands of justice. But this excludes the case of a borrower who "repays," in addition to the amount borrowed, gratitude or love, since to these an exact financial value cannot be assigned. A lender who receives only this kind of "interest" does not involve himself in the sin of usury,[76] for a debt may be repayed in one of two ways. Payment may be based on what sheer justice requires (*ex debito iustitiae*), to which one may be held by the terms of a contract. Here the quantity of the repayment will have to be proportional to the magnitude of the benefit received. Under these circumstances, the lender commits usury by requiring the borrower to repay more than he received. But when repayment is based not on justice but on friendship (*ex debito amicitiae*), the decisive consideration is not the quantity of the loan but the quality of the feeling in which it is offered and received. A debt of friendship may not be reduced to contractual arrangements, since this would be destructive of the spontaneity of the relationship on which it is based. The lender who merely appeals to the borrower's sense of gratitude does not implicate himself in the sin of usury. But Biel affirms Thomas's verdict against the lender who requires, as an explicit, contractual obligation, repayment in excess of the amount borrowed.[77]

Biel adheres closely to Thomas's argument when he grounds the prohibition against usury in divine, natural, and civil law. First he invokes Thomas's proof that usury is contrary to natural law, because it involves the sale of something that does not yet exist, namely, the borrower's use of what belongs to the lender. This leads to an inequality between value and price, in violation of what justice requires.[78] For the use of certain things (e.g., foods) is precisely their consumption, and the value of using any such item may not be assessed separately from the value of the thing itself. One who is given a bottle of wine is also given the right to its use. If he purchases the wine, it is inequitable to charge him, in addition, for its use. In the case of anything whose use is not distinct from its consumption, a loan has the effect of transferring its ownership to the borrower. It is clear, then, that one who sells the use of such an item apart from (or in addition to) the thing itself involves himself in injustice either by selling the same thing twice or by selling what does not exist. In just this way the usurer demands a double compensation: he requires, first, a repayment that is equal to the amount borrowed from him (i.e., the just price) and, in addition, a repayment that is equal to the value of the use of whatever was loaned (i.e., interest or usury). But since, according to Aristotle, money exists only for the purpose of facilitating exchange, it falls into the category of things whose use is their consumption.[79] The use of money is its alienation (consumption) in a commercial exchange. Hence it is unlawful to receive a price for its use over and above a price equal to the value of the principal of the loan.[80]

Not surprisingly, then, Biel agrees with Thomas's claim that divine law, no less than natural law, prohibits usury. In Luke 6.35, Biel reports, Thomas finds both a counsel (*mutuum date*) and a precept (*nihil inde sperantes*): we are not obligated, strictly speaking, to loan money to anyone, but if we do we are forbidden to make an unjust profit from the loan.[81] Similarly, Biel turns to Thomas (along with Alexander of Hales) for an exegesis of two passages in Deuteronomy, which seem to suggest that under some circumstances usury is not prohibited by the divine law.[82] Biel endorses Thomas's thesis that these texts are to be understood as concessions to the hardness of the Jews' hearts; they were permitted a lesser sin lest they commit an even greater one. (They were allowed to practice usury in relation to foreigners so that they would be less prone to exploit their own kinsmen.) Furthermore, since all men are brothers and neighbors, we may not exact usury from anyone. In the texts from Deuteronomy, then, the verb *feneraberis* ("you shall lend") must be taken improperly (as *mutuare*), without the connotation of lending only on the condition of receiving a repayment of both principal and interest.[83]

When Biel asks about the morality of paying usury, as opposed to extorting it from someone else, he avails himself of Thomas's distinction between actively inducing someone to lend money at interest (which is to share in his sin) and merely paying usury that the lender is already disposed to require.[84] Biel agrees with Thomas that it is unlawful to induce someone to sin by lending at usury, but he leaves Thomas's argument undeveloped when he turns to the more passive involvement in the usurer's sin (merely paying usury as demanded). While Thomas draws on Augustine's dictum that it is lawful to use another's sin for some good purpose (even as God brings good out of evil), Biel says only that to borrow at interest is licit if the end in view is a good one, but not otherwise. Something of the force of Thomas's argument is lost here, but the content of his opinion is correctly and favorably reported.

According to both Thomas and Biel, usury is an unjust profit and the usurer, by dealing unjustly with his neighbor, sins mortally. If he then seeks forgiveness through the sacrament of penance, he will be required to restore any profit derived from usury to the one from whom it was taken. Biel sides with Thomas, however, in claiming that the usurer is not obligated to divest himself of any additional profits derived from the investment of such ill-gotten gains, unless there was something illicit about the conditions of the investment itself.[85] But Biel is careful to note the way in which Thomas qualifies this conclusion. If the profit is something whose use is to be consumed, such as food or money, the lender is obliged to restore only the unjust profit and is permitted to retain anything additional that he may have gained by some honest use of it, for this subsequent profit is the product of his own industry rather than of the usury itself. But if usury is collected in goods that have a use distinct from their consumption, such as equipment or real estate, one must return not only the profit derived through usury but also any secondary profits arising from its use; if the use is distinct from the thing itself, restitution will not be complete until both are restored to the one from whom they were misappropriated. Profits derived from the use of such goods are not the product of the usurer's industry but are included in the unjust profit, which he must restore to its original owner.[86]

Since restitution is a mandatory work of satisfaction, Biel argues that rulers may not exact revenues from those who possess only profits derived from usury: to do so would render them incapable of making full restitution. In a rare misreading of Thomas in a social-ethical context, Biel attributes this opinion to Thomas. In fact, Thomas insists that such a person "must be punished by a financial penalty, lest he derive some benefit from his wickedness."[87] What may have misled Biel is Thomas's statement that any such penalty may not be retained by the civil authorities but must be devoted to some worthy purpose. When Thomas says that a fine may not be retained, Biel presents him as claiming that it may not be exacted at all.

Political-Judicial Ethics

Perjury. Because society is bound together by a web of promises and responsibilities, lying attacks the roots of human solidarity. Perhaps it is for this reason that Biel treats mendacity above all as a sin against the social body.

In the context of his treatment of the ethics of the courtroom, Biel outlines Thomas's view that since the act of lying is intrinsically (*ex genere*) evil, there are no circumstances under which a lie is not sinful.[88] After setting up the contrast between Thomas's opinion and that of Scotus (who makes the sinfulness of lying dependent solely on God's prohibition, which God is free to revoke), Biel defines his own position in such a way as to fall more nearly in Scotus's camp. His concern, like Scotus's, is to show that the ethical order is radically contingent upon the will and command of

God. By his absolute power, God could ordain that the act of intentionally deceiving through misrepresentation is not a sin—but in that case, according to Biel, it would no longer be a lie. Biel agrees with Thomas that there is always something inordinate about the act of lying, but while Thomas locates this defect in the nature of the act itself, Biel derives its sinfulness from the sheer fact of God's prohibition.[89] Thus Biel agrees with Thomas that lying is sinful; he further agrees that it is something inordinate about the act that accounts for its sinfulness. He diverges from Thomas, however, by denying that its inordinateness is intrinsic to the act itself (and thus somehow necessary). The inordinate—hence sinful—character of the act is extrinsic to itself and radically contingent upon God's precept. *Iustum est quia Deus vult!* It is clear that Biel gives "equal time" to Thomas and Scotus and tries to synthesize the best elements of both opinions, but in the end the voluntarism that he shares with Scotus has greater weight than his respect for Thomas's authority.

Before turning to the matter of truth-telling in judicial proceedings, Biel cites Thomas's analysis of the term "falsehood" (*mendacium*)[90] and associates himself with Thomas's observation that a falsehood may be committed with a gesture, for instance, as well as verbally.[91] Then he invokes Thomas's authority in support of his claim that anyone who is duly interrogated concerning a crime of which he is accused is obliged to answer truthfully.[92] Equally in remaining silent and in speaking falsely, he commits a mortal sin—even when he knows that by telling the truth he will ensure his own conviction in a capital case. For to violate some demand of justice is to sin mortally, and justice requires the defendant to obey his superior (the judge) in those matters to which his authority rightfully extends. Only when the judge clearly exceeds the limits of his own authority may the defendant refuse to respond to his questioning. Not even in this case, however, may he speak falsely without incurring mortal guilt for himself.

On the other hand, Biel joins Thomas in laying the basis on which an unjust sentence may be evaded.[93] In doing so, Biel again selects materials from Thomas's ethical writings to reinforce the view that disobedience to the state's demands, but never sedition or rebellion, can be lawful in some circumstances. He affirms Thomas's claim that one who is unjustly condemned to death may defend himself as he would against a common thief. Yet it is not lawful for a private person in such a predicament to defend himself by violent means. This would be to wage an unjust war: a war is justly waged only under the auspices of the one to whom the sword is lawfully entrusted.[94] But one who is sentenced to death, even justly, cannot be obliged to execute sentence upon himself. A man condemned to death by starvation would not sin by eating food smuggled to him by his friends: by declining to eat it he would become, in effect, his own executioner. Similarly he is not obliged to pass up a chance to escape from the place where he awaits his executioner. If he has no opportunity to escape, his duty is to offer no resistance but to suffer the penalty that is justly exacted of him.

In his allusion to Thomas's understanding of what constitutes a morally proper oath,[95] and in his discussion of Thomas's position in relation to the morality of oaths made heedlessly[96] or in jest,[97] Biel shows himself to be both conscientious and sympathetic in his use of Thomist materials. When Biel goes on to report Thomas's opinion that perjury is a more serious offense than murder, he records Thomas's argument at length and quite faithfully.[98] At once, however, Biel presents Richard of Middleton's critique of each element in Thomas's proof. While Biel does not explicitly commit himself to Richard's opinion, the total effect of his presentation is to leave Thomas's argument in shambles.

Finally, Biel turns to Thomas (and Augustine) for an exegesis of Leviticus 5.1, which permits him to avoid the inference that one who knows perjury is being committed must denounce the perjurer before the court.[99] Because the text does not specify to whom the perjurer is to be denounced, we may assume that his sin should be brought to the attention of those who would use this information to do him good rather than harm (such as a discreet priest or parents or friends). Since the text leaves room for a prudent judgment about the one to whom a perjurer must be denounced, the evangelical order (fraternal correction) is to be maintained, unless the perjury tends to harm some innocent third party.

The quest for justice. Biel cites Thomas in support of his claim that a frivolous or unjust appeal to a higher court is sinful, since it inflicts undue injury on the judge and on one's adversary by falsely impugning the justice of the judge's verdict and of the adversary's cause.[100] Biel further associates Thomas with the view that in such circumstances a defendant is obliged to make restitution for the damage thus inflicted by his appeal. Although Thomas does not pose the question of restitution in the text that Biel cites, the view attributed to Thomas is perfectly consonant with Thomas's inclusion of unjustified injury to someone's good name within the scope of the maxim concerning restitution.[101]

Biel joins Thomas in affirming that officers of the court are bound to make restitution to anyone victimized by acts of negligence or injustice on their part.[102] An instance of this sort arises when an attorney knowingly defends an unjust cause: in such a case he sins mortally, since it is unlawful to give active support to another's sinful deed (Romans 1.32). But if he agrees to defend what he believes to be a just cause and then comes to know otherwise, he will commit mortal sin only if he continues to aid in advancing what he now knows to be an unjust cause. He must desist from pleading his client's case, although he is not obliged to cooperate actively with the opposing party. The attorney who unwittingly defends an unjust cause is to be excused if his ignorance is not itself culpable (through negligence).

Finally, Biel sides with Thomas in maintaining that an attorney is not obliged to reveal information that is likely to prove detrimental to his client. Under no condition may such prudent silence verge into explicit falsehood, however.[103] On the other hand, Biel is correct in claiming Thomas's authority for his inference that a prosecutor sins by helping the defendant rather than making every reasonable attempt to secure his conviction.[104]

The sin of partiality. In grappling with the moral implications of simony and nepotism, Biel turns again and again to St. Thomas. His references to Thomas in this connection are unfailingly accurate (and highly favorable).

Biel finds in Thomas grounds for distinguishing between more important offices (involving the care of souls) and less important ones (which entail no such pastoral responsibilities).[105] In view of Thomas's claim that the sin of partiality is a more serious offense when it is committed in connection with religious affairs, Biel infers that Thomas would agree with his conclusion that while it is merely a venial sin to appoint the less-qualified person to a lesser office, it is a mortal sin to confer on him an office involving the care of souls. Biel's characterization is an inference rather than a direct citation, but it does no violence to the thrust of Thomas's logic. Thomas does say that it is a sin to appoint the less-qualified person to a pastoral office.[106] Biel correlates mortal/venial sin with greater/lesser office. Clearly he has done no violence to Thomas's intent, though he makes explicit what Thomas's language only suggests.

The relative importance of the applicants' technical competence, on the one hand, and their moral virtue, on the other, is a delicate issue on which Biel turns to Thomas for guidance.[107] He concurs with Thomas's opinion that an ecclesiastical office should never be conferred on one who is not good in a moral or spiritual sense (*bonus simpliciter*), regardless of any technical qualifications that he might possess. The sole reason for promoting someone to an office must be his ability to discharge its functions in a suitable manner. But an evil man is unfit to touch anything that is holy or spiritual.[108]

In dispensing ecclesiastical offices, it is never permissible to choose a good candidate in preference to one who is even better.[109] Thomas, indeed, concedes that "it is enough if a good man is selected; it is not necessary to choose the better man."[110] But the context makes it clear that Biel has not misrepresented Thomas's position. What Thomas has in mind here is moral goodness, whereas the dictum about always giving preference to the "better" candidate has to do with technical ability. Of two candidates, the first may be morally good and more competent, while the second is morally better and less competent. Since neither fails to meet the minimal standard of virtue, Thomas will not condone choosing a less competent moral hero in preference to a more competent person who is only relatively less virtuous. Biel is aware of the way Thomas uses this distinction between moral and technical goodness, and he finds it helpful.[111] After rendering this meticulous account of Thomas's opinion, Biel makes it clear that it represents his own solution as well, and he uses materials lifted from Thomas's discussion in disposing of objections designed to show that in some instances this solution does not hold.[112]

On this basis Biel adopts Thomas's argument against the sale of offices, though he makes it clear that Thomas objects to the practice not because it is in itself unlawful but because of the pragmatic consideration that simony renders the holder of a purchased office less accountable to his superior for negligence or malfeasance.[113]

Thomas's analysis of the sin of partiality (*acceptatio personarum*) figures prominently in Biel's discussion of the problem of nepotism, although he presents Thomas's comments in a context that is wider than the mere question of appointments to civil or ecclesiastical offices. He shows, first, how Thomas distinguishes between due honor or respect, on the one hand, and partiality, on the other.[114] Honor is appropriate only as a tribute to virtue. Yet it is not merely one's own virtue, but also that of another in whose place one stands, that must be considered: thus even wicked priests and prelates may be honored, if not for their own virtue, as representatives of God and of the community. "By the same token, parents and masters are to be honored by virtue of their participation in the dignity of God, who is the Father and Lord of all."[115]

Biel also invokes Thomas's way of showing, both by authority and by natural reason, that favoritism is sinful:[116] (a) Nothing is prohibited by divine law except sin; partiality is forbidden in Deuteronomy (1.16ff.) and Ecclesiasticus (42.1); therefore it is a sin. (b) Nothing is opposed to virtue except a vice; partiality is opposed to the virtue of distributive justice; hence partiality is a vice (sin).

Thomas's argument in favor of the second premise in (b) is cited in some detail, providing a glimpse into Thomas's typical way of grounding human virtues in a reference to corresponding divine perfections. To show partiality is sinful because it violates the norm of distributive justice, which in turn is binding upon human behavior because it imitates the justice of God himself. (Here is a rare instance in which Biel raises no objection when Thomas defines sin with reference to God's nature rather than to the dictates of the divine will.)

CLERICAL ETHICS

Certain responsibilities pertain to man not merely as a moral or as a social being but specifically as one who has been called to discharge some special function in the ministry of the Church. At several points, Biel grounds his discussion of a priest's obligation to his people, as well as his treatment of the norms regulating the cleric's secular involvements, in an appeal to insights gleaned from St. Thomas.

Priest and Parish

The flock makes certain rightful demands of its shepherd. Biel reports that Thomas holds each priest responsible for administering the eucharist to those who, free from all mortal sin, rightfully ask him to do so. (Nothing short of mortal sin forfeits one's right to receive the eucharist.)[117] Biel further reports (and endorses) Thomas's opinion that a priest may not abstain entirely from celebrating the eucharist, even if he serves in a strictly nonpastoral capacity.[118] Biel accepts certain elements of the argument by which Thomas supports this conclusion, but he objects to Thomas's use of II Corinthians 6.1 for this purpose. When Paul exhorts us to "receive not the grace of God in vain," Thomas observes that the celebration of the eucharist is opportune not only with regard to the people *for* whom it is offered but also with regard to God, *to* whom it is offered. Thus one who neglects to celebrate simply because there is no one for whom he must offer the eucharist overlooks the One to whom he is bound to offer it, and in this way the grace that he received is not allowed to bring forth its proper fruit; it is received "in vain." Both on exegetical and on logical grounds, Biel finds this argument unconvincing. He argues first that Paul's language ("*hortamur*") is appropriate to a counsel, not a commandment, and secondly that Thomas's argument leads to an absurdity: pushed to its limits, Thomas's logic in this case will suggest that the priest must celebrate the eucharist daily, so that there will never be a day in which the grace of his priestly office will have been received in vain. But Biel finds no fault with Thomas's appeal to I Peter 4.10 and to the authority of Gregory the Great in support of a conclusion that Biel and Thomas hold in common.

Biel states that this right to demand the eucharist from one's pastor, according to Thomas, does not pertain to notorious sinners[119] or to the mentally defective,[120] who might be prone to dishonor the sacrament in some way. With respect to the insane and feebleminded, Thomas's position is a bit more complex than Biel's report suggests. Thomas is concerned about the possibility of irreverence arising from psychological disorders, but he insists that the eucharist may still be offered to an insane person who, before lapsing into feeblemindedness, expressed some degree of devotion toward the sacrament. Thomas also grants that the eucharist may be offered to the insane at the moment of death. These qualifications are omitted from Biel's summary of Thomas's opinion.

The confidentiality of the confessional booth is another duty that the priest owes to his parishioners. Biel agrees with Thomas's claim that a legal oath cannot oblige a priest to reveal what someone has confessed to him. Thomas defends this conclusion by arguing that an oath obliges a priest to reveal only what he knows in a purely human capacity (*ut homo*), whereas he knows what is confessed to him not as man but as God (*ut Deus*). Therefore he can rightly claim that he (as a man) does not know what has been confessed to him (as God).[121] Here again Biel rejects Thomas's argument even though he accepts the view that it is designed to establish. Biel, like Scotus, is uneasy about the danger of blurring the distinction between God and his minister.[122] He insists, therefore, that rather than denying knowledge of some crime confessed to him, the priest must refuse any answer at all, on the grounds that an oath cannot oblige one to reveal what he is otherwise obliged to conceal.[123]

Biel acknowledges Thomas's teaching that the one who confesses to a priest is free to release him from the obligation of confidentiality.[124] He further reports (and endorses) Thomas's view that a priest who comes to know, apart from the confessional, what he already knew on the basis of someone's confession is not bound to confidentiality in the matter, so long as his language does not directly disclose what went on in the confessional.[125]

Prerequisites and Impediments

Biel associates himself with the rigorous moral standard to which Thomas holds the priest. Natural law requires holiness in one who handles holy things.[126] Divine law, too, makes it clear that to exercise a priestly function while in a state of mortal sin is to exercise it unworthily (and thus to commit still another mortal sin).[127] One may not celebrate the eucharist without partaking of the body and blood of Christ. In a state of mortal sin this is done only to one's condemnation.[128] So the primary prerequisite for priestly service is personal holiness; the most serious hindrance is mortal sin.

Because celebration always involves partaking of the consecrated elements, Biel feels justified in characterizing Thomas's view of unworthy celebrating on the basis of his comments about what constitutes the sin of receiving the eucharist unworthily. This is seen in Biel's discussion of the way in which some physical impurity (*immunditiam corporis*) may or may not disqualify a priest from celebrating the eucharist.[129]

One may partake unworthily by failing to meet any one of three conditions: purity of conscience, elevation of the mind, and cleanliness of the body.[130] Biel adheres to Thomas's way of relating the three: sin is the most important hindrance, secondly inattention, and finally physical impurity. Thomas proves especially influential in Biel's discussion of the ways in which nocturnal emission may pollute a priest in one or more of these respects, thus disqualifying him from celebration of the eucharist.[131] What seems most valuable about this discussion is that it provides Biel an occasion for expounding Thomas's emphasis on the fully conscious and voluntary nature of sin.[132]

Secular Involvements

At several points Biel makes it clear that there are ethical questions that concern essentially secular activities but impinge upon the clergy in a special way by virtue of considerations peculiar to the priestly office. In these contexts Biel turns to Thomas for guidance. The clergy's role in a just war, for instance, is assessed in light of Thomas's insistence that the priest may aid those who fight justly, but only by spiritual means (prayers, exhortations, absolutions): in no case may he take up the sword himself.[133]

Biel notes Thomas's general opposition to the practice of holding multiple benefices, but he goes on to report that Thomas is willing to consider exceptions based on "just necessity" or "pious usefulness," provided that these are understood in terms of common rather than private well-being.[134]

Biel shares Thomas's concern for the responsible stewardship of temporal goods committed to the Church's care. He correctly associates Thomas with his critique of bishops who divert such resources to their own use.[135] In this context Biel employs Thomas's discussion of three kinds of property held by bishops and the norms regulating the disposition of each.[136] Certain goods are strictly the bishop's own; these he may handle as he sees fit, within the boundaries of what is reasonable and proper. (In the use of his own properties a bishop, like anyone else, may sin by entertaining inordinate feelings toward them.) There are, in addition, two kinds of ecclesiastical goods of which bishops are the custodians and dispensers. (1) If he misappropriates goods that are designated for certain pious uses (*bona distincta*), he sins mortally and is obliged to restore them to those for whom they were originally intended. Other ecclesiastical properties are specifically intended for his own use. These he may use as if they were his own: he sins if he uses them immoderately or with avarice, but is not thereby obliged to make restitution. But (2) some properties are committed to his care in a more general way, with no specification of the uses to which they must be put (*bona indistincta*). Some of these may be used for his own benefit, but he commits mortal sin if he is immoderate in using them to sustain a lifestyle of luxury (Matthew 24.48–51). Yet Biel notes Thomas's reasons for holding that restitution is not necessary in this case.[137] In appropriating these goods to his own use (even excessively), the bishop commits no theft but simply makes them his own. He need not make restitution even when he sins in the misuse of what is his own.

CONCLUSIONS

Perhaps the most obvious pattern in the evidence is the sheer frequency with which Biel cites Thomas's opinion in ethical contexts. In addition, Biel only rarely misrepresents Thomas's position, and he usually agrees with him. Here as elsewhere, however, he is somewhat more likely to take issue with the reasons by which Thomas thinks a given opinion can be proved. A large part of what underlies this kind of critique is Biel's ethical positivism.

The prominent place of Thomas in Biel's ethics means that one who knows Thomas only as seen through Biel's eyes will be exposed to numerous examples of Thomas's style of ethicizing; in addition he will gain a substantial body of information about Thomas's solutions to various ethical questions. He will recognize the moderation that is typical of Thomas's approach to moral questions. He will be aware of Thomas's great sensitivity to the complexity of considerations impinging upon the moral evaluation of behavior. (A general "rule of thumb" is sometimes the most we can hope for. Prudence and common sense must then direct behavior toward achievement of the ends dictated by certain values, especially charity; but we are responsible for choosing the appropriate means toward such ends in light of concrete circumstances. The intention of the agent—in relation to that of the lawgiver—is the ultimate criterion, since only the will itself is formally good.)

Thomas is an exceedingly important source for Biel's social ethics. Biel depends on Thomas for his understanding of the role of law—divine, natural, or positive—in regulating the relations within the community. Thomas's way of restricting the state's rightful claims upon its citizens enters into Biel's analysis at a number of points, but nowhere more crucially than in relation to the doctrine of the just war. Yet Biel's presentation of Thomas's social theory is in one critical respect one-sided. He reports Thomas's use of Romans 13 to show that the sword is committed only to the magistrate, but he fails to acknowledge that, in Thomas's opinion, rebellion (not mere disobedience) is sometimes justified as a final resort against a prince who, by his unjust demands, has become little more than a robber. And when Biel reports Thomas's dictum that no one may be the judge in his own case, he provides another weapon that can easily be wielded against the victims of princely injustice who respond by resorting to violent means in their own behalf. Thomas's attitude toward revolution involves a delicate balancing of the prerogatives of legitimate authority, on the one hand, and the requirements of justice, on the other. Biel focuses on one theme to the neglect of the other: thus the balance is lost in favor of a one-sided emphasis on the sole right of the state to wield the sword.

The economic outlook that Biel borrows from Thomas (especially in connection with usury and the just price) is, to say the least, utterly medieval and anticapitalistic. Both politically and economically, then, Biel's appeal to Thomas is designed to reinforce a premodern, "reactionary" social ethic.

Finally, Biel uses Thomas as a resource for holding priests to a rigorous standard of personal holiness: by celebrating the eucharist in a state of mortal sin, a priest brings additional guilt upon himself, and he may not avoid the issue simply by refusing to celebrate. This kind of sacerdotal rigorism might easily provide the occasion for a bad case of "the scruples," especially since it is not balanced by Thomas's sense of the way in which divine grace enables one to live above mortal sin.

SIX

CHURCH, MINISTRY, AND WORSHIP

The preceding chapter has shown that Thomas's importance for Biel's theology centers largely in his analysis of certain duties arising from membership in a human community. Already it is clear that, for Biel and Thomas alike, the notion of Christendom is presupposed. In a Christian society, it is above all the Church that constitutes the community in which man exists ethically, that is, religiously. Divine law underlies human law. What is morally wrong is an offense not only against the neighbor or the state but also against the ultimate Sovereign: thus it is not only wrong but also sinful. This convergence of the ethical and religious dimensions defines the context in which Biel finds Thomas's insights most valuable.

The nature of the Church may be understood, in part, by comparing it to the Old Testament regime that it superseded and, in that light, defining the prerogatives of its ordained ministry.[1] The inner life of this Church finds its clearest focus in worship and prayer. After noting the ways in which Thomas helps Biel to unravel this complex of interrelated issues, we will be ready to examine Thomas's massive contribution to Biel's understanding of the community's sacramental life.

CHURCH AND MINISTRY

"If anyone says to you, 'Behold, here is Christ, or there,' do not believe him" (Matthew 24.23). Biel notes that Thomas interprets these words of Christ as a prophecy of the universality of his Church.[2] "Christ" must be understood in a broad sense as "the Catholic Faith." So when someone tries to restrict Christianity to some particular place—"here" or "there"—he is not to be believed. Furthermore, the Catholic faith is no secret teaching (in contrast to the heresies). Once proclaimed, it is like the lightning that comes from the east and appears even in the west (Matthew 24.27); it is both public and universal.[3]

This catholicity marks one of the most striking contrasts between the new community of faith and the old. Biel turns to Thomas at several points in his discussion of the relation of the Church to her Levitical predecessor. He treats the ceremonial law of the Jews, for instance, in great detail, borrowing Thomas's account of the derivation of the term "ceremony," and associating himself with Thomas's description of its function in Jewish religious life.[4] Originally the term arose either in connection with the gifts offered to the goddess of fruits, Ceres (*Cereris munera*), or from the cult that sprang up in the suburb of Rome, Caere, when the Romans' relics and icons (*sacra Romanorum*) were taken there for safekeeping during the siege of Rome by the Gauls. The term denotes exterior acts of worship by which one acknowledges one's submission to God. Thus Biel avails himself of Thomas's discussion only in very general terms. He invokes Thomas's etymology as well as his statement of the most basic function of ceremony in the religious life; he does not show how Thomas relates moral and ceremonial precepts or how he defines the purpose of each.

Biel follows Thomas in citing the words of pseudo-Dionysius (and of Hebrews 10.1) to show that the eternal benefits promised to a few during the time of the shadow are distinctly promised to all under the dispensation of the new law.[5] The superiority of the new economy to the old is further illustrated by Thomas's account of the sharp contrast between the law of fear and the law of love:

> The new law had its beginning in a manifestation of divine charity, because the new testament was sealed in the shedding of the blood of Jesus Christ, which was the sign of the most perfect

> love. But the old law had its beginning in the manifestation of divine power, which arouses fear. Even in the giving of this law terror seized the hearers because of the lightning, voices, and thunder, so that they said, "Let not the Lord speak to us, lest perhaps we should die." So also the old law induced men to obedience through the threat of punishment, but the new law through the expectation of the blessings which it offered.[6]

This contrast is grounded, Biel reports, in a consideration that lays the basis on which we may recognize a certain development in God's way of dealing with mankind. It was fitting that the human race in its infancy, so to speak, should be driven through a fear of punishment. Later on mankind was ready to progress toward the good on the strength of the motive power of love. "For just as fear is a path to love, so is the old law to the new."[7] (What hovers in the background of this citation, clearly, is the important hermeneutical principle that God's revelation is always accommodated to the capacities of those to whom it is given.)

Expressive of this fundamental difference between the old and new economies—between shadow and reality—is the denial of the power of the keys to the Old Testament priesthood.[8]

In addition to the jurisdictional power of the keys, priests under the new law possess a consecrational power with respect to the sacraments. These powers may be abused, but even so they are objectively inherent in the status to which ordination elevates the priest.[9] If a priest, for instance, intends to consecrate the eucharist in order to ridicule it or use it for some evil purpose, his sin does not eradicate his power to confect the sacrament.[10] Thus Biel reflects the anti-Donatist emphasis in Thomas's sacramental theology: the objective efficacy of sacerdotal powers is not dependent upon the morality of the priest.

Conspicuously absent from Biel's discussion is any thorough account of Thomas's interpretation of the authority and functions of the episcopacy. Only in passing, and in very general terms, does Biel allude to Thomas's belief that certain (unspecified) functions are properly reserved to the bishops.[11]

PRAYER AND WORSHIP

Far more thoroughgoing is Biel's account of Thomas's doctrine of prayer. He properly appeals to Thomas in defense of the claim that prayer is an act of the reason (not, e.g., of the appetitive powers).[12] Since prayer, in its broadest sense, is an appeal to one's superior, Biel joins Thomas in stipulating that prayer is appropriate to any being who has both a superior and the use of reason.[13] In the text that Biel is following (*S.T.* II–II q. 83 a. 10 *corp.*), Thomas's argument seems to exclude from the class of those to whom prayer is suitable only God himself and nonrational beings. (Although Psalm 146.9 speaks of the ravens who call upon God, Biel notes that Thomas interprets *invocare* here as a reference not to the specific act of praying but rather to the natural desire by which all things, including the subrational and even the inanimate, tend toward God.) Biel infers that Thomas does not mean to exclude even demons, who do, after all, meet these two conditions. Thomas does not speak directly to the question of whether prayer is an act appropriate to demons, but the evidence in his commentary on the third book of *Sentences* suggests that he would probably deny the view that Biel attributes to him. One of Thomas's reasons for denying that prayer is appropriate to dumb animals is his thesis that "they are not sharers in the blessed life, which is the main thing that is requested in prayer."[14] In view of Thomas's repudiation of Origen's claim that even the demons will eventually come to salvation, the same objection excludes demons as fit subjects of the act of prayer.[15]

Turning to the nature of prayer itself, Biel observes that Thomas distinguishes among four species of prayer (I Timothy 2.1): supplications, prayers, intercessions, and thanksgivings.[16] Three conditions are necessary for prayer. First, there must be an ascent of the mind to God, and this is implied by the term prayer (*oratio*) in its proper sense. Secondly, there must be a petition addressed to God, which may be definite (*postulatio*) or general (*supplicatio*). Thirdly, there is the reason for which the prayer is offered, and this again is twofold. With respect to God, the reason for praying is his holiness or perfection, which corresponds to the term supplication (*obsecratio*). With respect to the one who prays, the reason for praying is gratitude, which results in thanksgiving (*gratiarum actio*). By thanksgiving, in turn, we merit even greater benefits. Thus within the broader rubric of prayer (*oratio*) are included two kinds of intercessions, in addition to supplications and thanksgivings.

A comparison with the text that Biel is following suggests that his use of Thomas's schema is deficient in two respects. First, Thomas speaks of these four not as separate kinds but as parts of prayer. Secondly, Thomas uses the term "insinuation" as referring to an indefinite petition or to a mere statement of fact, and this drops out of Biel's summary altogether. Speaking of thanksgiving, on the other hand, Biel inserts the claim that we merit the preservation and increase of the benefits for which we give thanks; this point is not explicit in Thomas's discussion, but it is not by any means alien to his general thesis that by giving thanks for the benefits which we have received we merit even greater blessings. (The preservation or increase of one benefit seems to qualify as another—and greater—benefit.)

Prayer may be either silent or audible.[17] Thomas argues, according to Biel, that although purely mental prayer is sufficient as far as God is concerned, vocal prayer is useful for a number of reasons. The mind is excited to a more intimate knowledge and love of God by external signs. (Biel omits Thomas's warning that vocalizing one's prayer might turn out to be harmful rather than helpful and should, in that event, be discontinued.) Praying audibly helps to illuminate the mind and to hold it back from inattentiveness. Vocal prayer is a more complete response to the One from whom man receives not just his mind but everything he has—including his voice. Vocal prayer gives expression to a certain overflowing of devotion from the soul to the body. Finally, it is obvious that silent prayer cannot provide instruction for one's fellow worshippers, as can audible prayer.

Biel associates himself with Thomas's statement that prayer is answered only when its petition is made piously.[18] This condition includes all things that are required on the part of the one who offers the prayer, including—in addition to confidence, humility, and the right intention—attentiveness. Biel invokes Thomas's analysis of the three things that may be suggested by the term "attentiveness" in connection with prayer.[19] The one who prays may pay attention to the words of his prayer, or to their meaning, or to the immediate or ultimate end in view (the petition or God himself). In one sense or another, attentiveness is a necessary condition of efficacious prayer. If the mind wanders involuntarily, however, one's prayer is not deprived of its fruit.[20] Thomas's only exception to this maxim is that the refreshing of the mind is one effect of prayer that is prevented by inattentiveness. This exception is expressed in Biel's report that, according to Thomas, "actual" attention—not merely the power of the attention with which one originally began to pray—is necessary in order for the mind to be refreshed.[21]

How long should a prayer be continued? Biel responds to this question by citing Thomas's advice that it is useful to continue praying only to a certain point of diminishing returns, at which the act no longer has the effect of arousing interior devotion and desire toward God. Beyond this point, at which the distractions of fatigue become a hindrance to attentiveness, the prayer should not be continued.[22] (Prayer, after all, is not an end in itself.)

The exemplary prayer that Christ taught his disciples is interpreted in Biel's *Expositio* by the light of Thomas's exegesis. Biel appropriates Thomas's view of the way in which the sequence of petitions in the Lord's Prayer corresponds to the appropriate order of desires on the part of the one who prays.[23] First comes the end and then those things which are ordained for its sake. Now the end is God, to whom our affection tends in two ways. (1) Since God is the highest good per se, we love God in himself by willing his glory and perfection above all things. But (2) God is the highest good not only *in himself* but also *for us:* thus we are directed toward him, secondly, by our desire to enjoy the highest good. To love God in the first of these ways is to love him because it is just to do so; to love him in the second way is to love ourselves in him. The first thing to be desired is the end considered in itself: "Hallowed be thy name." The second is the means, by which we love ourselves in God (and thus affirm God not just as the end but precisely as our end): "Thy kingdom come. . . ."

We are directed toward this end, moreover, in two ways. (1) Intrinsically (*per se*), we are directed to God through the merit that is attached to obedience to God's commands: "Let your will be done— as in heaven, so on earth." And the means by which we are enabled to merit our final end is that which sustains life (in both its physical and its spiritual dimensions): "Give us today our daily bread." (2) Extrinsically (*per accidens*), we are directed toward beatitude by the removal of any impediments that would prevent us from obtaining it. Of these there are three. The first is sin, which directly bars one from the Kingdom: "And forgive us our debts as we also forgive our debtors." The second is temptation, which indirectly hinders the required obedience by leading the soul into sin: "And lead us not into temptation." Finally, we are held back from the kingdom by the present punishment of past sins, the distracting difficulty of earthly life: "But deliver us from evil."

In addition to this interpretation of the order observed in the Lord's Prayer, Biel borrows from Thomas's exegesis at two specific points. When we ask that God's will be done on earth as in heaven, he suggests, we are asking that just as every citizen of heaven conforms his will to God's, so may men do in their earthly dwelling.[24] And the request for daily bread must be understood both physically and sacramentally. By asking for corporeal bread, we ask for all things that are necessary to sustain the life of the body; by asking for the eucharistic bread, we ask for all the other sacraments that are required in order to preserve the life of the Spirit.[25]

The Christian's prayers are heard not only by God but also by the blessed in heaven, who are elevated to the ultimate dignity of sharing with God in the work of succoring those who cry out for divine help. Biel is correct in ascribing this view to Thomas.[26]

We have already noted, in connection with the modes of prayer, that Biel associates himself with Thomas's thesis that we should worship God in a manner suitable to the psychosomatic nature that we have received from him. The same theme recurs when Biel cites

Thomas's application of John of Damascus' dictum that we offer to God a twofold adoration (corporeal and spiritual) because we are composed of a twofold nature (sensible and intellectual). One kind of adoration is spiritual, consisting in an interior devotion of the mind, while the other is corporeal, consisting of an exterior humiliation of the body. In any act of adoration, what is internal is of greater significance than what is external; hence the external act is done for the sake of the interior, which it both expresses and arouses: "by the signs of humility which we exhibit corporeally, our affection is incited to be in submission to God, since it is natural for us to proceed from the sensible to the intelligible."[27] The importance of this citation lies not only in its vindication of a place for the physical in spiritual worship, but above all in its suggestion of the way in which the wholistic tendencies of St. Thomas's anthropology (and especially the empirical bent of his epistemology) can be used to safeguard the dignity of the body against the assault of Neoplatonic or Manichaean dualism.

Yet Biel, like Thomas, is concerned about the problem of superstition and idolatry in medieval worship, and he turns to Thomas for guidance in spelling out the boundaries beyond which adoration of the cross[28] or of the host[29] verges on idolatry.

Finally, Biel rightly associates with Thomas the view that each worshipper is bound to give an offering for the support of the priests. (In the same text, however, Biel claims that Thomas is among those who contend that bishops may enforce this duty, whereas in fact Thomas clearly states that voluntariness is part of what is implied by the term "oblation.")[30] This offering must not be something that has been obtained by lawless means; otherwise the Church's witness against sin would be compromised.[31] On the part of the worshipper, moreover, sin is involved in making any offering, such as a broken or counterfeit coin, that expresses irreverence toward the sacrament and contempt of its Author.[32] Biel's example is not Thomas's, but it is a fair application of Thomas's oft-repeated insistence that one may sin through irreverence, negligence, or contempt.

CONCLUSIONS

Biel's use of Thomas for liturgical purposes will not be fully apparent until we have examined Thomas's place in Biel's sacramental theology. On the basis of the evidence surveyed in the present chapter, two generalizations seem warranted.

First, Biel's portrayal of Thomas's ecclesiology is quite brief and superficial. The themes that Biel borrows from Thomas are, for the most part, utterly conventional—the notion of the Church's universality, the anti-Donatist conception of sacerdotal powers, the interpretation of Old and New Testaments in light of the shadow/reality motif, and so on. It may well be argued that, in an age of religious turmoil and uncertainty, what one most needs to learn from Thomas's doctrine of the Church is a clear notion of the authority of the ecclesiastical hierarchy, focused in the teaching office of the bishops. This could not be gained from reading Biel's academic theology. (Yet Biel's own understanding of ecclesiastical authority is by any standard quite conservative.[33] There is no reason to suppose that the virtual absence of Thomas from Biel's ecclesiology marks a gap that urgently needs to be filled.)

In connection with worship and prayer, secondly, what seems most striking about Biel's gleanings from Thomas is the wholism that undergirds their common insistence that one's corporeality may not be excluded from the totality of one's response to God. Biel correctly invokes Thomas's authority against any form of dualism that can find no positive role for the body in religious experience.

SEVEN

SACRAMENTS

In his inventory of authorities cited in each of the four books of the *Collectorium*, Wilhelm Ernst called attention to a certain imbalance in the distribution of Biel's references to St. Thomas. The frequency of Thomas citations rises from 37 in Book I to 39 in Book II to 77 in Book III; over half of the total number of references to Thomas, however, are found in Book IV, where Biel cites Thomas, according to Ernst's enumeration, 236 times.[1] In the present study this pattern is reflected in the length of chapters V and VII. The fourth book of Lombard's *Sentences* deals generally with the sacraments, and a wide variety of ethical problems comes up for discussion in connection with the sacrament of penance. It is in sacramental and ethical contexts, then, that Biel finds St. Thomas's insight most valuable in the *Collectorium*. A similar pattern may be discerned in the *Expositio*, where Biel calls on Thomas's help in expounding both the meaning of the liturgy and the moral prerequisites to a worthy celebrating or receiving of the eucharist.

Biel's sacramental theology is informed by Thomist perspectives[2] in five areas: (1) the nature of a sacrament as such, (2) eucharist, (3) baptism (in relation to circumcision), (4) penance, and (5) confirmation.

SACRAMENTS IN GENERAL

Biel begins his attempt to define the term "sacrament" by appropriating Thomas's analysis of the similarity between the sacramental sign and the grace that it signifies.[3] He invokes Thomas's authority in behalf of the thesis that the required "natural similitude" between a corporeal sign and a spiritual reality is not to be interpreted as a mutual sharing in the same quality: "for in this sense corporeal or sensible things are not similar to spiritual things, since no quality is the same in both according to species."[4] The similarity, rather, is one of proportionalities, such that the relation between *a* and *b* (both corporeal) is somehow similar to the relation between *x* and *y* (both spiritual). Yet there is no direct correspondence between *a* and *x* or between *b* and *y*. Biel illustrates this kind of similarity with Thomas's example: the role of water in removing corporeal stains is in a certain way like the cleansing function of baptismal grace in relation to spiritual stains.[5] The similarity is not between water and grace per se but between these two relations. Thus Biel correctly reports Thomas's opinion that some similarity between the sign (*signum*) and the thing signified (*res*) is implied in the very notion of a sacrament, and he is very precise in showing how Thomas defines this similarity by reference to the notion of proper proportionality ($a{:}b :: x{:}y$). In so doing, Biel makes contact with a basic component of Thomas's doctrine of analogous predication, but his develoment of that theme is, from a Thomist point of view, quite incomplete.[6]

Among sacramental signs, according to Biel, some are demonstrative (signifying things present), some are rememorative (signifying things past), while others are proleptic (signifying things yet to come). Biel claims to find these temporal references, implicitly (*sententialiter*), in Thomas's discussion.[7] In this way he makes it clear that he means to interpret Thomas's meaning, not just to quote his words. And it turns out that his interpretation is altogether justified. For the temporal distinctions to which he points are suggested, in the first place, by the prefixes of the terms that

Biel borrows from Thomas (*signa demonstrativa, rememorativa, prenostica*), and Thomas's examples for each kind of sign do conform to the temporal pattern that Biel sees implicit in the typology. Baptism is a rememorative sign, because it recalls the death of Christ. It is with reference to their present effect in the soul that sacramental signs are called demonstrative. And sacraments of the old law, in looking forward to the economy of grace, were totally prognosticative, while the sacraments of the new law retain a reference to the future insofar as they signify the end of the believer's sanctification, eternal glory.[8]

Such signs have an efficacy in bestowing on the soul the grace that they signify, and this is derived, in different ways, from three sources. Biel is able to ground this threefold schema in Thomas's teaching that God is himself the principal cause of the sacramental effect (justification), while Christ's passion is its meritorious cause, and the Church's faith, by linking up with the principal cause through a certain continuation of Christ's passion, becomes an instrumental cause of the sacraments' efficacy.[9]

While dismissing Thomas's attempted proofs, Biel agrees with his conclusion that to create *ex nihilo* is proper to God alone and is not communicable to anything created.[10] Yet there must be something about a sacrament that is causal in an active sense: just as a drug (*medicamentum*) is that by which something is drugged (*medicatur*) or an adornment (*ornamentum*) is that by which something is adorned (*ornatur*), so a sacrament (*sacramentum*) is that by whose action something is made holy (*sacratur*).[11] By definition, then, the sacraments must in some manner cause what they signify. Biel summarizes, in four sets of interrelated propositions, Thomas's understanding of the sense in which sacraments are the causes of grace.[12]

> (1) A sacrament is more than a *causa sine qua non* of the grace imparted through it, because such a cause by its presence removes an obstacle to the producing of the effect, but has no active role in producing it. The causality that enters into the definition of a sacrament, however, must be taken in an active sense: what is necessary but not active in the production of an effect

will be causal only accidentally (*per accidens*) and hence will not be part of the definition of the cause.

(2) Yet sacraments do not cause grace directly. What they immediately effect is not grace but a disposition that is required in order to receive grace. Two things result from receiving any sacrament. The first (*sacramentum et res*) is the sacramental character, or, in those sacraments that do not confer a character, some adornment of the soul analogous to a character. The second (*res tantum*) is grace. With respect to the first, a sacrament is an efficient cause, instrumentally though not principally. With respect to the second, however, it is only a "dispositive cause of grace" (*causa dispositiva gratiae*). What it directly causes is the requisite disposition (rather than grace itself). Even this limited causality, moreover, is instrumental, not primary.

(3) In order to serve in this causal capacity, the sacrament must have some spiritual power in addition to any power that it possesses naturally (as a material entity); a corporeal being can have no natural competence to produce a spiritual effect.

(4) Although this power is something that exists independently of that in which it inheres (*res absoluta*), it is a kind of incomplete being (*ens incompletum*), like motion. As an instrumental cause, its efficacy extends to that which exceeds its purely natural capacity; it acts not by virtue of its own form but merely as moved by God, whose instrument it is. Thus its causal virtue is not "fixed in its own nature" (*fixum in natura*) but must continually be received anew from the principal cause. (Biel adds that, according to Thomas, this supernatural power is given germinally [*inchoative*] in the institution of a sacrament and completely [*completive*] in its use.)

A comparison with the corresponding texts in Thomas's commentary on the fourth book of the *Sentences*[13] reveals that Biel's citations are scrupulously accurate, including lengthy passages that are quoted almost verbatim. Then Biel points to the contrast between Thomas's opinion and the doctrine that he ascribes to Bonaventure, Scotus, and Occam, among others, placing such emphasis upon God's will, ordinance, and covenant that little is left of sacramental causality as something inherent in the sacrament itself: even Thomas's notion of a restricted "instrumental" and "dispositive" causality finds no place in a doctrine that admits no causal medium, properly speaking, between the giver and the recipient of grace. Thus the sacrament becomes—not in itself but by virtue of God's ordinance—a cause only in the sense of a *causa sine qua non.*[14] Here, as Biel is himself aware, synthesis is out of the question: "The proof of one opinion is the disproof of the other."[15] And while some of Biel's conclusions are consistent with Thomas's view—he grants, for example, that sacraments cause the sacramental effect, but not by virtue of anything intrinsic to them naturally[16]—in the end his understanding of what is involved in this kind of causality leads him to reject two key elements of Thomas's teaching.

Biel denies, first of all, that what the sacraments effect is a prior disposition for the infusion of grace.[17] He notes that Thomas equates this disposition with the character imprinted upon the soul in the nonrepeatable sacraments (and with the "adornment" bestowed in the others). Then he argues that since the character or adornment may exist in one who lacks justifying grace (as in one who receives the sacrament insincerely or falls back into sin, or, even more dramatically, is one of the damned), and since grace may be bestowed without being preceded by such a character (as in circumcision under the Old Law), it makes no sense to say that the character effected by a sacrament is a necessary prior disposition for the infusion of grace.[18]

Biel denies, secondly, Thomas's thesis concerning the supernatural potency (*virtus*) by which sacraments are able to function causally with respect to the impression of a character (instrumentally) and then with respect to the infusion of grace (dispositively).[19] His massive argument against Thomas at this point includes a rebuttal of the claim that such a power is bestowed germinally in the institution but fully in the use of the sacraments. For at the time when Christ instituted the sacraments (prior to his ascension), the sacraments that we now celebrate did not exist, and what does not exist can receive nothing—germinally or otherwise.[20] And since "a certain form of words" is integral to the essence of the sacrament, Biel finds it equally impossible to specify the point in their "use" at which the power is bestowed. Until the last syllable of the consecration formula is uttered, the sacrament does not exist. But in the first instant after the last syllable is uttered, it passes out of existence; there is nothing left to be the subject of any such sacramental virtue.[21]

The incongruity of the second half of this argument is remarkable. If pushed to its limits, it seems to imply that the sacrament itself never exists at all, either because the consecrational formula has not been fully pronounced or conversely, and ironically, because it has been. When the last syllable is uttered, to be sure, the *words* no longer exist, but Thomas does not believe, as Biel presupposes, that the primary subject of the sacramental power is any word or words as such. It is rather the sacrament itself, which is effected by the instrumentality of certain words and on which, when it is used by the faithful, a certain supernatural power is conferred. Thus the fact that the words cease to exist at a certain point does not imply that nothing remains in which such a power may inhere. The first half of the argument—that this morning's eucharist, for instance, did not yet exist when Christ instituted the sacrament and thus could receive nothing, even "germinally," at that time—is only slightly less implausible. On Thomas's principles, future contingents are known by God in an eternal present.[22] Because it was principally as God, not as man, that Christ instituted the sacraments,[23] it may be said that this morning's eucharist already had a certain kind of existence at the time of the Last Supper—in potency, but also in the knowledge and intention of the one who instituted the eucharist as a sacrament.

Before discussing the way in which sacraments of the Old Law conferred grace, Biel reports what he claims is Thomas's manner of distinguishing between two ways in which a sign may confer its effect.[24] When grace is conferred by virtue of the sacramental sign itself (*ex opere operato*), all that is required of the recipient is that he place no obstacle (*obex*) between himself and the gift. But when grace is conferred sacramentally in view of something positive on the recipient's part (*ex opere operantis*), the mere absence of barriers will not suffice: in addition, he must exhibit a "good movement or inward devotion" (*bonus motus seu devotio interior*) toward God, which is in some sense meritorious of the grace bestowed.

In the immediate context, Biel does not characterize Thomas's position on the question at hand (whether Old Testament sacraments conferred grace *ex opere operato*). He merely cites Thomas's analysis of the two ways in which a sign may confer what it signifies, and he admits that Thomas's handling of that distinction is not entirely satisfactory (*licet satis obscure*). Perhaps that is why Biel renders Thomas's opinion in light of Scotus's dictum that "a sacrament . . . confers grace by virtue of the work performed (*ex virtute operis operati*), so that no good interior motion is required, which would merit grace: but it is enough if the one who receives it places no obstacle in the way."[25] In the text that Biel claims to be following, Thomas's distinction is hardly recognizable as the basis of Biel's claim that a sacrament, as an *opus operatum,* confers grace apart from any subjective movement of the soul toward God. As one term of a purely logical distinction, of course, *opus operatum* makes no reference to inner faith and charity; yet, in following Scotus, Biel obscures Thomas's emphasis on the actual sacramental bond between the *opus operatum* (considered objectively) and the *opus operantis* (considered subjectively)—or between outer work and inner faith. In the text that Biel claims to be citing, Thomas does not suggest that the mere absence of obstacles is sufficient for the bestowal of sacramental grace *ex opere operato.* With the sole exception of circumcision, which is a special case because of its continuity with Christian baptism, Thomas denies that sacraments of the Old Law conferred grace *ex opere operato.* Here, as he typically does, Thomas speaks of sacramental efficacy *ex opere operato* not as a way of getting around the need for some inner movement toward God (except in the case of infants, who are beneficiaries of the Church's faith), but rather as a way of refuting Donatist attitudes concerning the efficacy of sacraments performed by evil priests.[26]

Here it is clearly not a question of the lack of some subjective prerequisite on the part of one who *receives* the benefit conferred by a sacrament. Biel misrepresents Thomas's opinion, then, because he reads Thomas through the eyes of Scotus, although Scotus himself does not claim to be offering an interpretation of Thomas at this point.

When Biel correlates the number of the sacraments with the various kinds of benefits that they confer, he avails himself of the alternative formulae reported by Thomas.[27] These materials are of considerable interest in their own right, but since Biel does not reveal which schema Thomas prefers, this text adds little to his composite account of Thomas's teaching.

The chief benefit of the sacraments is the remission of sin. In connection with the "sacraments of the law of nature" (*sacramenta legis naturae*), which were in force during the interim between Adam's fall and the giving of the Mosaic law, Biel gives a very close account of Thomas's undestanding of the relative functions of faith and sacrament in the remission of original sin.[28] Thomas, as Biel reports, holds that "faith alone without any external sign" (*sola fides sine exteriori signo*) was sufficient for children, but what was required was not just a habit but an act of faith in the child's behalf. (This was most appropriately done by the parents to whose care the child was committed and through whom, after all, he contracted original sin.) Even in adults faith was sufficient, although genuine faith always sought to express itself in external works. But the remission of guilt was effected by virtue of this inner faith, not by virtue of the outer works to which it gave rise. External signs were, accordingly, expressive of the individual's devotion or zeal for God's glory; they were not included in what was strictly required by the precept.

Parallel to this treatment of what was required of one who received the sacraments of the law of nature is Biel's discussion of one way in which Thomas categorizes the sacraments of the New Law.[29] In some of the sacraments no overt act on the part of the recipient is required (beyond the removal of impediments to the sacramental effect); baptism, confirmation, eucharist, ordination, and extreme unction fall under this heading. The validity of such a sacrament requires, in addition to the proper form of words, the use of some material element (bread and wine in the eucharist, water in baptism, chrism in confirmation and ordination). In the other sacraments (penance and matrimony), the sacrament's validity depends in part upon some definite act by the one who receives its benefit. In these two sacraments, the act of the recipient functions as the sacramental matter; no additional material element is required in order for the sacrament to be valid.

In discussing whether the grace bestowed sacramentally differs from the grace of the virtues and gifts, Biel traces the main outlines of Thomas's way of conceiving the relationships between the essence and powers of the soul, on the one hand, and between grace and the virtues, on the other.[30] What is bestowed by the sacraments is justifying grace (*gratia gratum faciens*), which Thomas, according to Biel, distinguishes from charity both in itself and with respect to its subject.

> For according to him grace inheres in the essence of the soul and charity in its affective power, which is really distinguished from the essence of the soul. Consequently he says: "Just as the powers flow from the essence, so do the virtues (which are in the soul's power) flow from grace (which is in its essence), and they are distinguished according to the various acts which perfect the powers." Consequently he says that from the grace which is in the soul's essence flow certain virtues to correct defects arising from sin, and these are called sacramental graces, since it is to these that the sacraments are directly ordained. And since grace, which has to do with the essence of the soul, cannot be without the virtues, but can be without sacramental grace, it follows that the grace which the sacrament contains differs from the grace which is in the virtues and gifts.[31]

Biel's paraphrase is quite faithful to Thomas's intention (and, at several points, even to the precise language in which Thomas expresses himself). But he rejects both Thomas's distinction between the soul's essence and powers and—therefore—his distinction between grace and charity. The powers of the soul, in Biel's view, constitute its essence; justifying grace is the same in reality as charity.[32]

What one receives from a valid sacrament is not only grace but also—at least in those that are not repeatable—a character impressed indelibly upon the soul. Biel associates himself with Thomas's opinion that the sacramental character is an absolute quality of the soul (not merely a relationship in which it stands).[33] But he insists that this conclusion is based not on rational arguments but on the authority of Church and Scripture.[34]

Conferring such benefits, the sacraments may be instituted only by God. The Church has no power to institute additional sacraments or to change the ones that were instituted by Christ.[35] Biel is correct in associating Thomas with the view that only Christ (in his divinity) possessed the power to institute the sacraments of new economy. For some reason, though, he is confused about Thomas's position regarding the promulgation of the sacraments.[36] He claims that Thomas joins Scotus, among others, in holding that all sacraments were not only instituted but also promulgated by Christ. In the text that Biel seems to have before him, however, Thomas clearly argues that, while all sacraments were instituted by Christ, the promulgation of some of them (extreme unction and confirmation) was reserved to the Apostles.

EUCHARIST

Among the seven sacraments, the eucharist is central to the worshipping life of the community and thus to Biel's theological concern. Since Biel invokes Thomas's authority more frequently in relation to eucharistic questions than in his treatment of any other sacrament, we will look first at Thomas's contribution to Biel's understanding of what happens when the faithful gather at the Lord's table.

The Eucharist as a Sacrament

Biel makes use of Thomas's interpretation of the various names of this sacrament.[37] The etymology of "eucharist" (*eu* = *bonum, charis* = *gratia*) makes it clear that not only is grace made manifest in this sacrament but the fount of grace—Christ himself—is contained in it. The terms "sacrifice" and "host" recall both the sacrifice at Calvary and the reoffering of the Son to the Father in the mass. "Synaxis" (or "communion") points to the fact that the same Christ is consumed by all the faithful. Biel goes beyond Thomas in his exegesis of the term "viaticum" (provision for the journey of life, understood especially as a provision for the wayfarer's journey from this life to the next). Thomas is somewhat more forceful in relating the eucharist to the last end of man—beatitude—which is to be attained through the power of the blood of Christ contained in the eucharist. Biel explains further that this sacrament is called *viaticum* both because of its Author (who has already entered the Father's presence) and because of its recipient (the *viator* who is about to follow Christ into heavenly beatitude). Biel's interpretation is not exactly Thomas's, but it is hard to see how Biel can be accused of doing violence to Thomas's intention. Thomas refers *viaticum* to the last end to be attained by means of what the sacrament offers; Biel does not err in understanding this end as the bliss into which Christ has entered and toward which the Christian pilgrim (*viator*) moves in the strength provided by the heavenly food of the eucharist. Indeed, Biel's elaboration is a faithful gloss on Thomas's formula. The only discrepancy in content is found in Biel's allusion to the bread as that by which the *viator* is sustained on his journey; Thomas speaks rather of the shed blood of Christ. But since Thomas believes that the whole Christ is present under either species,[38] Biel's shift of emphasis here does not destroy anything that is essential to the point Thomas wants to make.

Biel very carefully summarizes the four arguments (*rationes*) by which Thomas tries to show that the eucharist was instituted at the most appropriate time.[39] Biel agrees that the timing—after the Supper and immediately before the Passion—was indeed the most fitting, and he reports Thomas's reasons precisely and in detail. But in the end Biel's voluntarism gets the best of him again. At best, he concludes, Thomas is playing at child's games; his arguments are really quite beside the point. The divine will was pleased to have the sacrament instituted at that particular point, but not *because* it was the most suitable. The case is precisely the converse: the appropriateness of the time of the institution is constitued by the sheer fact that it was pleasing to the divine will. As Biel puts it: "We must seek no prior cause of the divine will."[40] At best, then, Thomas's proofs are secondary; ultimately they are irrelevant. His conclusion is affirmed, but his method strikes Biel as fallacious. (This exemplifies a now-familiar pattern in Biel's response to Thomas.)

On the other hand, Biel is open to Thomas's logical analysis when it is applied to what we may call the human side of such questions: what evokes his critique of Thomas's method is any suggestion that God's sovereign acts toward us are conditioned by the force of some logic to which his will is subject. For instance, Biel is glad to associate himself with Thomas's analysis of the "reasons" why the sinner needs a sacrifice (at Calvary and in the eucharist), but he makes it clear that what is at stake is not a norm that binds the divine will but an account of the benefits available only through the sacrifice freely ordained by God. For the initial remission of guilt, for preservation in the grace by which he continues to adhere to the Source of his peace and salvation,and finally for the total union of his spirit with God, fallen man needs a sacrifice.[41] At this level, Biel makes Thomas's "reasons" his own.

Ex parte sacerdotis: Consecration

At a number of points the role of the priest who confects the eucharist provides an occasion for Biel to draw on Thomas's insights. He endorses Thomas's analysis of the four constituents of a valid consecration.[42] In order to consecrate the bread and the wine, there must be a suitable minister: only a priest may consecrate. "Suitable" is not to be construed as "good" or "worthy," however. Biel makes it clear that neither he nor Thomas wishes to deny the power of even an evil priest to consecrate a valid sacrament.[43] Secondly, there must be the due intention on the priest's part: he must intend to consecrate the bread and wine for sacramental purposes. Thirdly, the requisite matter—bread and wine—must be used. Finally, the form instituted by Christ—"This is my body"—is indispensable. If a priest uses this formula and the appropriate matter, with a proper intention, he confects the eucharist, even if the remainder of the liturgy is omitted. (Liturgical forms, after all, vary according to time and place, but the words of Christ—"*Hoc est corpus meum*"—are used universally.) But Biel joins Thomas in holding that although the eucharist may be consecrated without observing the entire liturgy, the priest sins gravely in such a case by showing contempt for the Church and its rite.[44]

What Biel places in sharp relief is Thomas's commitment to a high view of the instrumental efficacy of the consecrational formula. He notes that Thomas rejects the opinion of those who claim that the power of the priest's words is to be understood not as something inhering in the words themselves but as a power extrinsic to them (such that, by the terms of God's ordinance, the formula serves only as a *causa sine qua non* of the consecration).[45] On the contrary, as Biel reports, Thomas holds that the words of Christ, when used by a priest with the requisite intention, possess an active (though instrumental) power to convert the elements of bread and wine into the body and blood of Christ. In the other sacraments, as Biel has already made clear, Thomas affirms that there is a supernatural power that contributes instrumentally to causing the sacramental effect (e.g., the character or adornment of the soul, which serves as a prior disposition for the reception of grace). In the eucharist, this power is bestowed, instrumentally, by the words of consecration. They are the words of Christ, after all; they are spoken in the person and at the command of the One from whom they receive this instrumental efficacy.[46] Biel's summary is flawless, but he rejects Thomas's opinion on the basis of an argument similar to the one he uses to refute Thomas's more general claim that there is a power in each sacrament by which its effect is produced.[47] Here again Biel's concern is to safeguard the unique causality of God in directly producing the sacramental effect. Biel repudiates Thomas's notion of an intermediary (the instrumental potency of certain words) between the principal Cause and his effects, because he fears that such a doctrine will call into question the sole efficacy of the divine power. In this particular case, Biel argues that no created power could effect the eucharistic conversion, which involves the annihilation, both materially and formally, of the bread: to destroy in this radical sense—no less than to create *ex nihilo*—is proper to the uncreated power of God alone.[48]

Biel agrees with Thomas, however, in excluding the words "take and eat" (*accipite et comedite*) from the scope of the formula for consecrating the bread.[49] For these words pertain not to the bread's transubstantiation into Christ's body (which is essential to the sacrament as such) but rather to the subsequent use of the sacrament after the consecration is completed. "Take and eat" presupposes that transubstantiation has already occurred and thus cannot be part of the formula by which it is effected. A valid confection of the eucharist, therefore, does not require that the priest add the words "take and eat" after saying "this is my body." The eucharist is confected when the priest applies the shorter formula to bread and wine with the requisite intention, even if the faithful do not then "take and eat." The use (or nonuse) of a sacrament is irrelevant to its validity.[50]

Similarly, Biel turns to Thomas for guidance in determining the boundaries of the formula for consecrating the chalice.[51] The words, "of the new and eternal covenant which is poured out for you and for many for the remission of sins," are integral to the formula ("This is the chalice of my blood"), since they constitute a series of determinations of the predicate, "my blood." Hence the omission of these words renders the consecration itself defective. But the clause beginning with the words "As often as you do this" pertains not to the consecration but to the use of what has already been consecrated. (Biel interprets the phrase "new and eternal" by means of a distinction borrowed from Thomas.[52] With respect to God's predestination, the covenant is called "eternal," because it was ordained and prepared from all eternity. But with respect to the execution of God's eternal decree, the covenant is rightly called "new," because it was made manifest only in the passion of Christ.)

At a more practical level, Thomas helps Biel to unravel a number of procedural issues confronting any priest who is about to celebrate the eucharist. Biel follows Thomas, for instance, in his insistence that not just the bread and wine but everything pertaining to the sacrifice must be consecrated. The priest himself must be consecrated, because the sacrament that he is about to confect contains the Holy of holies—Christ, who makes all things holy.[53] Yet the same bread may not be consecrated more than once, presumably because—as in the case of the prohibition against the same person being baptized twice—a second consecration seems to cast aspersions upon the validity of the first.[54] (In any case, after the first consecration the requisite matter, bread and wine, no longer exists and thus cannot be reconsecrated. What now exists under the sacramental species is not bread or wine but the body and blood of Christ, which need not—indeed cannot—be "made" holy.) In order to avoid reconsecrating the elements, Biel deals at great length with defects that the priest may notice before or after the words of consecration have been spoken. How should he proceed, for instance, if he notices that a spider has fallen into the chalice? The answers to such questions are fairly complex, and in these contexts Biel often cites Thomas's opinion fairly and extensively, even when he disagrees with Thomas or feels that his conclusions can be accepted only with some qualification.[55]

One of the four constituents of any valid consecration is the appropriate material element.[56] In discussing whether the bread must be made of wheat (rather than, say, of rye or barley), Biel reports Thomas's view that at least the greater portion of what goes into the bread must be wheat; else the requisite matter is lacking and the consecration remains incomplete.[57] Biel, however, is unconvinced. He insists that neither reason nor the Church's authority supports the view that specifically wheaten bread is essential to the sacrament.[58] Yet Biel grants that a priest sins if he violates his Church's rite by using some other kind of bread (not because there is anything defective about his consecration but simply because he is guilty of contempt and disobedience).[59] Similarly, Biel reports Thomas's opinion that natural water should be used, although the use of artificial (e.g., distilled) water in a moderate amount does not prevent the consecration from taking effect. Yet a priest who knowingly proceeds in this way sins gravely, for what *may* be done (without destroying the sacraments' validity) is not always what *ought* to be done (in order to avoid incurring guilt in some other way).[60]

Ex parte Christi: Real Presence

Biel cites Thomas, among others, in order to show that the pronoun "this" (*hoc*[61] or *hic*[62]) in the formula for consecrating the eucharistic elements is used in a demonstrative sense. When the priest says, "This is my body," or, "This is the chalice of my blood," he is doing something more than merely reciting the words of Christ or reporting what Christ said. He is rather pointing to the body or the blood of Christ existing under the sacramental species. Biel goes on to show how Thomas understands the referent of the demonstrative: "this" (*hoc*) must be construed as "what is contained under this" (*contentum sub hoc*).[63] But "what is contained" must be understood indeterminately: the meaning of the statement is neither that the bread is Christ's body (which would be absurd) or that Christ's body is Christ's body (which would be merely tautological). The words of consecration do not cause the bread to be Christ's body or Christ's body to be itself. *Hoc,* rather, refers to what is successively common to both the bread and Christ's body, namely the substance underlying the species of the bread. At the highest level of abstraction, *hoc* points to this undifferentiated, unspecified reality, which used to be the substance of bread but is now converted into the substance of the body of Christ.[64] Biel makes it clear that Thomas's eucharistic teaching leaves no room for the view that the substance of the bread continues to exist *along with* the substance of Christ's body (impanation). He reports that Thomas finds such a doctrine not only inappropriate (*inconveniens*) but altogether impossible and heretical.[65] It is (a) unfitting because, first of all, it is incompatible with the reverence owed to Christ as he exists under the species of bread. Adoration (*latria*) could not be properly exhibited to what is contained under the species if the substance of bread remained, for then the eucharist would become an occasion for idolatry. Secondly, the first thing signified in the eucharist should be Christ's body. But if the substance of the bread remained, the sacrament would point first to the bread and only then to the body of Christ.[66] Thirdly, the use of the sacrament as spiritual food shows that truly corporeal bread (whose substance is not displaced by the substance of Christ's body but merely coexists with it under the species) is out of the question. Biel then shows how Thomas argues, further, against (b) even the possibility of any such coexistence. Nothing can begin to be where previously it was not except by some change in itself or by the change of another into itself. Hence, if the substance of the bread remains intact, it would follow that the body of Christ is changed (moved) locally. This is impossible, however, since at any given moment the body of Christ may be confected on altars in various places, so that contrary motions would have to be predicated of a single subject at the same time—which is, by definition, absurd. Finally, Biel takes note of the argument by which Thomas proves that (c) such a doctrine is heretical. Any teaching that contradicts the clear witness of Scripture is *ipso facto* heretical, and Jesus clearly said, "This is my body." But if the substance of the bread remained, Christ would have said "here (*hic*) is my body," rather than "this (*hoc*) is my body." Thus the notion of a coexistence of two substances—bread and body—is excluded by the authority of Christ's own words.

But after reciting Thomas's arguments in such detail, Biel follows Scotus in dismissing each as inconclusive.[67] In the end Biel shares Thomas's conclusion that the substance of the bread is entirely displaced by the substance of the body of Christ, but he claims that this truth can be known only on the basis of the Church's decisions and the authoritative witness of the saints.[68]

After reviewing Thomas's account of alternative positions on whether the whole Christ is present in each part of the host, Biel suggests that Thomas is among those who claim that the whole body is present both in the entire (unbroken) host and in each of its parts.[69] Thomas holds, according to Biel, that although the body is wholly present under each part before the breaking of the host, it is not actually but only potentially present more than once under its undivided parts. For the unity of anything is a function of its being: "Now the parts of any homogeneous continuum do not actually have being before the divisions, but only potentially; thus none of them has its own unity in act. Hence their multiplicity (*numerum*) is understood not as actual but only as potential, but after the division they are made multiple in act."[70] Biel deems this argument implausible. Before the whole is divided, he argues, its parts exist, which is to say that they are already in act. Otherwise the whole would be composed of what does not exist, since "*whatever is* is in act, and *what is not in act* simply is not."[71] Therefore Biel opts for the alternative solution advanced by Alexander of Hales: the body of Christ is in the host both once (in the whole) and repeatedly (in the parts).[72]

Similarly, Biel presents and immediately rejects Thomas's understanding of the body (into which the bread is transubstantiated) as a composite informed by the intellective soul in its capacity as the giver of corporeal being.[73] Perhaps Biel senses that to affirm Thomas's opinion at this point would give Thomas aid and comfort in his attempt to show by rational proofs that the substance of the bread is entirely replaced by the substance of Christ's body. The text that Biel cites forms part of Thomas's argument to that effect. Since Biel wants to remove this matter from the rational arena,[74] it is not surprising to find that he ends up refuting Thomas's claim that one part of what enters into the composition of the body of Christ as present in the host is the intellective soul. Thomas's opinion, he contends, "cannot be maintained, because the substance of the bread is converted into the same body that was in the tomb, or at the Supper and on the Cross; but that body did not include the soul, since the soul of Christ was not in the tomb."[75]

In order to explicate the mode of Christ's presence in the eucharist, Biel asks whether the body of Christ is in the elements quantitatively. He notes that the crucial issue is whether quantity is an absolute reality, objectively distinct from its subject (whether substance or quality). Some *doctores,* he reports, answer in the affirmative; of these, some hold that the reality of Christ's presence in the sacrament includes the quantitativeness by which his body is extended—that is, occupies space—in heaven: "For they assert that wherever any substance is, there too, necessarily, are all the absolute accidents inherent in it. Consequently they say that in the sacrament the body of Christ is not extended locally by that quantity, since the quantity of Christ is not there in its own mode, i.e., in a quantitative mode, but in the mode of substance."[76] The quantitative dimension of the body, in other words, is present in the host, but not quantitatively. It is present, according to this theory, only "by a natural concomitance to the substance" (*per concomitantiam naturalem ad substantiam*) in which it inheres. The conversion is terminated at the point of *substance:* what replaces the substance of the bread is not the quantity but the substance of Christ's body, and any accidents of that body are present in the host only by way of a real concomitance with their proper subject. (Just as whatever has whiteness is white, so is anything quantitative that has quantity.) Yet the nonquantitative way in which the quantity of Christ's body is present in the host can be seen from the fact that the *whole* body (not just some portion) is in each part of the broken host.

After outlining this argument in great detail, Biel associates it with Thomas and Giles of Rome, but he chooses his words carefully: he does not say that this is Thomas's opinion but rather that Thomas and Giles lean (*declinant*) toward this way of handling the question.[77] In fact, it turns out that the argument that Biel has summarized in this way does bear a close resemblance to Thomas's treatment of questions dealing with the quantity and dimensiveness of Christ's eucharistic body.[78] But Biel himself seems to lean toward the Occamist alternative to Thomas's opinion (though he also seems eager, as usual, to find whatever common ground there may be between them). After sketching Occam's view, Biel cautiously associates himself with it. Ordinarily Biel, like Thomas, tends to express his own opinion with the passive periphrastic (*dicendum*): "It must be said that . . ." In this case he seems a bit more tentative: "It is said (*dicitur*), therefore, . . ." It seems likely, though, that Biel must be regarded as reluctantly excluding Thomas's opinion in favor of Occam's: "the body of Christ (as in the sacrament) is not extensive, because it does not have one part after another, but all of its parts coexist at the same time at each point of the sacramental species."[79]

Implicit in Thomas's opinion regarding the quantitativeness of Christ's eucharistic body is his dictum that no local change or movement is implied in Christ's beginning to be present bodily where he previously was not. Here again Biel faithfully reports Thomas's opinion[80] but then follows Scotus in subjecting it to a thoroughgoing critique.[81]

By contrast, Biel has no quarrel with Thomas's claim that the body of Christ remains in the host so long as its species of bread are not destroyed. (One practical consequence of Thomas's view, as Biel notes, is that it is a punishable irreverence to allow the consecrated host to putrify: any part of it that is not used in the eucharistic service must be reverently preserved or consumed.)[82] The sacramental species, by virtue of their (now displaced) substantial form, continue to exhibit the same accidents; the species, in other words, continue to relate to the substance of bread and wine as the end of their acts, since they retain the same being (*esse*) both before and after the moment of substantial conversion.[83] Biel notes the criticism of this opinion by Scotus, but in the end he invokes the authority of Alexander of Hales in support of a formulation closely akin to Thomas's.[84]

A parallel concern is to ascertain the relation between the species of an image appearing around the host—flesh, blood, or even a child—and the species proper to Christ's own body. Biel discusses Thomas's solution in a lengthy (and almost verbatim) citation.[85] Sometimes such an apparition is merely a function of some change within the visual apparatus of those by whom it is seen, with no corresponding change in the elements per se. This is what happens when the change is only momentary or when it is apparent only to one or to a few. Even in this case no deception is involved; as St. Augustine suggests, it is not deceptive to use even an optical illusion in order to signify a truth (in this case, the fact that Christ is truly present under the species). In the case of an apparition that proves not to be transient and is accessible to more than just a few, Biel reports that Thomas rejects the opinion of those who regard the species of the image as the proper species of Christ's own body. "For according to him, the body of Christ may not be seen except in the one place in which it is circumscriptively contained. Since, then, it is seen in its own species in heaven, it is not seen in that manner in the sacrament or on earth."[86] In addition, as Biel observes, Thomas rejects this view on the basis of biblical evidence indicating that Christ appears to the faithful in his resurrected body only for brief periods before passing again from their sight. "But what appears under the species of flesh remains for a long time; sometimes, indeed, we read that it is enclosed and, at the decree of many bishops, is reserved in a small casket, which would be horrible to contemplate as being done to Christ in his own species."[87] What is seen, rather, is an image formed miraculously, either in the eyes of the onlookers or even in the sacramental matter, for the purpose of attesting the true presence of Christ in the eucharist; but when this change takes place in the element, its dimensions remain the same despite any changes in its other accidental qualities. (When the sacramental dimensions no longer remain, after all, the body of Christ ceases to be present in the bread.)

Biel's solution to the problem places him in sharp disagreement with Thomas. Here again he associates himself with Alexander of Hales, who emphasizes that such apparitions may be not of divine but of human or demonic origin, and who observes that Christ is able to appear when, where, and however he pleases.[88] Biel remains uneasy about the element of falsity surrounding an apparition that seems to be Christ's own body but in fact is not. He argues, against Thomas, that the appearance of flesh or blood other than Christ's cannot have the effect of confirming faith (as opposed to credulity).[89] He also shares Alexander's desire to safeguard the power of Christ to make himself present in his own species wherever he pleases.[90] When Thomas says that Christ is present in his own species only in heaven, Biel responds that this is ordinarily but not always the case. In order to strengthen faith—or for any other purpose that he finds suitable—Christ sometimes makes himself visible to the eye in the elements (*sub sacramenti velamine*) or even apart from them (*in se et nude*). And the modes of such an appearance, Biel argues, need not be the same for different persons: at any given time, Christ may reveal his flesh to one in the elements and to another apart from them. "This is not impossible to God, since even an angel in his assumed body shows himself to one and not to another who is equally present . . . (Daniel 10.7). . . . What an angel, therefore, may do in an alien body Christ may do in his own body."[91] To a large extent, what we have here is yet another example of the way in which a zeal for divine omnipotence leads Biel to part company with Thomas.

Biel goes on to acknowledge Thomas's teaching that the body that Christ gave his disciples was of the same character as the one that he possessed at the time of the Supper: this body was both passible and mortal.[92] Among those who received Christ's body, Biel observes, Thomas numbers Judas.[93] Christ offered his body to the whole college of disciples, to which Judas still belonged when the eucharist was instituted. Christ does not exclude Judas from the privileges of discipleship, although, by later withdrawing from the fellowship, Judas effectively excludes himself.

Already it is clear that Biel makes abundant use of Thomas's insistence that Christ is truly and substantially present in the eucharistic elements. Biel joins Thomas in affirming, with the orthodox medieval tradition that culminated at the Fourth Lateran Council in 1215, that the presence of Christ in the eucharist is objectively real, not dependent on the inner condition of those who partake of the sacramental bread and wine. Against this background, Biel and Thomas must confront an issue that proved to be a recurrent concern in medieval eucharistic theology: does the real presence of Christ imply that his body and blood may be consumed not only by sinners or unbelievers (*manducatio peccatorum aut infidelium*) but even by a dumb animal who by chance eats bread that has been duly consecrated (*manducatio brutorum*)? Reverence for Christ and a concern for his dignity combine to make such an inference unpalatable, to say the least. Yet a consistent eucharistic realism seems to point in this direction.

Biel has already noted Thomas's claim that Christ remains corporeally in the consecrated elements so long as their species remain intact.[94] This opinion gives special urgency to the question of the *manducatio brutorum.* Proper care or disposition of the consecrated host becomes a matter of great concern if the host is not entirely consumed by the faithful, for the body of Christ will be contained in even a crumb of the consecrated matter so long as it exhibits the species proper to bread. And if that crumb should find its way into the stomach of a church mouse, the true body of Christ will have been eaten by a mouse. Biel makes it clear that Thomas does not shrink from such a conclusion.[95] By whomever or whatever it is consumed, the body of Christ remains in the bread so long as the species of bread remain. For the power of the consecration—to render Christ corporeally present in the substance of the bread—is directed to the species; it does not cease to be operative until the species no longer exist.[96]

Biel thus outlines both Thomas's opinion on the question at hand and the argument by which Thomas seeks to establish it. Biel's immediate source is Alexander, not Thomas. He omits some of the premises of Thomas's argument, but its general structure is clearly presented. Thomas battens down the hatches, for instance, by inserting a premise to the effect that the species of the bread remain in each part of the consecrated host so long as the substance of bread would have remained, had it not been displaced. Biel omits this premise, but the omission hardly obscures the larger thrust of Thomas's logic.

Biel reports that St. Bonaventure is troubled about Thomas's willingness to grant that the body of Christ could be eaten by dumb animals. Bonaventure argues, according to Biel, that Christ is present under the sacrament only insofar as it is ordained to human use.[97] But in the mouth or stomach of a mouse, the consecrated bread ceases to be humanly edible. So at that point it ceases to be a sacrament at all: upon being eaten by a mouse, the bread receives again its own substance, and the substance of Christ's body ceases to be there. But Biel shows how Thomas refutes Bonaventure's position:[98] (1) Up to the moment at which the species of bread are destroyed, it is not absurd to suppose that the bread could be retrieved from an animal's stomach and put to human use. (Our revulsion need not obscure the point that is at stake for Thomas: nothing less than the total destruction of the species can break the substantial bond between the consecrated bread and the body of Christ.) In addition, (2) from the fact that something is ordained to a certain end it does not follow that it passes out of existence whenever it can no longer be used in pursuit of that end.

Many of the same considerations are reflected in Biel's account of the way in which Thomas deals with the problem of the *manducatio peccatorum.*[99] The decisive point is Thomas's belief that the substance of Christ's body is objectively present in the consecrated host so long as the species of bread remain. And the species can be changed by nothing less than what would be required in order to change the substance of the bread (if it were still there). This is effected not by the lips or the teeth but only by the complete process of digestion. It is irreverent, then, to say that the body of Christ ceases to be present as soon as the host is touched by a sinner's lips. The reality contained under the species (and bound irrevocably to them) is the substance of Christ's body and blood. The sinfulness of one who partakes unworthily is not enough to dissolve the bond between the sacramental species and the reality of Christ's corporeal presence. Otherwise the instrumental efficacy of the words of consecration—and thus the reliability of Christ's promise to make himself savingly present in the consecrated host—would be placed in jeopardy.

After making such a detailed presentation of this aspect of Thomas's doctrine of the real presence, Biel aligns himself with Thomas. He makes Thomas's opinion the basis on which he attempts to refute the arguments in favor of several alternative solutions.[100]

Ex parte suscipientis: Use and Misuse

The benefit of the eucharist for those who receive it in the proper way is manifold, according to Biel. He turns to Thomas for corroboration of his analysis, especially in the two most crucial respects. (1) The first fruit from the tree of life (the Cross) is mediated by the Lifegiver, who is sacramentally present in the eucharist: the principal benefit of the eucharist is the gift of spiritual life (*vivificare*). By coming visibly into the world, Christ makes possible the life of grace, which the world could otherwise never know. By coming sacramentally to everyone who receives the eucharist, Christ makes possible a new life of the soul.[101]

(2) Receiving the life of grace involves the forgiveness of all past sins: the second fruit on the tree of life is the forgiveness of sins (*relaxare peccata*). Biel points to Thomas's distinction between the two ways in which the saving efficacy of the eucharist may be considered.[102] (What comes to expression here, clearly, is Thomas's more general distinction between *opus operatum* and *opus operantis.*)[103] Considered in itself, the eucharist derives from the passion of Christ a power to effect the remission of any sin whatever. In relation to the one who receives the eucharist, however, this power may be thwarted by the presence of subjective obstacles to receiving its full effect. Perhaps the most serious of such obstacles is an unforgiven mortal sin of which one is aware even while receiving the consecrated elements. Unforgiven mortal sin renders one spiritually dead and thus unable to receive spiritual nourishment. So long as he is inclined to remain in his sinful condition, he cannot be united to Christ, who is the fount of life and the forgiver of sins. This forgiveness is not effected in one who knowingly receives the eucharist in a state of mortal sin. Such an obstacle, rather, will mark him as one who receives the body of Christ unworthily. But in order to be sinful such contempt of the sacrament must be fully conscious: a mortal sin of which one is not aware will be forgiven by the grace received in the eucharist.[104] Thomas's example, cited by Biel, is that of one who comes reverently to the eucharist assuming that his

mortal sins have already been forgiven, whereas in fact (though he does not realize it) his contrition has been defective. In the eucharist such a person will receive the grace of charity, which in turn will perfect his contrition and effect, therefore, the remisison of the mortal sin of which he is still unwittingly guilty.[105]

Biel joins Thomas in arguing that the eucharist can effect the remission of all venial sins.[106] There can be such a fervor of devotion that all venial sins (past and present) are forgiven and one is enabled, at least temporarily, to be free from all venial sin. Thomas realizes, says Biel, that this is not always the case, since the forgiveness of venial sin is in proportion to the intensity of one's devotion. For the forgiveness of venial sins is a secondary effect of the eucharist. Its primary effect is to transform the recipient by joining him to Christ in a union of fervent love; venial sin is incompatible with an intensity of love (though not, like mortal sin, with love itself). Sometimes, though, venial sins may hinder one from receiving the inner refreshment that is a further benefit of the eucharist. Biel quotes Thomas's dictum that whenever a person comes to the eucharist distracted by venial sins, he receives an increase of charity but not this refreshing of his spirit.[107]

In addition to the remission of past venial sins, Biel reports—and affirms—Thomas's belief that a further effect of the eucharist is to help guard against any lapse into mortal sin in the future.[108]

In both the *Collectorium*[109] and the *Expositio,*[110] Biel appropriates the argument by which Thomas shows that the benefit of the eucharist is made available to all those who receive it, both as a sacrament and as a sacrifice. But even for those who do not partake of it, the sacrament may be beneficial—not as a sacrament, of course, but as a sacrifice. (Thus Christ says that his blood is to be shed not only "for you" who partake but also "for many" who do not.) As a sacrifice, the eucharist may have a vicarious effect—not in those *to* whom but in those *for* whom it is offered. In these it presupposes spiritual life potentially, but not actually. If they are disposed to receive the benefits of a mass celebrated in their behalf, one effect of the eucharist will be the remission of their mortal sins. As a sacrifice, the mass obtains grace by virtue of Christ's passion. This grace brings about contrition, which in turn leads to remission of all mortal sins in those for whom the eucharist is offered. (Biel follows Thomas in refuting an objection to this view on the basis of Augustine's teaching that Christ's body is offered only for those who are members of his body. "It is to be understood," according to Biel and Thomas, "that it is offered for the members of Christ when it is offered so that some may become members of Christ.")[111]

The benefits of the eucharist are not available to one who receives it unworthily; on the contrary, he thereby incurs the guilt of yet another mortal sin. But Biel invokes Thomas's authority in defense of the claim that one who merely fails to receive spiritual nourishment (through an increase of grace) does not incur the additional guilt of an offense against the body of Christ.[112] In the text that Biel claims to be following, however, Thomas's concern is quite different from Biel's. He is dealing with the narrower pastoral issue of sinful acts committed ignorantly and the ways in which such acts do (or do not) make one unworthy to receive the eucharist. Thomas's point is that one who commits a sinful act because of some ignorance that is not itself culpable does not become a sinner in so doing. Presumably what cannot make him a sinner cannot deny him the spiritual nourishment that is offered in the eucharist. Biel's example is not parallel to the case that Thomas has in mind. The view that Biel attributes to Thomas is, in fact, incompatible with Thomas's suggestion that nothing prevents one from receiving the grace of the eucharist except mortal sin (which alone renders one spiritually dead and thus incapable of receiving spiritual nourishment).[113]

Biel is more careful in summarizing Thomas's discussion of the relative gravity of the sin of receiving the eucharist unworthily.[114] Biel rightly claims to be true to Thomas's intention in distinguishing between two basic points of reference for the assessment of the seriousness of any sinful deed. First we must look at the act per se; then we must consider the circumstances under which it is done.[115]

In the first way (*ex genere*), sins are committed either against God or against a creature, and a sin against God—all other things being equal—is the graver of the two. Within this category fall sins against the humanity of Christ, which may be against his visible, incarnate humanity (as when the Romans crucified him) or against the humanity concealed under the sacramental species. And it is a more serious offense to crucify his incarnate body than to consume his eucharistic body unworthily. Absolutely speaking (*essentialiter, ex genere*), the sin of partaking unworthily is more serious than any offense against the neighbor, in view of the greater dignity of Christ's humanity against which, primarily, this sin is directed. But a sin against his divinity or against his humanity *in carne* will be a graver offense than the sin against his sacramental body that one commits by partaking unworthily.

In order to prevent the irreverence that might result from a careless handling of the chalice, Thomas sanctions the practice of withholding the cup from the laity, as Biel notes.[116] Several elements of Thomas's argument are overlooked, however. It is crucial to Thomas's argument that Christ is fully present under either species. Thus a layperson receives the whole Christ when he consumes the host; the denial of the cup does not in any way deprive him of access to the saving presence mediated by the eucharist.[117] Biel's account of Thomas's justification for communion in one kind omits this consideration, although it is implied, as we have seen, in his account of Thomas's understanding of Christ's presence in the eucharist.[118] Here Biel uses Thomas to reinforce his own warnings about the practical dimensions of the question. In contrast to bread, wine is relatively unstable and thus easily spilled by those who are very young or senile or infirm. To spill the blood of Christ is a serious offense, which the denial of the cup to the laity helps to prevent.

Another offense against the dignity of the eucharist is committed when a person knowingly receives it from an evil priest.[119] But we have already seen how Biel makes use of Thomas's anti-Donatist insistence that a priest's sin does not nullify his power to administer valid sacraments.[120] Now he turns to Thomas for an analysis of the way in which the benefits of a mass for the dead may be hindered by the sin of the priest.[121] *Ex opere operantis,* the eucharist is celebrated by a minister who acts principally not in his own person but in the person of the one who endowed this particular mass: its fruit is derived form the merit of the Church, which in turn arises from the devotion of its members and especially of the one who ordains that the mass should be said for some soul in purgatory. But insofar as he acts in his own person, the evil priest cannot benefit others by celebrating the eucharist. Biel joins Thomas in tempering this conclusion with a reminder that one who is thought to be an evil priest may have recently turned from his sin: his true inner condition may be hidden from those who call him evil. But generally speaking the mass of a good priest is to be preferred over that of a priest whose integrity is not above question; for then the mass will be beneficial not only by the power of Christ's institution and the Church's merit, but also by virtue of the minister's own piety.

CIRCUMCISION AND BAPTISM

Like Thomas, Biel is heir to a tradition that seeks to define the meaning and value of Christian baptism, in part, by a comparison with its Hebraic predecessors, circumcision and the baptism of John.

Circumcision

The sacraments of the Old Law, including circumcision, have a number of benefits; Biel reports that one of these, in Thomas's opinion, was to effect a ritual cleansing from bodily impurities.[122] The aim of the Old Law was to lead men to the fear and reverence of God, drawing them gradually from the carnal to the spiritual. Since "familiarity breeds contempt," God set up numerous kinds of uncleanness by which men could be barred from the sacramental life of the Jewish community. These impediments comprised the "filthiness of the flesh" which, according to Hebrews 9.13, was removed by the sprinkling of the blood of goats and the ashes of calves. By removing the obstacle to participation in the cult, Old Testament sacraments are said to purify the flesh; symbolically this cleansing is expressed in the requirement that the Levitical priest wash his hands at frequent intervals in the liturgy, lest he unworthily touch holy things. His own need for purification places the priest under the burden of the law along with his people, thus guarding against the temptation to grow proud in his priestly office. (By the same token, this need for ritual purification is a reminder that, in relation to the exceeding holiness of what is contained in the Christian sacraments, priests of the new economy should always consider themselves unworthy.)[123]

Beyond this negative function of purification, the sacraments of the Old Law in some manner bestowed grace. Biel claims to be following Thomas's example when he asserts that this was accomplished not by the power of the sacrament itself (*ex vi sacramenti sive opere operato*) but by virtue of some merit on the part of the one participating in the sacrament (*per modum meriti ex opere operante*).[124] Biel fails, however, to note that Thomas makes one significant exception to this rule: circumcision alone, among the sacraments of the Old Law, conferred grace *ex opere operato.*[125] This omission is quickly corrected, however. In discussing the benefits obtained through the sacrament of circumcision, Biel turns to Thomas for a summary of four alternatives available in the medieval tradition. (Here again Thomas serves as a kind of theological encyclopedia.) Then Biel claims that Thomas, along with Alexander of Hales, leans toward the view that circumcision, *ex opere operato,* both blotted out original sin and bestowed grace, though these negative and positive effects were not as powerful as in Christian baptism.[126] But while Biel leaves no room for doubt about Thomas's belief that circumcision conferred grace *ex opere operato,* he lacks precision in characterizing the way in which Thomas contrasts the benefits bestowed in circumcision and in baptism. Thomas's claim is not, as Biel suggests, that the same blessings are bestowed in both sacraments, but more intensely in baptism. Thomas teaches, rather, that in circumcision grace was fully bestowed as far as its negative effect (the removal of guilt) is concerned; some of its positive effects (ordering the soul and rendering it worthy of eternal life) were conferred, but others (restraining concupiscence and thus enabling one to act meritoriously) were not.[127] Yet, in Biel's defense, it will be noted that he speaks carefully when he says only that Thomas's opinion resembles the one that he associates with Alexander. By comparison with the other alternatives presented in the context, Thomas's view can indeed be said to bear a closer resemblance to Biel's fourth solution than to any of the others. And Biel's own solution is clearly modeled after Thomas's (and Alexander's).[128]

The contrast between baptism and circumcision is suggested in Thomas's teaching that no sacramental character was imprinted upon the soul of one who received circumcision. Biel notes one of the primary considerations underlying Thomas's opinion.[129] As a sacrament of the Old Law, circumcision is carnal, whereas the character is spiritual. Thus circumcision imprints a character in the body but not in the soul.[130] Biel contrasts Thomas's view with that of Scotus, but in the end he concludes that neither is supported by conclusive arguments. Either of the two opinions, therefore, may be affirmed.[131] But Biel proceeds to use Thomas's opinion as part of his own attempt to refute Thomas's doctrine of the dispositive causality of the sacraments. For even on Thomas's premises, he argues, circumcision is a means of justifying grace, although it imprints no character on the soul. It is clear, therefore, that grace can be imparted without the character, which Thomas, however, identifies as the prior disposition necessary for the infusion of grace. Hence it follows, according to Biel, that what the sacraments effect is not some prior disposition, as Thomas believes. Thomas's teaching concerning circumcision, then, is deemed incompatible with his own doctrine of dispositive sacramental causality.

At the point of its institution baptism superseded circumcision as the basic vehicle of the grace by which one may be incorporated into the chosen community. Biel summarizes Thomas's understanding of the religious value of circumcision in terms of a threefold time schema.[132] (1) In the interim between the institution of circumcision and the passion of Christ, the law enjoining circumcision remained fully in effect: hence circumcision was necessary for salvation. (2) Between the passion and the proclamation of the Gospel, circumcision was permissible, but it was neither necessary nor beneficial. When Jesus cried out, "It is finished" (John 19.30), he signified the end of the Levitical economy of salvation. During this period one could be circumcised and still be saved, but in such a case salvation resulted not from the power of circumcision as a means of grace but from faith in Christ's sacrifice. (3) But after the Gospel had been proclaimed, circumcision was no longer merely a matter of indifference as far as salvation is concerned. Now it is death-dealing: "If you be circumcised, Christ will profit you nothing" (Galatians 5.2). Biel's summary is scrupulously fair to Thomas's intention, although he follows Scotus in rejecting several major elements of Thomas's argument.[133]

The Baptism of John

Biel explicates the relation between John's baptism and Christ's in light of Thomas's analysis of the form,[134] recipients,[135] and benefits[136] of John's baptism of repentance. Because Biel agrees with Thomas that John's baptism did not confer grace, he joins Thomas in arguing (against Lombard) that all who received John's baptism needed to be baptized again with the baptism of Christ.[137] For if John's baptism did not bestow grace, it could not suffice for salvation, even in those who received it in faith, putting their confidence in God rather than in John's baptism itself. In representing the alternative to Lombard's opinion, Biel adheres closely to the main lines of Thomas's argument; when he formulates his own conclusion, Biel aligns himself with Thomas's position.[138]

The Baptism of Christ

At a number of points, Biel's doctrine of baptism reflects a careful (and largely sympathetic) use of materials borrowed from St. Thomas. Biel uses Thomas not only as a sourcebook for outlining alternative solutions to certain problems,[139] but also as an authority invoked in behalf of his own solution. For instance, Biel associates himself with Thomas's claim that the full Trinitarian formula is essential to any valid baptism.[140] A counterargument—based on the Apostolic practice of baptizing in Jesus' name only—is refuted by means of Thomas's explanation that the Apostles baptized in Jesus' name as part of their initial task of making his name known to the world. For this purpose, a dispensation from the triune form was granted, but as soon as this purpose was achieved, the reason or cause for the dispensation (and thus the dispensation itself) were nullified. So one who is baptized today in the name of the Son only would need to be rebaptized in the name of Father, Son, and Spirit. Biel notes Scotus's objection to this opinion, but he refutes Scotus's argument by applying Thomas's maxim that an effect ceases when its cause ceases: the silence of Scripture (concerning revocation of the Apostolic dispensation from use of the Trinitarian formula) need not cast doubt upon Thomas's claim that the dispensation reflected in Apostolic practice is no longer in effect.

Biel makes use of the argument by which Thomas shows that immersion is but one of several ways in which baptism may be received. Baptism is a washing of the body, in whole or in part; one may be baptized by pouring or sprinkling, provided only that in some way the body comes into contact with water that is applied by an appropriate minister with the due intent and the requisite formula.[141] This is what informs Thomas's belief that a fetus entirely enclosed within the mother's womb may not be baptized.[142] But if the birth process has already reached the point at which the head or the breast of the infant is accessible (without harm to the mother), a valid baptism may be administered; if the infant then dies, his salvation will have been insured. If the head or breast, the seat of reason or will, is not accessible when the fetus's survival is in doubt, will a foot or a hand suffice? Biel reports Scotus's opinion that, since the whole soul is in each part of the body, it is proper to baptize by applying water to any part of the body; then he associates Thomas, in a rather general way, with Scotus's way of handling this issue.[143] In fact, however, Thomas does not share this particular premise in Scotus's argument, although he agrees that it is best to go ahead and baptize in such a case: it can do no harm, after all. And if the infant survives, he should be rebaptized only in terms of a condition appended to the baptismal formula: "If you are not already baptized, I baptize you. . . ." Biel's summary, then, is somewhat imprecise.

Biel's use of Thomas's teaching about the minister of baptism parallels, in some respects, materials that we have already examined in connection with the eucharist. Only two additional emphases demand our attention here. First, Biel avails himself of Thomas's teaching that, because baptism is the most essential of all the sacraments for man's salvation, no human being is ineligible to baptize.[144] For the sacrament that is most indispensable, both the matter (water) and the minister (any person) must be most readily available. In an absolute sense, any rational creature, including angels and demons, may receive the power of serving as the minister of baptism. In fact, however, this happens only in extraordinary circumstances. For Biel, as for Thomas, it is crucial to leave open the possibility that God might choose to bestow this power on angels or even on demons: just as God's saving power is not circumscribed by his own sacraments, neither is he bound to any particular class of ministers (even a class as broad as humanity itself). But Biel follows Thomas in showing why, as a matter of fact, the ministry of baptism is ordinarily reserved to men. Christ, who instituted the sacrament, was a man, and it is fitting that its ministers should be found among those who share in the "amphibious," psychosomatic character of his humanity. The act of baptizing, moreover, is an act of the Church militant, from which angels and demons are excluded.[145]

Secondly, Biel makes use of the argument by which Thomas proves that the proper ministerial intention is what unites minister, form, and matter into a single cause of the sacramental effect.[146] In view of the indispensability of baptism, this emphasis on the minister's intention—an elusive, subjective factor—poses the question of the assurance of salvation. The baptized cannot know the minister's intention with certainty; does it follow, then, that he remains unsure of his baptism and thus in doubt concerning his own salvation? In the case of those who die in infancy, such an inference would suggest that there is something imperfect about God's provision for human salvation: such an infant would be damned in spite of the Church's best efforts to make the means of grace available to him. Biel invokes Alexander's argument to show that adults can be sure that the baptism of fire will supply whatever may be missing due to the minister's lack of the requisite intention: for those who die before reaching the age of discretion, God himself (*summus sacerdos*) will make up anything that is missing from the sacrament. (His power, again, is not bound to the sacraments.) Biel associates Thomas with Alexander's argument at this point,[147] and he goes on to show how Thomas vindicates God's justice even on the assumption that such extrasacramental salvation were not made available: God is no man's debtor.[148] Biel is happy to concur with Thomas in defending God's freedom with respect to both the end (salvation, which God owes to no one) and the means (the sacraments, to which his power is not limited). Yet Thomas's position is not, in fact, exactly the same as Alexander's. In his commentary on the fourth book of the *Sentences,* Thomas merely presents that opinion as one of two possible ways of approaching the problem, without committing himself to either of them. In the *Tertia pars* of the *Summa theologiae,* he does not exclude this interpretation entirely, but he clearly prefers an alternative that emphasizes that the baptizing minister speaks in the person of the whole Church, whose intention makes up whatever may be lacking in his own intention.[149]

Except for Christ and Mary, who lacked nothing that might have been received in baptism, everyone who is baptized receives the baptismal character, which is imprinted on the soul.[150] The ultimate effect of baptism is a total remission of guilt. Biel notes the way in which Thomas uses the image of baptism as a burial with Christ in order to show that in being baptized one is put in touch with the total saving efficacy of his passion. Not only all guilt but all punishment as well is remitted, therefore, in baptism.[151] This effect can be hindered by mortal and venial sin in which the baptized wills to remain or that he intends to commit in the future. But, as Biel notes, Thomas makes a significant distinction here.[152] Mortal sin, freely embraced by the recipient of the sacrament, cannot coexist with the justifying grace that is offered in baptism: a single mortal sin, if it is still the object of one's delight and intention, is enough to prevent the forgiveness of sins altogether. But venial sin is not incompatible with the presence and operation of the grace mediated by baptism. One who receives baptism while willing, by act or by intent, to remain in venial sin will thereby commit an additional sin (i.e., that of willing to continue sinning), which will not be remitted by the grace bestowed in baptism: the means of dealing with this particular sin is not baptism but subsequent penance. This will not prevent the baptismal forgiveness of all other sins, however, since forgiveness is effected by grace, which venial sin does not exclude.[153]

One who receives baptism insincerely, on the other hand, will receive the sacramental character, but his insincerity constitutes a barrier to his receiving the full effect of the sacrament, which is the forgiveness of his sins. Biel notes the contrast between Thomas and those who contend that when such insincerity is later removed, forgiveness is effected not by the power of baptism but rather by the power of penitence and contrition. He reports that Thomas believes, on the contrary, that when this insincerity is removed, all guilt and punishment for sins committed prior to baptism are remitted by virtue of the baptism, but the sin of insincerely receiving it must be dealt with separately in the sacrament of penance.[154] Biel omits the argument undergirding Thomas's opinion at this point. That argument involves the notion of the baptismal character as an immediate, dispositive cause of the infusion of justifying grace—a notion that Biel, as we have seen, finds unpalatable.[155]

PENANCE

Beyond the age of discretion—in the vast majority of cases, at least—the sacramental remedy for sin is not baptism but penance. Baptism is administered primarily, though not exclusively, to infants. Unlike baptism, moreover, penance may be repeated as often as it becomes necessary to deal with the consequences of the persistence of the tendency toward sin after baptism. The special problems posed by one who receives baptism insincerely or without turning from every venial sin has already shown one of the ways in which Biel, like Thomas, finds it necessary to point from the baptismal font to the confessional.

Biel follows Thomas's interpretation of the sense in which penance may be called the basis (*fundamentum*) of the new life in grace.[156] Penance is somehow similar to the foundation of a house. The foundation of any building is the first part of the structure to be set in place, but it is also that by which the other parts are supported. Now in the spiritual realm the priority of one thing to another may be considered with respect to both what must be known in Christian doctrine (*scienda*) and what must be done in Christian practice (*agenda*). The logical priority of knowing over doing means that faith, which has to do with the intellect, is the "first foundation" (*primum fundamentum*) of the spiritual life. The *agenda* of Christian practice include both the avoidance of what is evil and the pursuit of what is good. Negatively, fear is a *fundamentum*, because it is what first of all leads one to draw back from sin (present or future), while penitence is also a basis on which one draws back from sins already committed.[157] Positively, the foundation of Christian life in its practical dimensions is charity (Ephesians 3.17). The foundation supporting the whole structure, finally, is humility (*in prosperis*) or fortitude (*in adversis*). In this context, clearly, Biel and Thomas are thinking of penance (*paenitentia*) as a virtue, not as a sacrament, although the virtue of penitence is involved in the contrition that is essential to the sacrament.[158]

Biel's account of Thomas's teaching on contrition leaves much to be desired. He is correct in associating Thomas with the view that the principal requirement of the penitent is contrition.[159] The depth and complexity of Thomas's argument are not fully reflected in Biel's summary, but Biel does not err in his claim that Thomas accords a distinct priority to contrition over confession and satisfaction. Thomas makes it clear that forgiveness of sins in the sacrament of penance always presupposes actual contrition, whereas the mere intention to confess and to do works of satisfaction can sometimes be sufficient.[160] When Biel attributes to Thomas the definition of contrition as "a grief for sin, voluntarily assumed, with the intention of confession and making satisfaction," the only respect in which he goes beyond Thomas is in the addition of the adverb, "voluntarily." Strictly speaking, Biel is on solid ground: obviously Thomas does not believe that the requisite grief for sin is assumed involuntarily. Biel's interpolation takes on a deeper significance, however, when it is viewed in light of what he has omitted. For in contrast to Biel's rather one-sided emphasis on the involvement of the human will, Thomas is careful to maintain the priority of divine initiative in disposing the will to assume the grief of contrition.[161]

When Biel discusses the place of contrition in the process by which sins are forgiven in the sacrament of penance, he begins by outlining the views of Lombard, Scotus, and St. Thomas.[162] Lombard holds that sins are forgiven solely by virtue of the sinner's contrition, which precedes absolution: thus the priests' words of absolution do not effect the remission of sins but merely acknowledge what is already a *fait accompli.* Scotus, on the other hand, sees a need to safeguard the doctrine that the sacraments of the new economy confer grace *ex opere operato:* one who receives the sacrament of penance without contrition but only with a mild sorrow for sin because of the threatened punishment (*parum attritus*) may yet receive justifying grace through the mediation of the sacrament. Against this background Biel presents Thomas's opinion as an intermediate between the views of Lombard and Scotus.[163] According to Biel, Thomas approaches Lombard's position when he insists that some inner movement of the sinner's intellect and will is absolutely required if the sacrament is to have its full effect. When this inner disposition does not fall short of genuine contrition, grace is infused even before confession is made or absolution received. But Thomas, Biel continues, approaches Scotus's position by allowing that sins are sometimes remitted by the power of the sacrament itself: when the sinner's inner disposition is not sufficient, the sacrament supplies what is deficient in his attrition and transforms it into contrition. (In order for this to happen, the penitent must merely place no obstacle in the way.)

So Thomas believes, according to Biel, that the sacrament of penance confers justifying grace *ex opere operato* only in those whose inner disposition falls short of contrition. This is Biel's inference, and it is entirely sound. For Thomas holds (1) that true contrition effects the infusion of grace prior to actual confession and absolution;[164] on the other hand, he argues (2) that remission is granted to those who lack perfect contrition when they sacramentally confess and receive absolution.[165] For those who come to the confessional after grace has been infused on the basis of their contrition, what is bestowed by the sacrament is obviously not the first (justifying) grace but rather an increase of the grace that is already possessed. For those who still lack contrition at the moment when the priest utters the words of absolution, Thomas believes that remission of sins is granted by means of the sacrament itself. This forgiveness is by an infusion of grace, which for them will be the first grace (as opposed to an increase of grace already possessed).

Biel is clearly wrong, however, when he includes Thomas among those who hold that the "insufficient disposition"—i.e., attrition—is transformed into contrition by the power of the sacrament. Thomas explicitly refutes this view in his commentary on Book IV of the *Sentences.*[166] Biel's presentation of Thomas's doctrine of contrition, then, is defective, not only in obscuring Thomas's insistence that contrition is itself an effect of God's prior operation in the soul, but also in misrepresenting Thomas's way of dealing with the suggestion that the sacrament of penance may effect a transformation of attrition into contrition. By omission as by commission, Biel fails to do justice to Thomas's teaching at this crucial point.

Biel associates himself with Thomas's dictum that genuine contrition already includes the intention to make confession to a priest.[167] When Biel addresses the issues involved in the case of one who is insincere in his confession, he carefully describes the way in which Thomas views the problem.[168] Thomas, Biel reports, holds that confession, as a part of the sacrament, can exist in one who is not inwardly contrite but who is externally submissive to the Church's spiritual jurisdiction. Until his insincerity passes away, he will not receive the benefit of the sacrament. But if this barrier is later removed, the benefit of the sacrament will be applied to all of the penitent's sins except that of receiving the sacrament insincerely (which has never been confessed, after all). After renouncing his insincerity, therefore, the penitent is not obliged to repeat his original confession, but he must confess his sin of insincerity in order to be absolved from it.

Biel finds Thomas's logic unconvincing. He argues, against Thomas, that either the penitent confesses his insincerity as part of his original confession, or he does not. In the first case, his irreverence toward the sacrament would infect any priest who went on to absolve him in spite of his insincerity: both would thereby sin and the absolution would be nullified. In the second case, his confession would be incomplete and therefore ineffective.[169] Furthermore, Biel thinks it is unreasonable to treat the sin of insincerity (*fictio, simulatio*) as if it were in a class apart from all other sins.[170]

In general, according to Biel, Thomas holds that more than one confession of the same sin is not required for salvation.[171] This conclusion forms part of the basis on which Thomas helps Biel to deal with a familiar pastoral problem posed by those overscrupulous souls who are unduly preoccupied with their own sins. For such persons the possibility of a lapse of memory is a matter of great concern. Some medieval theologians taught that by forgetting to confess one sin, a person would render the entire confession defective: if that sin were later recalled to memory, it would be necessary to reconfess all those that were confessed originally, in addition to the sin that was omitted. Biel notes that Thomas rejects this opinion, although the impact of his appeal to Thomas is weakened by his failure to take account of the reasons undergirding Thomas's position.[172] There is one case, however, in which Biel and Thomas believe that reconfession of the same sins is necessary: when one confesses to a priest sins that are reserved to the confessional jurisdiction of the priest's superior, it will be necessary to make another full confession to the superior.[173]

In addition to contrition and confession, the penitent is obliged to perform appropriate works of satisfaction. Biel affirms Thomas's view that satisfaction must be something above and beyond mere restitution for damages wrongfully inflicted.[174] (Satisfaction is addressed to God, restitution to the neighbor.)

At one point Biel's treatment of penitential satisfaction gives him an occasion for discussing various elements in Thomas's doctrine of grace. In both the *Expositio* and the *Collectorium,* Biel pays considerable attention to Thomas's position regarding the question of whether a work of satisfaction loses its efficacy when it is performed apart from charity[175] or, to put it differently, in a state of mortal sin.[176] In the *Collectorium,* Biel associates Thomas with Alexander of Hales, who believes that since satisfaction implies acceptance by God and reconciliation with him (on the basis of charity and justifying grace), one who lacks charity can do no more than to prepare himself for making satisfaction; works of satisfaction performed by such a person will be valueless as far as the sacramental remission of sins is concerned. Because we cannot be sure of our worth before God, it behooves us to remain in a perpetual state of penitence. If one is unaware of any defect in his works of satisfaction, they need not be repeated, even though the mortal sin of which he is unaware will render those works sacramentally null. But if he searches his conscience and makes every attempt to prepare himself to receive the infusion of charity, he does not commit a further sin by doing works of satisfaction while not in a state of charity.

Biel asserts that Thomas "imitates" (*imitatur*) Alexander in this way of dealing with the problem of satisfaction performed apart from charity. A close examination of the corresponding text in Thomas's commentary on the fourth book of the *Sentences* shows that Biel's report faithfully reflects a number of Thomas's emphases. Thomas stresses the role of satisfaction in restoring the ruptured friendship with God (corresponding to Biel's *reconciliatio*). The equality of this restored friendship is based not on some equivalency between God and man but rather on God's acceptance of man (corresponding to Biel's *acceptatio*). Thomas argues that works performed apart from charity are not *satisfactoria* at all; so Biel concludes that, for Thomas as for Alexander, such works must be repeated if their sacramental benefit is to be realized. Thomas is, as Biel suggests, in harmony with Alexander's restriction of the term "satisfaction" to works of punishment for sin insofar as it is considered not as an injury to the neighbor but as an offense against God. Like Alexander, Thomas counsels continuous penitence in view of our inability to know with certainty that our charity is genuine (or, therefore, that our works of satisfaction are acceptable). Thomas agrees that one who attempts to do works of satisfaction while unwittingly in a state of mortal sin (i.e., apart from charity) is not obliged to repeat them when he later comes to be in a state of charity. Nor will he incur additional guilt in this way (just as one who comes to the eucharist while unwittingly in a state of mortal sin is not thereby made guilty of receiving Christ's body unworthily). But Biel is clearly wrong when he suggests that Thomas speaks of satisfaction as removing the entire penalty owed for sin, not just some part of it.[177] Thomas speaks of the removal of the penalty as an effect of the whole sacrament of penance rather than as an effect of satisfaction per se. But he is careful to insist that not all guilt (*reatus*)—which he defines as what is worthy of punishment (*meritum poenae*)—is done away with in penance.[178]

Biel's response to Thomas's teaching at this point undergoes a complete reversal, as a comparison of the relevant passages in the *Collectorium* and the *Expositio* makes clear. In the *Collectorium* Biel finds Thomas's opinion too harsh and complains that it seems to foster an anxious scrupulosity on the penitent's part, "because a man cannot know conclusively whether or not he has made satisfaction, even though . . . he performs everything commanded him."[179] Biel endorses, instead, Scotus's claim that a work that is performed outside the state of charity remits the penalty for sin, even though it does not merit any positive reward. For Biel is convinced that Scotus's milder verdict is more in keeping with divine mercy than the rigorism that he sees implicit in Thomas's opinion.[180] In the *Expositio,* however, Biel—while commending Scotus's leniency—seems to give a cautious nod of approval to the more rigorous view. Scotus's opinion is more merciful, but Thomas's is "more secure and less doubtful. For it is sure enough that prayers offered by one who is in grace . . . are profitable." But the efficacy of works performed in a state of mortal sin is at best open to question.[181]

In light of the sinner's contrition, confession, and satisfaction, the priest exercises the power of the keys and absolves him of his sins. Biel makes use of Thomas's analysis of the three senses of the term "power" (*potentia*) in this context.[182] On one critical issue, he clearly misrepresents Thomas's teaching. Biel claims that Thomas associates Christ's judicial "power of preeminence" (*potentia praecellentiae*) with his foreknowledge of human merit and demerit. In fact, however, what is decisive for Thomas at this point is not man's (foreknown) merit but Christ's own. What makes Christ a fit subject of this power is not his foreknowledge of man's merit but rather the merit that accrues to Christ himself. Here again, on a crucial issue involving the question of the sinner's justification before God, Biel's reliability as a guide to Thomas's teaching falls short of the high standard to which he usually holds himself.[183]

CONFIRMATION

The handful of texts in which Biel refers to Thomas in connection with the sacrament of confirmation includes important indications of the way in which Thomas handles a number of significant theological questions. For instance, the fact that there is no clear biblical account of this sacrament's institution by Christ or the Apostles raises the issue of how the silence of Scripture is to be understood. Also at stake here is the extent of the Church's authority. Biel follows Thomas's summary and refutation of two opposing views of the institution of confirmation as a sacrament.[184] Some, he reports, hold that confirmation was instituted neither by Christ nor by the Apostles, since (1) we have no Scriptural warrant for thinking otherwise, and (2) what little evidence we do have suggests that they did not use the matter and words of the sacrament but merely employed the laying on of hands. A second opinion holds that the sacrament was instituted not by Christ but by the Apostles who were, after all, pillars of the Church (*bases ecclesiae*). Biel follows Thomas in rejecting both of these views. Thomas's argument against the *sola scriptura* position is a good deal more potent than Biel's,[185] but Biel does make it clear that Thomas does not regard the silence of Scripture as a decisive consideration, at least in this case. And he adheres closely to Thomas's logic in refuting the second opinion: the Apostles, though pillars of the Church, were not its lawgivers. Biel's expansion is entirely consonant with Thomas's intention: the only one who is competent to institute a sacrament is the one who gives the sacrament its efficacy—and that is God alone.

The pope's power of bestowing on whomever he will the power of administering the sacrament of confirmation is affirmed by Thomas, as Biel acknowledges. Biel argues against this view on the grounds that bishops were designated by Christ as the ministers of this sacrament, and the Church has no more authority to change the sacraments than to institute new ones. This would involve the Church in a legislative function which, Biel notes, Thomas himself has already denied her.[186] (Here Biel points to what he thinks is an inconsistency on Thomas's part in order to show that he is rejecting Thomas's answer to a specific practical question in the name of fidelity to the thrust of Thomas's teaching at a deeper level.)

Biel cites Thomas's authority in support of his claim that baptism is a prerequisite for receiving the sacrament of confirmation.[187] In the eucharist, there is no such prerequisite for receiving either the sacrament or the reality (grace) conveyed by it. For the validity of the eucharist is utterly independent of any reference to the one by whom it is received. The body of Christ is truly received by anyone (whatever his status or disposition) who partakes of the consecrated host. Confirmation, by contrast, is perfected as a sacrament only when it is brought to bear on its recipient. An indisposition on his part—such as the lack of the baptismal grace and character—will mean, therefore, that he does not receive the sacrament of confirmation at all.

CONCLUSIONS

With one crucial exception, Biel is only rarely mistaken or hostile in his use of Thomas's sacramental theology. Yet the force of his appeal to Thomas is often diminished by his omission of the arguments (*rationes*) with which Thomas believes his conclusions may be established. Indeed, Biel's relatively rare disagreements are typically at the level of *ratio* rather than *opinio*. Here as elsewhere Biel sharply contracts the sphere of reason's religious competence. To a large extent, Biel's critique is based on the nominalist-voluntarist emphasis on divine will, freedom, and power. The absolute immunity of God's will to any rule, logic, or necessity external to itself is expressed in Biel's impatience with Thomas's attempts to explain why God acts as he does in the sacraments.[188] But whenever he can, Biel makes common cause with Thomas's own vindication of God's freedom[189] and justice.[190]

For the most part Biel's voluminous citations from Thomas's works have the effect of presenting Thomas's thought in a very favorable light.[191] The major exception to this rule is Biel's treatment of Thomas's doctrine of sacramental causality. Although he presents Thomas's opinion fully and fairly, Biel seems to fear that to regard sacraments as dispositive causes of grace is to cast aspersions upon the exclusively saving power of God himself.

As the vehicles of justifying grace, sacraments are God's own instruments—not the Church's or the minister's. A close reading of Biel's treatment of the sacraments provides numerous insights into the anti-Donatist emphasis of Thomas's sacramental theology.

Only in one major area does Biel seem inclined to make a systematic misrepresentation of Thomas's teaching. It is not without significance, however, that the questions on which Biel's interpretations are least faithful to Thomas's intention mark the precise spot at which the dissolution of the medieval synthesis reached its most fateful denouement in Germany on the eve of the Reformation. We have seen how Thomas's doctrine of justification undergoes substantial distortion as a result of what Biel says—and what he leaves unsaid—about Thomas's teachings on contrition, satisfaction, merit, and grace. This is a tendency on which we shall have occasion to comment further in the following chapter. It is not incongruous, however, that this pattern should be reflected first in Biel's treatment of the sacraments; for the primary importance of the sacraments—especially baptism, the eucharist, and penance—lies in their role as the means by which justifying grace impinges on the sinner's predicament. From the standpoint of an analysis of the religious roots of the Protestant schism, Biel's frequently maladroit handling of Thomas's teaching on these points is of considerable significance.

In the context of his sacramental essays, Biel takes note of several tendencies in Thomas's thought that have special relevance to the theological situation in the sixteenth century. We have noted Biel's indications of the way in which Thomas handles certain issues related to the question of the certitude of salvation, for instance, and to the radical use of something approaching a principle of *sola Scriptura.* Above all, one cannot read Biel carefully without gaining a distinct image of Thomas's doctrine of the real, substantial, and bodily presence of Christ in the eucharist.

It is of great interest that Biel offers a very close account of Thomas's arguments against the doctrine that the substance of Christ's body exists in and with the substance of the consecrated host. This doctrine—often labeled "impanation"—bears a close resemblance to Luther's teaching that the substance of Christ's body is "in, with, and under" the substance of the consecrated host. For the present we simply note that Luther's understanding of Christ's real presence in the eucharist is emphatically refuted by Thomas's teaching as reported—and embraced—by Biel. (Even though Biel deems Thomas's arguments inconclusive, he summarizes them with great fidelity and embraces the conclusion that Thomas uses them to establish.)

More positively, one who looks at Thomas primarily through Biel's eyes will encounter a wealth of information about Thomas's way of understanding what it means to receive the sacraments unworthily. He will also find in Biel's interpretation of Thomas resources supporting a eucharistic realism that does not flinch from admitting that Christ's body may be consumed by sinners or even by dumb animals. The *manducatio peccatorum* and the *manducatio brutorum* were hotly debated issues during the age of the Reformation. A careful study of Biel's theology highlights resources in Thomas's thought bearing on those questions.

EIGHT

JUSTIFICATION

By the middle of the sixteenth century, the impact of the Reformation extended to Christology, anthropology, ethics, sacraments, and beyond—touching, within a single generation, the total spectrum of theological concerns. Yet it is hardly an exaggeration to say that in Germany, at least, the crisis initially had its roots in certain late medieval developments with respect to the doctrine of justification. Once the flame was ignited, a broad range of issues came up for criticism and reformulation. But the original spark came from an encounter with the semi-Pelagian tendencies that were at work at several points in the theological ambiguity of the late medieval period. The controversy over indulgences, for instance, carried an explosive potential that it would not have had except for the urgency of its implications for a number of issues related to the question of man's justification before God—faith and works, merit and charity, free will and grace.

Nowhere is this pattern seen more clearly than in Gabriel Biel's soteriology and Martin Luther's response to it.[1] And we have already seen how Biel's treatment of soteriological issues in a sacramental context involves a remarkable degree of insensitivity and distortion as far as his interpretations of St. Thomas are concerned. When Biel discusses these critical issues in a more general way, it again becomes clear that his skill as an interpreter of Thomas is far less impressive here than the evidence reviewed in our previous chapters might have led us to expect. Even here—statistically speaking—Biel is generally both accurate and sympathetic in his handling of Thomas. But a close analysis will show that the points at which he either distorts or attacks Thomas's opinion involve what are actually the most crucial terms of the discussion. Even when Biel endorses what he claims is Thomas's view, it sometimes turns out that Thomas himself would hardly recognize in Biel's language a position that he could unreservedly call his own.[2]

THE CAUSES OF JUSTIFICATION: GOD'S GIFT AND MAN'S CHOICE

Although Biel ignores the arguments underlying Thomas's views on the role of free will in the processes of justification, he makes it clear that Thomas sees a certain motion of the human will as a requisite predisposition for the infusion of grace.[3] What he fails to note is Thomas's conception of the will itself as being disposed or prepared by the prior operation of grace.[4] On the other hand, Biel does take note of Thomas's view of servile fear as something given by the Spirit in order to move the sinner toward repentance.[5] (Although it is given by the Holy Spirit, Biel obeserves that, in Thomas's view, servile fear is not a gift of the Spirit in the strict sense. For the term "gift" connotes an infused habit, which is even more excellent than a virtue; furthermore, one cannot receive a gift of the Spirit without at the same time receiving the Spirit himself, who cannot be received apart from charity—which, in turn, the very definition of servile fear excludes.)[6]

Two lengthy passages—one in the *Collectorium* and one in the *Expositio*—are absolutely crucial to Biel's presentation of Thomas's doctrine of grace. Central to Denifle's critique of Biel's competence as an expositor of the medieval tradition is the famous *locus* in Book II, distinction 28 of the *Collectorium.*[7] Here Biel claims to distill the teaching of Aquinas's *Summa theologiae* I, question 109, regarding man's need for grace (both before and after the Fall) to enable him to love God above all things. Because this text is quite long and complex, it may prove helpful to label the following sets of propositions alphabetically so that each may be analyzed separately and in the context of the argument as a whole.

According to Biel, Thomas claims that (A) since all motion is traceable to the Prime Mover, nothing can accomplish its own act without first being moved by God. Hence the act of any created being—including the human intellect and will—depends upon God both as the source of its inherent perfection (by which it acts) and as the one by whom it is moved to act at all. Therefore, Biel continues, Aquinas holds that (B) the human intellect needs divine assistance in order to know any truth whatsoever; by means of this assistance, the intellect is moved by God to its own act. This does not mean, however, that in each instance the intellect needs additional resources beyond what its own nature provides, although it does require a fresh illumination in order to know certain things that exceed the scope of natural knowledge. But sometimes, conversely, God graciously imparts knowledge that is otherwise available through the normal mechanisms of human knowledge: sometimes he does miraculously what can be done naturally.

(C) Now the will is subject to a similar condition (*sic habet et voluntas*). For in both states of human nature—both in its primal integrity and in its present corruption—God as Prime Mover must concur in order for anyone to will and to do a work that is proportionate to his own nature; this is the good of acquired virtue. But the superabundant good (*bonum suprexcedens*) is the good of infused virtue, which alone is meritorious. For this, even in its integrity, human nature needed the power provided by grace. But in its corruption, grace is needed first in order to heal man's nature and then (as before the Fall) to make it capable of doing a meritorious work.

(D) Apart from the assistance of grace, human nature in its fallenness can do many good things by virtue of God's general activity as the cause and sustainer of the cosmos. But it cannot do all that Adam could do in this way before his lapse into sin. In his unfallen state a "general divine motion"—apart from any special "gift of grace"—was all he needed in order to be able to love God above all things merely by exercising his purely natural faculties. In his fallen condition, this is no longer the case. Because of the corruption of human nature, the will seeks a deficient good unless the lost wholeness of its nature is restored through grace. Hence a sinner must have the benefit of healing grace (in addition to God's general help as Prime Mover) before he can love God above all things.

(E) The corollary is as follows. In his original integrity man was able to fulfill all the precepts of God's law so far as their substance or content is concerned (apart, Biel implies, from any gift of grace in addition to God's general sustaining influence). He was unable, however, to fulfill them in the requisite manner—meritoriously, that is, in a state of infused charity. But in his fallen condition, apart from the healing influence of grace, he cannot fulfill all the precepts even with respect to the substance of the acts that they enjoin. For he lacks the natural capacity to fulfill the first and greatest of the commandments: apart from an additional gift of healing grace he cannot love God above all things.

(F) In each status (integral or corrupt) man needs the general assistance of the Prime Mover in order to do anything at all. "Thus in order to prepare himself to receive some benefit from God, he needs not another gift of grace but [simply] God as the one who moves him" to prepare himself.[8]

(G) Man cannot rise from sin apart from grace, for this rising is not merely to cease from sinful acts but also to be renewed in that which is lost through sin—that is, grace. Yet (H) he can avoid mortal sin without grace, because it is not necessary that he should be continually in the act of sinning. Hence, all mortal sins, considered as separate acts, are avoidable. Over a long period of time, however, one cannot avoid all of them without the aid of grace. For the commandment to love God above all things cannot be fulfilled apart from the enablement of grace; to violate this greatest of all precepts is to fall into mortal sin. (I) Venial sins, considered as separate acts, can be avoided apart from grace, but the unengraced person cannot avoid venial sin altogether.

A comparison with the text that Biel claims to be paraphrasing reveals that he is quite faithful to Thomas's intention in items (A) through (E).[9] With (F), Biel's exposition becomes more problematical. At a most crucial juncture in the argument—dealing with Thomas's assessment of what the sinner is able to do for himself before his nature has felt the impact of healing grace—Biel's expertise as an interpreter of Thomas seems to desert him. He suggests that Thomas reduces the help that one needs in order to be able to prepare oneself for grace to nothing more than the *concursus generalis* by which the Prime Mover is ultimately involved in every creaturely act. Such a position is excluded by Thomas's insistence that to prepare oneself for grace is to be turned toward God, which happens only as a result of God's inner working in the sinner's faculty of free choice (Jeremiah 31.18, Lamentations 5.21).[10] Since the *concursus generalis* is universal in its scope, Biel's interpretation will stand only if it can be shown that Thomas means to claim that God works inwardly to turn *every* sinner toward himself. Clearly Thomas does grant that God's influence as Prime Mover leads everything, including the will of every person, to tend finally toward God in seeking whatever is its proper good: each thing in its own way seeks to be "like" God, and this is a consequence of the fact that he is the First Mover. But Thomas goes on to make it clear that God's work in the soul, by which he turns its faculty of free choice toward himself, is distinct from this more general help by which he enables every creature to be and to do what is proper to itself. Otherwise it would make no sense for Thomas to speak, as he does, of God's directing certain men (but not all men) to himself as to a *special* end.[11] It is true that Thomas seeks to avoid an infinite regress by conceding that the grace by which one is enabled to dispose oneself for receiving the gift of habitual (sanctifying) grace is not the same as habitual grace itself.[12] But Biel—ignoring this critical distinction between habitual grace and special gratuitous help—makes use of Thomas's language as a pretext for claiming that Thomas sees no need at all for a special gift of predisposing grace.

Although Thomas argues the points in greater detail, there is nothing in (G),[13] (H),[14] or (I)[15] that is unfair to Thomas's intention.

Now Biel's language becomes very cautious. After summarizing what he takes to be the clear thrust of Thomas's teaching, Biel suggests, somewhat tentatively, that "blessed Thomas seems to think" (*videtur beatus Thomas sentire*) that (1) in either status—integral or corrupt—man needs the gift of infused grace in order to act meritoriously. But (2) for acts that are good but not meritorious, the natural faculty of free choice is sufficient. God's general sustaining influence as Prime Mover is always presupposed, however; for that matter, good (but nonmeritorious) works may be further enabled by infused grace. This is not necessary, however: free choice and the *concursus generalis* are sufficient to account for such good works. (3) Without infused grace the sinner can abstain from all acts of sin, but only for a certain period of time (*ad tempus*). (4) Without infused grace, furthermore, he can prepare himself to receive grace. But (5) he cannot rise from sin without first receiving the gift of infused grace.

Narrowly construed, there is nothing here that Thomas would find offensive.[16] Several significant omissions, however, may be noted. Item 4 is technically correct. As we have seen, Thomas grants that infused grace cannot be its own precondition (lest an infinite regress be implied). But by failing to note Thomas's insistence that the will itself must be prepared by God prior to the infusion of sanctifying grace, Biel's analysis reinforces the misleading impression that is already apparent in his earlier discussion of Thomas's way of dealing with the whole question of preparation for grace (F).

The same tendency is seen in what Biel omits from item 5. Biel is correct, of course, in claiming that, on Thomas's principles, one cannot rise from sin without infused grace. In fact, Thomas is even more emphatic; he insists that the sinner depends upon God to provide not only the "habitual gift" (corresponding to Biel's *gratia infusa*) but also the inner movement by which his soul is prepared to receive it. In the context of Thomas's threefold analysis of what is lost by sin and restored only by grace, the effect of this emphasis is to underscore the sinner's helplessness and radical dependence on God's special intervention through the predisposing operation of grace.[17] The moral heroism of Biel's own—semi-Pelagian—soteriology may be what prompts him to soften the impact of Thomas's Augustinianism at this point.

Biel goes on to claim that, in Thomas's opinion, the sinner can fulfill some of the precepts (according to the substance of the deeds) without the gift of infused grace, though not without the *concursus generalis.* This reflects Thomas's teaching that each sinful act, considered individually, is avoidable, even though the sinner's corrupt nature renders him unable to avoid all of the sinful acts to which he is inclined. Biel's language also takes account of Thomas's insistence that every creaturely act presupposes the *concursus generalis.*[18] Then Biel shows how Thomas grounds the sinner's need for God's help in a certain poisoning of the flesh,[19] darkening of the mind,[20] and perversion of the will.[21]

The pivotal element in Biel's exposition lies in his claim that Thomas is unclear about whether the help that fallen persons need is anything more than the *concursus generalis.* Biel bases this comment on article 9 of question 109 in the *prima secundae.* Thomas's statement is that, in addition to the infusion of grace, the sinner needs some further help of grace by which God moves him to act righteously. This additional help is required both for the general reason that every creature acts by virtue of God's creative-sustaining motion and for the special reason that human nature has been corrupted (as indicated above) through sin. Biel seems to sense that Thomas's language is amenable to either of two interpretations. (a) The general and special reasons may be two reasons for needing the same kind of help: in that case the *concursus* would be the most likely candidate. On the other hand, (b) these two reasons may correspond to two different kinds of help—the general help by which God sustains the creature in existence and the special "gratuitous" help by which he moves the soul to act righteously. It is fair to say that Thomas's language in article 9 is open to either of these interpretations. He does not specifically endorse or exclude either of them; there lies the ambiguity that Biel is careful to leave unresolved. In light of Thomas's earlier teaching on the soul's preparation for grace (which Biel, as we have seen, unfortunately misrepresents), we are in a position to infer that (b) is a more faithful reflection of Thomas's intention. After all, the distinction between general and special corresponds precisely to the contrast between the *concursus* of the Prime Mover and the inner work by which

God, through grace, moves the soul—specifically the will—to act righteously.

In fairness to Biel, one must remember, first of all, that Thomas's language in article 9 does not resolve the issue with the kind of finality that would make Biel's gloss clearly inappropriate. We recall, secondly, that Biel stops short of claiming that Thomas identifies the requisite assistance of grace with God's *concursus generalis*. He merely claims that Thomas leaves the question unanswered.[22] So there are two things that must be said about Biel's mistake at this crucial point. First, it is not a crass inversion of Thomas's real opinion. Biel does not claim that Thomas affirms what he in fact denies; he seeks, rather, to be sensitive to a real ambiguity in an exceedingly subtle text. If we consider only the specific text that he claims to be following, Biel's interpretation has at least a *prima facie* plausibility, even if it is not the best of all possible interpretations. But we must go on to acknowlege, secondly, that Biel's exegesis is decisively conditioned by his prior misinterpretation of the way in which Thomas understands the grounds of the predisposition of the soul for receiving the gift of infused grace.

Finally, Biel points to Thomas's view that human nature, in its fallen status, is incapable of loving God above all things apart from the healing influence of grace. On the less urgent question of how man in his primal integrity was able to love God above all things, Biel correctly notes that Thomas does not posit a need for healing grace; in his wholeness, man did not need to be healed. (Biel, it is true, overlooks Thomas's insistence that even before the Fall man needed God's help in moving him inwardly to the act of loving God above all things. This omission does not throw Biel's larger analysis out of balance, however. In the more immediate and existential question of fallen man's natural incapacity for loving God above all things, Biel leaves no doubt where Thomas stands.[23]

It is important to note that Biel applauds Thomas's position, at least insofar as it transcends Gregory of Rimini's claim that in the fallen state, one cannot even do what is morally good without the special assistance of God. Biel's presentation of Thomas's opinions begins with the statement that "blessed Thomas seems to speak more moderately" (*beatus Thomas . . . videtur temperantius loqui*). What is remarkable about Biel's apparently sympathetic treatment of Thomas is that the text that he has before him includes Thomas's denial of what is usually regarded as a favorite theme in Biel's doctrine of justification: one who reads Biel carefully will find a close and sympathetic rendering of Thomas's views concerning the sinner's inability to love God above all things by the exercise of his purely natural faculties (with the help only of the *concursus generalis*). It is clear, moreover, that Biel in this context does not misinterpret Thomas's language as referring only to the *concursus;* the grace that is required in order to love God *super omnia* is described as "the grace that heals [man's] nature" (*indiget homo auxilio gratiae naturam sanantis*). Now it is true that Biel does not endorse Thomas's opinion in every particular. It is difficult to know with certainty which elements of Thomas's position he means to commend when he says that Thomas "seems to speak more moderately." Clearly Biel prefers Thomas's opinion to that of Gregory of Rimini with respect to a natural human ability to do works that are morally good but not meritorious. Whether he means to suggest that his sympathies extend to Thomas's teaching about the need for healing grace as a precondition for loving God above all things is not entirely clear in the present context. But at least it should be noted that Biel registers not a single word of dissent, and his own conclusions (in the second article of distinction 28) reveal no sharp contrasts between Biel and Thomas on this question.

So Biel's error—which Denifle found unforgivable—is to claim that, according to Thomas, the sinner can prepare himself for grace without any divine assistance beyond the *concursus generalis.* Heiko Oberman recently attempted to vindicate Biel's integrity as an interpreter of Thomas by suggesting that Biel's rendering may have been rooted in Thomas's early *Sentences* commentary, where Thomas has sometimes been accused, in contemporary scholarship, of giving aid and comfort to just the kind of semi-Pelagian error that Biel ascribes to him. While acknowledging that Biel's interpretation is at variance with Thomas's mature doctrine as expressed in the *Summa theologiae,* Oberman points to the dispute between Johann

Stufler and Henri Bouillard as to whether Thomas's teaching in the *Sentences* commentary approaches semi-Pelagianism in this respect.[24] If modern scholars find the evidence debatable, Oberman suggests, we should not judge Biel too harshly:

> Before Biel is accused of ignorance in this matter, it might be pointed out that along with Biel, a significant group of late medieval theologians not only regarded Gregory's position as too extreme, but also felt that they had Thomas on their side. Capreolus' thesis that the authority of the *Summa* was to be more highly esteemed than that of the *Sentences* had to gain general acceptance before their claim could be rejected.[25]

Oberman's defense of Biel is unconvincing for two reasons. The more obvious is that Oberman overlooks Biel's bibliographical reference: Biel explicitly claims that his source is question 109 of the *prima secundae,* and in all other respects Biel's summary is indeed faithful to the thrust of Thomas's teaching in the *Summa.* At a more general level, Oberman's thesis founders on our observation that this particular distortion is but part of a syndrome. Even when Thomas's language is not, as in this case, ambiguous or obscure, Biel consistently exaggerates his claim for the competence of the unaided free will, and he consistently minimizes (or omits) Thomas's sense of the sinner's utter dependence on God's gracious initiative as a precondition for even the most minimal human movement toward God. What we must recognize here is something very close to a systematic distortion, even though Biel struggles valiantly to remain within the bounds of plausibility in interpreting the text that lies before him. The point of Biel's consistent misrepresentation is *not* the question of some natural ability to fulfill the first commandment apart from the special enablement of grace. It is rather the question of a natural ability to prepare oneself for receiving the habitual grace that alone will create the possibility of loving God above all things meritoriously. Precisely at the point of determining the basis on which the sinner prepares himself to receive the gift of justifying grace, Biel is clearly guilty of reducing Thomas's *auxilium gratiae* to nothing more than the *concursus Dei generalis.*

In Lecture 59 of the *Expositio,* Biel outlines five propositions that he claims to find, at least implicitly, in question 114 of Thomas's *prima secundae.*[26] The issue at stake is the place of personal merit in the dynamics of justification, and here gain—at yet another crucial juncture—Biel's competence as an interpreter of Thomas's thought falls far short of the ideal.

(1) As Biel intimates, Thomas denies that any human work, considered according to its intrinsic value apart from grace, is meritorious of eternal blessedness. No one receives grace as a result of some work performed by the sheer exercise of one's innate moral powers. "For according to the order of his wisdom, God has ordained that no one should be glorified in heaven without first being engraced in this life. But [he further ordained] that he will not reward any act with heavenly bliss unless its origin is the grace received in this life."[27] A comparison with the corresponding text—article 2—in question 114 reveals that the opinion expressed in Biel's first proposition is indeed Thomas's, but there is a significant development in Biel's use of the argument by which Thomas seeks to defend it. For Biel makes the necessity of grace, as a precondition of merit, largely a matter of divine fiat: that a human work cannot merit blessedness unless it is performed in grace is merely a consequence of what God has ordained. Thomas too speaks of God's ordinance:[28] he grants that human merit "depends on the divine preordination" (*meritum hominis dependet ex praeordinatione divina*). But Thomas transcends Biel's voluntarism by proceeding to show how God's ordinance is appropriate to human finitude (before and after the Fall) and sinfulness (after the Fall). Biel, to be sure, grounds the ordinance in divine wisdom (*secundum ordinem sapientie sue*), but by failing to pursue Thomas's argument in depth, he manages to convey the impression that the basis of God's decree is, if not sheer fiat, at least something hidden forever from our inspection. Thomas, on the contrary, advances an argument that focuses on the radical ontological deficiency of any finite creature—whether integral or fallen—with respect to the merit of an infinite reward. In Thomas's opinion, what God ordains is that eternal life will be bestowed on the condition of the performance of certain acts if—and only if—

the principle of those acts is truly commensurate with such a reward. Admittedly, Thomas invokes a "law of divine providence" to the effect that every act must be in proportion to its agent's powers. But a law of providence is far more general than the kind of *ad hoc* ordinance that Biel's language seems to imply. A law of divine providence, after all, will be applicable to every creature in all respects, whereas the kind of ordinance Biel has in mind is relevant only to the specific issue at hand. On Thomas's principles, the contrast between a finite work and an infinite reward means that divine providence already requires the addition of an infinite power to one's natural endowment; only this power can serve as the principle of acts to which an eternal reward is promised. Biel completely disregards this basic ontological element in Thomas's argument.

In addition, Biel overlooks Thomas's emphasis on the effect of sin as an impediment that prevents the sinner from meriting an eternal reward. The result of this omission is a shift in the basis on which infant baptism is sanctioned. In Biel's rendering, Thomas is portrayed as justifying pedobaptism primarily by appealing to an external ordinance of God. In fact, however, Thomas's argument focuses immediately upon the sin that the infant contracts from Adam; God's decree is presupposed, but Thomas thinks it is worthwhile to show how the ordinance is tailored to fit the requirements of the human condition.

It should be clear, however, that Biel's modifications of Thomas's argument are largely matters of emphasis or nuance. The fundamental proposition that he attributes to Thomas is one with which Thomas is in full agreement. Even the argument (*ratio*) contains nothing that cannot be affirmed by a consistent Thomist, although Biel's emphasis on the divine ordinance would probably have to be subjected to certain qualifications along the lines suggested above.

(2) The second proposition that Biel attributes to Thomas introduces the notion of condign merit. For both Biel and Thomas, a work has the merit of condignity if its intrinsic value is equal to the reward. If, on the other hand, its intrinsic value falls short of this standard, it is only semimeritorious; it has the merit not of condignity but of congruity.[29]

Thomas claims, according to Biel, that a morally good act performed apart from grace merits nothing condignly, since condign merit presupposes a certain worthiness in the agent, which in turn cannot be present unless he has received the grace that removes him from a state of mortal sin. A close reading of the texts that Biel is following here shows that his summary is indeed faithful to Thomas's intention.[30]

But (3) Biel goes on to claim that Thomas agrees with him in allowing that the sinner can merit grace *de congruo.* The most generous of all judges, Biel argues, will allow no good work to go unrewarded. Apart from grace, the sinner's work may be morally good (as Thomas clearly grants). In itself (i.e., condignly) such a work is meritorious of nothing (as stated in the first proposition). But out of his own liberality, God's covenant with the sinner ("Draw near to God, and he will draw near to you," James 4.8) bestows on it a value in excess of its intrinsic worth. A sinner's work is thus meritorious—not of justification or heaven but only of the grace that inserts him into the position of being able to merit such a reward. What the sinner merits is not the eternal reward but the grace that makes him capable of meriting it. Biel makes it clear that the sinner's merit is strictly *de congruo;* it is more a reflection of God's liberality than of any inherent goodness in the sinner or his work. But the proof-text from James—Biel's favorite—provides him an occasion for expounding a doctrine based on the maxim that God helps those who help themselves. Biel claims that "by doing what in him lies" (*faciendo quod in se est*) the sinner merits grace *de congruo.* And this is part of what he lays at the feet of St. Thomas.

It seems likely that Biel bases his claim on a passage in article 3 in which Thomas speaks of man's meritorious act in terms of condignity and congruity: "If it is considered according to the substance of the work and insofar as it proceeds from free choice, there can be no condignity, on account of the exceedingly great inequality. But there is a congruity, on account of a certain equality of proportion. For it seems fitting that God, according to the excellence of his own power, should reward a man who does his best."[31] Biel infers, then, that Thomas shares his own view that by doing his very best—*faciendo quod in se est*—the sinner merits, *de congruo,* the grace by which he is justified. In fact, however, Thomas categorically denies (in acticle 5) that the first grace can be merited. He leaves the negation unqualified; he does not seem to believe that the distinction between condignity and congruity is relevant in this context. He points to Paul's language in Romans (4.4 and 11.6) to buttress his claim that any kind of merit will be excluded by the very concept of grace. This will hold true, according to Thomas, both from the perspective of grace itself (as a free gift) and from the perspective of what is offered to the sinner by means of grace (in view of his own finitude and sinfulness).[32]

Earlier in the same question (article 2, ad 3), Thomas argues that no one can merit anything from God except by means of his gift (*per donum ejus*). In this context *donum* clearly means something more than the *concursus generalis* and one's natural endowments. For Thomas is addressing an argument that seeks to exalt the religious value of purely natural human capacities prior to the inner transformation effected by grace. Thomas insists, on the contrary, that there can be no merit at all on the part of one in whom sanctifying grace is not already operative. Thus when Thomas speaks of congruity in connection with "man's meritorious work" (article 3, *corpus*), he is not—as Biel supposes—talking about the works performed while one is still in a state of mortal sin. This becomes unmistakably clear, as we have seen, in article 5.

Perhaps Biel was misled by Thomas's attempt to show, in article 1, that the human person—whose character it is to act in a manner that is both rational and voluntary—is the kind of being to whom a meritorious act is both possible and appropriate.[33] Here Thomas employs language that invokes the image of the human agent as rational and free—and thus, in some limited sense, self-moving. Indeed, Thomas's discussion in article 1 contains not a single word about man's need for some enablement by grace as a precondition for his meriting anything from God. If article 1 were Thomas's final word on the subject, Biel's error might seem less blatant. But even in article 1, it is clear that Thomas's concern is with a question that is logically prior to Biel's concern about the sinner's congruous merit of justifying grace. Thomas asks (in preparation for his discussion of the issues at stake in Biel's question) whether it is possible for man to merit *at all*, with or without the help of grace. It is only after emphasizing, in article 2, man's radical dependence on grace as the basis of *all* his merit that Thomas goes on to speak, in article 3, of man's meritorious work. In article 1, he posits the faculties of rationality and free choice as necessary (though not as sufficient) conditions for man somehow to move himself to do what he ought to do. But in articles 2, 3, and 5, Thomas makes it abundantly clear that these purely natural faculties are insufficient, apart from the healing influence of grace, to make the sinner capable of meriting anything at all from God.

Biel's misrepresentation conveniently reinforces his earlier distortion of Thomas's views concerning the sinner's ability to prepare or dispose himself for receiving the gift of justifying grace. In both cases what he falsely attributes to Thomas is an excessive, semi-Pelagian estimation of what the sinner can contribute to his own salvation merely by virtue of his natural endowments as a rational and moral being. By now we are in a position to recognize that we are dealing with a fundamental, programmatic distortion that enables Biel to claim Thomas's authority in behalf of his own view of the human situation.[34]

(4) Biel's fourth proposition is little more than a restatement of the first: considered in itself even a work performed in a state of grace is not meritorious of an eternal reward *de condigno.*[35] Biel buttresses this conclusion with a number of proof-texts which, while not explicit in Thomas's argument, are entirely consistent with its logic. Then Biel points to the fact that, by definition, there must be a certain proportion or equality between a condign merit and the reward that is proper to it. But between a temporal work and an eternal reward there can be, strictly speaking, no equality. This argument, as we have seen, finds a close parallel in articles 2 and 3 of Thomas's *prima secundae,* question 114.

(5) Finally, Biel associates with Thomas a certain analysis of the way in which good works performed in a state of grace may, nonetheless, be meritorious *de condigno.*[36] With respect to (a) the grace

that cooperates with the human faculty of free choice, (b) the inner moving of the Holy Spirit by whom grace is bestowed, and (c) the promise by which God ordained an eternal reward to works performed in grace, such works have a merit of condignity. For the requisite equality is found in comparing the source of the meritorious act (ultimately the Holy Spirit, proximately grace) with the reward corresponding to it (ultimately God himself, proximately the beatific vision). Up to this point, the opinion and the argumentation—including several of Biel's proof-texts—correspond very closely to Thomas's presentation in article 3 of question 114.

Biel goes on, however, to introduce the notion of God's fidelity to his promise as a basis of the justice that is suggested by the very notion of condign merit. The emphasis on the priority of God's will central to Biel's value theory is curiously interwoven with his insistence that it is just for God to keep his promise by rewarding a meritorious work:

> On the part of God, who made the promise, there is justice in giving the reward. For it is just that a promise be kept. Hence it is said to the laborer: "Take what is yours" [Matthew 20.14]. Now it would be unjust not to give him what is his own. But this justice is not from the nature of the act but from the most generous promise of God who willingly made himself a debtor. By his own will he obligated himself to render such a reward for such a work, and thus condignity arises from the truth of him who promises. For as long as the promise of the Lord stands, it is just to give it and unjust not to give it, although that justice depends solely on the most liberal will of God, who promised such rewards.[37]

Several observations are in order. First, Biel's commitment to a voluntarist value theory—"*iustum est quia Deus vult*"—may not be so thoroughgoing as it is often assumed to be. Although Biel labors mightily to show that God's will is the norm of his justice in keeping a specific promise that he has freely made, in the end he seems to take it for granted that the obligation of promise-keeping per se is binding even upon God, entirely apart from his decision that it is unjust to break one's promise. God promises freely, but thereafter not even God may violate his own promise without making himself the transgressor of a law that is, apparently, independent of the divine will. Biel seems to assume that it is intrinsically unjust to fail to keep a promise—even for God. He did not have to make the promise at all, but having made it, he is no longer free to violate it without committing an act of injustice.

Secondly, it is significant that no form of the noun *promissio* (a promise) or of the verb *polliceor* (to promise) occurs in question 114 of the *prima secundae.* "Promise" is simply not one of the rubrics under which Thomas accounts for the condignity of human merit in the text that Biel claims to have before him. Thomas's rubric, above all, is that of *ordinatio.* God has ordained that beatitude should be given as a reward for condign merit, and it is just that his ordinance should be executed: there lies, according to Thomas, the justice that is essential to the very notion of condignity. Biel's *promissio,* on the other hand, has a conditional, bilateral connotation. He understands God's promise, above all, in light of James 4.8: "Draw near to God and he will draw near to you"—or rather, "*If* you draw near to God, *then* he will draw near to you." This bilateral emphasis Biel imports into Thomas's doctrine of condign merit. Again the effect of this interpretation is to associate Thomas—wrongly, as it turns out—with certain semi-Pelagian tendencies in Biel's view of how the sinner is actively involved in meriting his own justification.

THE GROUNDS OF JUSTIFICATION: FEAR, CHARITY, AND MERIT

When Biel assesses the place of charity and merit—and the relation between them—in the dynamics of justification, his use of materials lifted from Thomas includes numerous examples of his skill as an interpreter of Thomas's theology. But at several critical points his summaries are clearly misleading. As a composite, Biel's image of Thomas is, at best, of mixed value.

In view of his mistake about Thomas's assessment of the sinner's ability to merit grace *de congruo,* it is of great interest to note other texts in which Biel acknowledges that Thomas posits charity as a precondition for human merit before God. Servile fear, for instance, cannot be meritorious, since it springs from a love of self rather than of God.[38] There is a kind of servile fear, according to Biel, that does not already include the notion of willing to continue in sin except for the threatened punishment. Here he rightly invokes Thomas's authority in behalf of the thesis that such fear may be good, though not meritorious, inasmuch as it may lead to the fear of God that prompts one to forsake his sin. In that case, servile fear becomes indistinguishable from the natural fear by which we shrink back from anything that is threatening or harmful. Such fear is in itself good, because it is natural.

But what is purely natural cannot be meritorious in God's sight. Biel associates himself with Thomas's view that since everything acts in a manner proportional to its own nature, no one can merit eternal life without first receiving a supernatural gift by which his nature is elevated and made commensurate with an eternal reward.[39] Apart from charity, unreconciled to God, in a purely natural fallen state, one can merit nothing from God condignly. Before he can act meritoriously, he must be the recipient of God's reconciling grace. Biel makes it clear that Thomas regards grace and charity as prerequisites for any meritorious act, and the context leaves no doubt about Biel's desire to affirm Thomas's position in this respect. We should be cautious, then, about making a too-easy assumption that Biel's semi-Pelagian soteriology puts him in conflict with Thomas at this point. Clearly, however, what is at stake here is the question of condign merit (by which the justified person merits eternal life), not congruous merit (by which the sinner merits the infusion of justifying grace). At this point, Biel finds himself in harmony with Thomas's teaching.

Like Thomas, Biel is concerned about the question of merit with special reference to the case of one who falls back into mortal sin after having been justified. Like Thomas, he asks whether one who exists in a state of grace can merit for himself restoration from any subsequent lapse into sin.[40] Biel follows Thomas in adducing Augustine's interpretation of Psalm 70.9 as a possible basis on which the question might be answered in the affirmative, but then he shows how Thomas arrives at the opposite conclusion. For a single act of mortal sin erases all merit and righteousness as far as one's standing before God is concerned. "Therefore nothing is owed to the lapsed by virtue of the good works which he did while in a state of grace, and all his merits perish because of his mortal sin."[41]

Biel's summary, although it omits certain key elements of Thomas's argument, is, on the whole, fair to Thomas's intention. Thomas's approach to the question is, to be sure, more complex than Biel's summary suggests. Biel simplifies the discussion by omitting Thomas's separate subarguments against the possibility of meriting restoration either *de congruo* or *de condigno.* But the core of Thomas's argument is the claim that a lapse into sin has the effect of cancelling the merit of all previous good works—which cannot, therefore, impinge upon the new status in which one is placed by an act of mortal sin. This hard core of Thomas's argument is reported clearly and succinctly by Biel.

That Biel has read Thomas carefully becomes even more apparent in his own response to the *dubium.* Thomas's distinction between merits of congruity and of condignity is central to Biel's response, although Thomas's solution to the problem proves to be only partially acceptable. Biel affirms Thomas's opinion with respect to condign merit but rejects it with respect to the merit of congruity. For Biel reasons that even one who exists in a state of mortal sin can merit *de congruo* by disposing himself to receive grace, even though his works as such are dead, because they are performed apart from the state of grace. How much more, then, will he merit *de congruo* by works performed in charity, even if they are afterwards rendered lifeless by his sin?[42] Biel suspects that Thomas's view unduly constricts the range in which God's liberality and freedom are operative: God remains free to ordain that the grace of rising from a lapse into sin will be given only in view of good works preceding the fall. In that case the gift would arise from God's sheer liberality, but previous good works would be a necessary (though not a sufficient) condition for receiving the gift. Since previous good works, then, are a prerequisite to receiving the grace by which one may subsequently be restored, they are in some sense meritorious; but since they are not sufficient in themselves, depending rather upon God's generosity, theirs is a merit of congruity, not of condignity. Biel argues, accordingly, that the Scriptural passages cited by Thomas must be understood as referring only to the *meritum de condigno.*[43]

In his discussion of the relation between works, merit, and satisfaction, and in his refutation of the radical Augustinian view of morally good acts performed apart from the state of charity, Biel presents interpretations of Thomas that are, respectively, a fair inference from Thomas's language[44] and a close report of major elements in Thomas's *opinio* and *ratio.*[45] In the first case, however, Biel lays at Thomas's feet only the distinction between *opera satisfactoria* and *opera meritoria.* This distinction serves as Biel's point of departure for a development for which he claims Thomas's authority only implicitly (*sententialiter*).[46] He does not go on to show how Thomas himself uses the distinction between the two kinds of works in relation to the question at hand (viz., whether works done by one person may be of benefit to another). In the second text, something of the complexity of Thomas's argument is lost, but Biel is correct, strictly speaking, when he claims that, in Thomas's view, one who fulfills a divine precept according to the substance of the deed commanded does not sin merely by failing to fulfill it according to the Lawgiver's intention, that is, in charity. ("Else one who honors his parents out of a natural piety would sin thereby, and one who is not in a state of grace would sin by not murdering."[47] Biel's claim is only that this position is in keeping with Thomas's intention; although, in the text that Biel cites, Thomas does not deal with the question under the rubric of substance/intention, the main point he wishes to make is that the mode of charity is not integral to what God's law requires.[48]

Biel does not report the other element of Thomas's argument, which points to the fact that God's law also enjoins charity: the greatest of the commandments, and likewise the second, cannot be fulfilled apart from charity, since charity is precisely what they command. But this omission does not have a distorting effect in the context of Biel's presentation. He merely lists examples of the kinds of precepts that can be fulfilled, "according to the substance of the deed," apart from charity without incurring the guilt of violating the specific precept in question. When he attributes this view to Thomas, he is on solid ground.

In a Christological context, Biel calls on Thomas for a number of very general comments regarding merit and charity. In part Biel's references to Thomas are fair enough. He shows, for instance, how Thomas defends the possibility of Christ's meriting in the first moment of his conception. The notion of merit, after all, includes no reference to temporal succession.[49] But Biel's rather ambiguous attribution[50] seems to imply—incorrectly—that Thomas shares Biel's usage of *caritas* as a synonym for *gratia.*[51]

Biel's reference to Thomas's discussion of the ways in which the merit of one person may—or may not—be applied to another is terse to the point of obscurity. He completely overlooks Thomas's distinction between the benefit that is predicated on the claims of justice (*per viam meriti*) and that which arises from an appeal to God's unmerited liberality (*per modum orationis*). But the principal defect in Biel's report is his suggestion that Thomas leaves open the possibility of a merit that arises not from one's present condition but has to do, rather, with something following from his current disposition.[52] Biel seems to confuse *valere* (to be beneficial) with *mereri* (to merit), which Thomas is careful to keep distinct. So Biel makes the mistake of claiming that, according to Thomas, a work may be meritorious (not just beneficial) without regard to one's present condition (*non ex dispositione quam iam habet*). It seems likely that Biel should be regarded as attempting to express Thomas's claim that the benefit of human works may extend not only to an eternal reward (blessedness) but also to the resultant temporal relaxation of penalties. Elsewhere, as we have seen, Biel shows an awareness of Thomas's teaching that merit arises from charity on the part of the one who does good works. But Biel's language is unfortunate, to say the least; the point he ends up making is not Thomas's at all.

THE PREREQUISITE OF JUSTIFICATION: FAITH (IMPLICIT, EXPLICIT)

In the third book of the *Collectorium*, there are six citations in which Biel provides generally faithful and sympathetic accounts of major elements in Thomas's teaching concerning faith. Biel correctly associates Thomas with the claim that since the time of Adam's fall an explicit faith in the Mediator has always been necessary for the salvation of anyone who has reached the age of discretion.[53] In connection with his own attempt to show that everyone is without excuse before God (Romans 1.17), Biel addresses the case of one who is outside the sphere of Christian culture (e.g., *in silva natus*) and who therefore is never exposed to the teaching or preaching of the Gospel. Biel, like Thomas, is eager to avoid the inference that such a person is incapable of coming to explicit faith, since this would be to accuse God of failing to make adequate provision for human salvation. So he resolves the question by citing Thomas's dictum that "in those things which are necessary for salvation, God was not and is not unavailable [*numquam . . . deest vel defuit*] to anyone who seeks salvation, except through his own fault."[54] God will either send a preacher or make a direct revelation to anyone who is otherwise incapable of knowing what he must believe (*credenda*).[55]

Biel follows Thomas in holding that what must be believed explicitly if one is to be saved is above all the doctrine of the redemptive-mediatorial work of Christ.[56] He cites Thomas's words very carefully:

> Explicit faith is necessary in order to direct our intention toward the ultimate End. And because through sin man had drawn away from that End, he could not be led back except by the mediator of God and men, the Lord Jesus Christ. After sin, therefore, it was necessary to have explicit knowledge of the Redeemer, and especially of those things by which he leads us back toward the End after conquering the enemy who used to hold us captive. [For this purpose] four things were required. First, that our de-

> fender should be appointed, and this took place in the nativity. Second, that he should fight for us, and this was done in his passion. Third, that he should be victorious, which happened in his resurrection, when after conquering death he opened a way of access into eternity. Fourth, that he should make all of his own to be sharers in his victory, which will take place in the judgment, when he renders good to the good and evil to the evil.[57]

The only significant respect in which Biel alters Thomas's language is seen in his substitution of a form of the verb "to believe" (*credantur*) for Thomas's use of a form of the verb "to know" (*scirentur*). A slight nuance, perhaps—but one senses that Biel's qualified fideism may be what makes him uneasy about speaking of the *credenda* as *scienda*. Thomas holds that faith is a kind of knowledge, but Biel's modification has the effect—if not the intent—of obscuring that emphasis. (The plausibility of this conjecture is reduced, however, when we note that in other citations Biel retains the knowing-language employed by Thomas.)[58]

In addition to this fourfold analysis of what must be believed (or known) explicitly, Biel appeals to Thomas in support of his claim that no one can be saved without having an explicit faith in the mystery of the incarnation—and in the mystery of the triune God, which it presupposes. Then Biel associates himself with Thomas's emphasis on the special obligation of those who hold certain offices—priests, prophets, doctors, preachers.[59] Such persons are obliged to be ready to make a complete explication of the Church's faith as far as the clear substance of each article is concerned. At a deeper level "to explicate" means to probe the implications of what is affirmed explicitly. This is a task that can be completed only in heaven (*in patria*). But one whose office gives him a share in the Church's ministry of teaching and defending the faith must be able to expound to those committed to his care what is only implicit in the articles of the Creed. Biel adds that this special obligation extends no further than the practical limits set by the capacities of those to whom the teaching ministry is directed.[60]

To speak of the apologetic function is to broach the question of the relation between faith and reason. We have had several occasions to note Biel's failure to present a comprehensive statement of Thomas's views on that issue. In the third book of the *Collectorium*, however, Biel provides a meticulous summary of the way in which reason, according to Thomas, may or may not diminish the merit accruing to explicit faith in the Church's creed.[61] Thomas distinguishes, says Biel, between reason as a prior basis for the act of faith (without which one would not dare to believe) and reason as a means of deepening one's faith or communicating it to others. In the first case, an unanswerable proof will have the effect of destroying the merit of faith altogether, because it renders the act of believing less than fully voluntary. When a proposition is proven rationally, the option of *not* believing it is taken away; one simply may not withhold his assent. But no act can be meritorious unless it is voluntary. In the second case, however, the will to believe (on the basis of authority or revelation) precedes the appeal to reason. Here it is a matter of "faith seeking understanding," not vice versa, in order to defend the faith and to be of service to others. So long as the priority of faith is not threatened, the use of reason in this second way does not diminish but rather increases the merit of faith.

But when Biel points to Thomas's contrast between knowledge (*scientia*) of what is visible and faith (*fides*) in what lies beyond the reach of the senses, he seems to be confused about Thomas's use of the terms "faith" and "theology."[62] For Thomas feels free to speak of theology as a science even in passages where his principal intention is to remove the *credenda* from the realm of *scientia*.[63] But Biel misrepresents Thomas as claiming that theology can never be a science for the *viator*.[64]

CONCLUSIONS

By far the most intriguing result of our argument in this chapter is that Biel seems to be unaware of the conflict between himself and St. Thomas on the question whether man in his present condition (*homo viator*) is naturally capable of loving God above all things apart from grace (*ex puris naturalibus*). Biel carefully reports Thomas's opinion that with Adam's fall human nature was rendered incapable of loving God above all things merely by exercising its purely natural faculties. He makes it clear that—in Thomas's view—the sinner needs more than the "general influence" of the First Mover; his nature must be healed (not just sustained) before he will be able to love God above all things. In view of Biel's subsequent declaration that the wayfarer is indeed capable of loving God above all things *ex puris naturalibus*,[65] it is remarkable that Biel does not go to the trouble of disavowing Thomas's opinion. Indeed, by all indications, Biel presents Thomas's opinion in a relatively favorable light, although he stops short of an explicit endorsement.

How could Biel remain insensitive to the contrast between himself and Thomas at this point? His mishandling of Thomas's distinction between God's special help and the *concursus Dei generalis* might offer an obvious clue if it were not for the fact that his summary of Thomas's opinion leaves no doubt about the sinner's need to receive the healing grace that alone can enable him to love God above all things. Perhaps Biel just assumed that Thomas was speaking of the love of God not according to the substance of the act but rather according to the mode (i.e., *ex gratia*), which was included in God's intention when he established the first and greatest of the commandments. For in that case there would be no conflict between Biel and Thomas; Biel believes that man, *ex puris naturalibus*, can love God above all things as far as the sheer, objective content of the deed is concerned, but he acknowledges that the precept is not fully obeyed until the deed is done in the way the Lawgiver intended—in grace. We must admit, however, that nothing in Biel's paraphrase of Thomas clearly points toward such an explanation.

Perhaps, then, Biel would seek to reconcile his view with Thomas's by pointing to his own claim that the infusion of grace is simultaneous with the *viator*'s act of loving God above all things (in the act of contrition).[66] This enables Biel to claim that he, no less than Thomas, is unwilling to posit the act of loving God above all things in one who is not engraced. No one, on Biel's principles, loves God above all things apart from grace, since grace is infused at precisely the moment in which he loves God above all things. Yet it is by purely natural means that this act is elicited. In this way Biel puts himself in a position to claim that although the requisite act may be produced without the external aid of grace, there will never be a single moment in which such an act exists in one who is not also a recipient of grace. Thus Biel might claim to find a harmony between his view and Thomas's: both deny that anyone can love God above all things without the infusion of healing grace. Biel, of course, reverses the logical priority observed in Thomas's teaching that one loves God only on the condition that he first receive the gift of healing (enabling) grace. Biel teaches that the *viator* may receive grace—no longer healing so much as decorative or, at most, invigorating—only on the condition that he love God above all things *ex puris naturalibus.* Biel uses the notion of simultaneity to eliminate the clearly Pelagian taint of a temporal priority of man's love to God's gift, although his logical priorities are clear. Perhaps he hopes that the absence of a temporal succession will be enough to render his doctrine compatible with Thomas's.

Again, however, the speculative, post hoc nature of this solution must be acknowledged. Just on the basis of the internal evidence, the simpler answers may be (1) that Biel's reference to Thomas's "moderation" implies approval only of his position regarding man's natural ability to do morally good—but nonmeritorious—acts, or (2) that Biel simply took the contrast between himself and Thomas (on the *ex puris naturalibus*) for granted, sensing no need to underscore the obvious.

The second pattern that is worth emphasizing is Biel's tendency to portray Thomas as making greater claims for the sinner's ability to dispose himself for grace than Thomas himself would actually countenance. By preparing himself—again *ex puris naturalibus,* with the additional help of only the *concursus generalis*—fallen man (in Biel's rendering of Thomas's doctrine) can merit for himself the first grace, not condignly but at least congruously. What is so intriguing about this particular misrepresentation is that it coheres with Biel's general tendency (noted, for instance, in the previous chapter) to lay at Thomas's feet a doctrine bearing noticeable resemblance to elements of his own analysis of the sinner's ability to take at least a minimal first step toward God.

It should be noted that this view of Biel's doctrine of grace is challenged by some students of late medieval theology. Recently, for instance, A. E. McGrath has attempted to vindicate Biel's soteriology against the accusation of Pelagianism (or semi-Pelagianism). Both in a 1981 article and in the first volume of his *Iustitia Dei*, published in 1986, McGrath argues forcefully against the thesis, articulated by Heiko A. Oberman in particular, that Biel is to be regarded as a spokesman for resurgent Pelagian (or at least semi-Pelagian) perspectives in late medieval theology.[67] The decisive category for Biel, as McGrath notes, is that of covenant (*pactum*): "Biel and the *via moderna* operate with a concept of *covenantal* causality, by which the relationship between man's action and the divine response is a consequence of the divine ordination, rather than the nature of the entities in themselves."[68] The active role of the *viator* in the early stages of the process of justification—prior, that is, to the infusion of justifying grace—is in no way proportional to the infinite reward granted freely to those who do their very best (*facere quod in se est*). The fact that the sinner possesses the ability to assume an active role in meeting the conditions of the covenant—and the fact that God has bound himself to bestow an infinite reward upon all who do their (finite) best—must be understood as expressions of God's gracious, utterly free generosity in creating human beings with freedom, conscience, synderesis, and reason, on the one hand, and in establishing his covenant with fallen humanity, on the other. When God created human beings with such marvelous moral endowments, and when God entered into covenant with mankind to repair the consequences of the fall into sin, God acted freely, liberally, graciously.

It is, above all, the notion of *pactum*, McGrath suggests, that safeguards Biel's doctrine of justification from the taint of Pelagianism: "Gabriel Biel interprets the axiom *facienti quod in se est* to mean that God is under obligation to give the first grace to the man who desists from sin. However, this does not mean that man is capable of remitting his own sin. As Biel emphasizes, the link between doing *quod in se est* and the remission of sin is provided by the covenant, rather than the entities in themselves."[69] Biel teaches that "it is God, and God alone, who remits sin"[70]—and McGrath seems to think that this observation shows that Biel is not a Pelagian in his doctrine of salvation.

Even a thorough going Pelagian, however, need not hesitate to affirm that God alone remits sins: the crucial issues have to do with the conditions under which remission takes place and the extent of the sinner's ability—and responsibility—to do certain things on his own (*ex puris naturalibus*) in order to meet those conditions.

Biel's use of the notion of what McGrath terms "imposed" (as contrasted with "intrinsic") value—a notion that loudly echoes the Scotist doctrine of the *divina acceptatio*—is regarded as an additional safeguard against any suggestion that one can be the source of one's own salvation or that justification is a debt owed by God rather than the gift of God in his graciousness and radical freedom.[71]

McGrath further argues that Biel's doctrine of predestination is not as vacuous or as irrelevant as it is deemed to be by Oberman, who holds that Biel teaches a Pelagian doctrine of justification.[72] According to McGrath, the charge of Pelagianism arises only when Biel's doctrine of predestination is read anachronistically: Oberman's mistake, in McGrath's view, is to evaluate Biel's teaching not by the norms of the kinds of Catholic theology that had emerged by the late fifteenth century but rather in terms of the concerns and conceptualitites of a later era.[73]

It is of considerable interest, however, that after vigorously defending Biel against allegations that the soteriology of the *via moderna* is tainted by a Pelagian view of the human situation before God, McGrath cites Biel, along with Scotus, as a prime example of the late medieval tendency to misunderstand the Augustinian doctrine of justification because of a reliance on collections of "sentences" from Augustine's writings rather than on the works of Augustine himself. Isolated statements, taken out of context, were inevitably distorted and misunderstood. In this way, McGrath observes, Scotus and Biel "both manage to achieve a complete inversion of Augustine's teaching on the relation between grace and free will by confusing an image used by Augustine himself with a similar image found in the pseudo-Augustinian *Hypognosticon*."[74] If Biel effects "a complete inversion of Augustine's teaching on the relation between grace and free will," it is difficult to see why it is misleading to characterize his position as Pelagian or semi-Pelagian.

Yet the really important question is not whether Gabriel Biel was a semi-Pelagian in the strictest sense of that term. The relevant question is whether his optimism about the human capacity to contribute actively to one's own justification before God had the effect of setting up a theology of self-reliance that leaves the *viator* subject to a potentially terrifying sense of responsibility to merit God's grace (even if only *de congruo*) by disposing himself for grace (*faciendo quod in se est*) without any additional assistance or enablement beyond his purely natural endowment as a moral and rational creature (*ex suis naturalibus*). The crucial question is not whether Biel meets the strict definition of what it means to call a theologian or his doctrine Pelagian but whether Biel's analysis of human abilities and responsibilities (apart from any special enablement by grace) leaves the sinner in virtually the same predicament, psychologically and spiritually, as would be the case under Pelagian or semi-Pelagian assumptions.

It is possible, after all, to use Augustinian terminology to make an essentially Pelagian point. It is possible to appropriate the rhetoric of *gratia* in such a way as to emphasize human competence, initiative, and responsibility for taking the steps that are pivotal in determining one's own destiny. It is plausible to view the Gabrielist doctrine of grace as an instance of just such a pattern. For all his emphasis on God's graciousness in arranging the possibility of salvation, the ultimate effect of Biel's vision of the *viator*'s situation before God is not to heighten the sense of helplessness and radical dependence on divine assistance. Its religious effect, on the contrary, is to enhance a mood of self-reliance. According to Biel, God has already acted graciously in establishing the covenant, but now the response to God's initiative depends decisively on the unassisted movement of the human will. If that is not a Pelagian view of the human predicament, it might as well be.

As Oberman has shown, it is possible for a doctrine to be Augustinian in its outer structure but Pelagian at its inner core.[75] That is precisely the case with Biel's doctrine of justification. The doctrine of the *pactum* allows Biel to thematize the graciousness of the whole economy of salvation; Biel's final word, however, is not an invitation to cast oneself on divine mercy but rather a challenge to rise up and actualize the possibilities that have been set before each human being through God's work in creation and in the establishment of the covenant. In sovereign freedom and graciousness, God created the world as the stage on which human destiny unfolds, endowed human beings with awesome moral and spiritual capacities, and bound himself, by the terms of the covenant, to bestow his grace on anyone who does his very best: now the burden is on the sinner to win God's favor (*de congruo*) by doing "what in him lies" (*quod in se est*), thereby making an appropriate response to the opportunities so graciously afforded him. Regardless of one's view on whether it is fitting to characterize this blend of optimism and activism as Pelagian (or as semi-Pelagian), Biel's doctrine of justification clearly does involve a major shift away from the mature Augustine's (and Aquinas's) view of the sinner's radical dependence on the activating, enabling effect of grace upon the soul. For Biel, the *viator* is capable of loving God above all things (thus fulfilling the law and meriting the gift of grace) without the benefit of any supernatural assistance beyond the *concursus generalis* by which all things are preserved in existence and moved toward their natural end. At this point one is justified in speaking of an anthropological optimism that is foreign to the mature Augustine (and to Aquinas). What is more, Biel is convinced that if the *viator* it to receive God's justifying grace, he *must* do what he *can* do for himself. Here lies the basis on which one may speak of Biel's moral heroism or activism. Again the contrast with the perspectives of both Augustine and Aquinas is unmistakable.

For our present purposes, the most important implication of this discussion lies in the fact that Biel's appropriation of Thomas's teaching on justification involved a systematic distortion in the direction of Biel's own optimism about what the *viator* can do for himself. Other interpreters of St. Thomas during the late medieval period—including self-avowed Thomists, such as Cajetan—made much the same mistake with regard to St. Thomas's doctrine of grace.[76] Our point is not that Biel is to be censured as an exceptionally inept or insensitive interpreter of Aquinas; by the standards of his contemporaries, Biel seems to have been no worse an interpreter of the Thomistic doctrine of the preparation for grace than were many of those who, unlike himself, regarded themselves as disciples of St. Thomas. The fact remains, nonetheless, that Biel appropriates Aquinas's doctrine in a way that both reflects and reinforces his own tendency toward moral activism and anthropological optimism.

NINE

ESCHATOLOGY

Few questions were more crucial to the development of patterns of dissent and protest in the early sixteenth century than were those dealing with death, purgatory, prayers for the dead, and indulgences. The religious crisis out of which the Protestant Reformation was born found its decisive focus in criticism of the abuses that had arisen in the context of late medieval uncertainty about the theology of indulgences. Widespread religious anxiety made the issues at stake in the controversy over indulgences urgent and critical to the evolution of spirituality during the transition from late medieval to early modern Christianity in Europe.

In this chapter, we will not speak to the question of Biel's total treatment of issues relating to the use and misuse of indulgences. We will look, rather, at a number of texts that illustrate Biel's use of St. Thomas as a resource for his own eschatology. Since the bulk of these texts deal with the question of intercession for the dead, this body of evidence will put us in touch with certain elements of Thomas's teaching that were directly relevant to the controversy over indulgences.

POST MORTEM: THE ABODE OF THE DEAD

We already have had occasion to note the fourfold topography of the afterworld that Biel borrows from Thomas.[1] It is true that Biel does not paint a complete picture of Thomas's doctrine concerning the abode of the soul between death and the resurrection. He does make it clear, however, that Thomas shares the medieval Catholic conception of purgatory as an extension of history—a kind of half-way house—in which redeemed souls, on their way to glory, remain until all penalties and works of satisfaction still outstanding at the time of death have been resolved.[2] But what Biel places in sharpest relief is Thomas's emphatic rejection of the claim that no soul goes to its ultimate abode until the time of the last judgment: except for those in purgatory, Biel and Thomas insist, souls go directly either to heaven or to hell. For the merit or demerit of the souls is like the weight of bodies. "Hence just as a body is immediately carried to its place because of its lightness or heaviness, unless it be held back, so also when the bond of flesh is dissolved . . . the soul immediately attains its reward or penalty unless something hinders it."[3] The hindrance is a matter of penalties that must be suffered in purgatory before some souls will be allowed to receive the reward of blessedness.

Biel gives a close and sympathetic reading of several arguments by which Thomas supports this conclusion.[4] For instance, the bodily continuity resulting from our common descent from Adam (Acts 17.26) is contrasted with the radical discontinuity of souls, which are created one at a time. Thus it is fitting that all of the just should be glorified in their bodies at the same time (in the resurrection), but the same congruency does not apply to the glorification of their souls. The glory of the body, moreover, is of far less moment than that of the soul. To defer the souls' glorification until the time of the resurrection would be to impose on the saints a great and unwarranted loss.[5]

PRO DEFUNCTIS: INTERCESSION FOR THE DEAD

It is well known that Johann Tetzel's activities as a merchant of indulgences were motivated by the need to raise funds for the renovation of St. Peter's in Rome. Biel speaks to a similar case when he asks whether the dead can receive any benefit from indulgences purchased in their behalf by their survivors.[6] After reviewing the arguments to the contrary, Biel notes that Thomas's answer is affirmative but with a certain qualification (*sub quadam distinctione*). Thomas notes, according to Biel, that an indulgence may be conferred under one of two conditions. It may be granted (1) to those who perform certain works of piety or (2) to those for whom such works are done. In the first case, an indulgence is of no benefit to the deceased, who is incapable of doing the requisite works. (No one can, on his own authority, transfer the benefit of such an indulgence from himself to someone else; he is not competent, in himself, to dispose of the Church's *thesaurus spiritualis.*) But in the second case, an indulgence may be of benefit to the dead if the requisite works of piety are applied to the dead by the intention of the one who secures the indulgence. (Such an application, Biel observes, is in harmony with the intention of the one who grants the indulgence.) Biel quotes Thomas's conclusion that "there is no reason why the Church may transfer the common merits, on which the indulgences depend, to the living but not to the dead."[7] He goes on to note one other argument adduced by Thomas in support of this position. The merit of the whole Church is more efficacious than the merit of one person. But because personal merit on the part of the living may be of benefit to the dead, much more may the Church's corporate merit be brought to bear in their behalf.[8]

The good works of the living impinge upon the dead only when the living are united to the dead in charity;[9] thus it is already clear that the beneficiaries cannot be the damned but are, rather, redeemed souls in purgatory.[10] This transference is effected by the intention of the one who does a certain work specifically for another who happens to be deceased.[11] Because the bond of charity is presupposed in any efficacious work of vicarious satisfaction, it is above all the eucharist (in which Christ, the fount of charity, is present) and the giving of alms (as an effect of charity) that are suitable as works to be performed for the benefit of the dead.[12] But since the direction of the intention is always involved in such works, prayer is equally suitable: "by definition [prayer] involves a reference not only to the one who prays . . . but more directly to the one for whom the prayer is offered."[13] Other works, such as fasting, are not intrinsically referred to the benefit of another; they can be done in charity, however, thus acquiring an extrinsic intentionality toward the deceased and qualifying as works performed in his behalf. For any work whatever can be performed in love and directed toward the benefit of others.[14]

The impact of such a work is not restricted to the person for whose benefit, in particular, it is done. Biel endorses Thomas's suggestion that a prayer for one soul in purgatory will be of benefit to all others, for every soul in purgatory exists in a greater or lesser state of charity, which makes all things common.[15] Thus the Church's intercession will be more efficacious for one whose charity is greater, even if the intercession is not offered especially for him. For his own charity ensures that he will experience a greater joy in the good that befalls another.

But the benefit of vicarious intercession is limited to the remission of temporal penalties.[16] The prayers of the living cannot be brought to bear upon the ultimate *status* of the deceased (eternal damnation or blessedness).[17] For the eternal destiny of each person is determined in accordance with his own intrinsic worth (*secundum mensuram accipientis*), which is an effective disposition of the soul for either heaven or hell.[18]

With Thomas, Biel affirms that the Church's intercession may benefit the dead both *ex opere operato* and *ex opere operantis.*[19] In the latter respect, a work may be considered in either of two ways, that is, in relation to its principal author or in relation to a secondary agent commissioned by him. *Ex opere operantis,* a work is beneficial to others, including the dead, only to the extent that it is done by one who is in a state of charity. But Biel joins Thomas in arguing that this requirement must be understood only in relation to the principal agent. The charity of one who endows a mass for his deceased father is not rendered ineffectual by a lack of charity on the part of the priest who celebrates it. But if the principal agent is not in a state of charity when he ordains the celebration of the mass, it will not benefit the deceased, regardless of the celebrant's piety. Aquinas, on the other hand, insists that while works of mercy performed for the deceased by one who is still in a state of sin (*servus in peccato existens*) are to some extent efficacious, such works are even more beneficial when provided by one who is himself in a state of grace and charity (*Magis tamen valerent si in caritate essent*).[20]

Biel makes common cause with Thomas in refuting the claim that it would be unjust for the souls in purgatory to be in the position of suffering great loss through the negligence of others. (If the living should fail to pray for them, after all, they would suffer—through no fault of their own—a postponement of their release from purgatory.) Here the decisive consideration, according to both Biel and Thomas, is that intercession for the dead is effective only for a temporal good (such as the shortening of the years to be spent in purgatory). If the failure to pray for the dead had any bearing on someone's eternal destiny, the objection would stand. Sometimes a person may be deprived of temporal goods through the fault of others. "But no one can be deprived of an eternal reward except through his own guilt."[21]

As hinted earlier, Biel associates himself with Thomas's critique of the claim that not even the damned are entirely beyond the reach of the Church's intercession. He gives a very close account of several arguments by which Thomas refutes this view. The damned, first of all, are irrevocably *in termino.* A soul in purgatory is still somehow a *viator,* but the damned are no longer *in via* at all. They, no less than the saints in glory, have arrived at their final destination (*terminus*). As the glory of the blessed is irrevocable, so is the misery of the damned. "Hence their penalty cannot be diminished, just as the reward of the saints cannot be increased."[22]

Biel notes, secondly, that Thomas alludes to one possible way in which prayers might benefit the damned.[23] Some have suggested, he says, that although the penalties of the damned cannot be interrupted or diminished, still the Church's prayers might eliminate one cause for additional grief: at least the intercession of the living will spare them the terror of seeing themselves so absolutely forsaken that no one cares for them at all. But Biel joins Thomas in foreclosing this possibility on the authority of St. Augustine, who teaches that the spirits of the damned are totally oblivious to anything that is done by the living. So Biel cites Thomas's conclusion: "They do not know when prayers are made for them, unless in exceptional cases [*supra communem legem*] it should be revealed to some of the damned, which is altogether uncertain. Hence it is safer to say simply that prayers do not benefit the damned, nor does the Church intend to pray for them."[24] Although Biel does not explicitly add his own endorsement to Thomas's argument, the context includes no rebuttal or caveat; since Biel has already made it clear that he shares Thomas's conclusion, the total effect is that of an implicit acknowledgment of the value of Thomas's analysis.

Finally, Biel and Thomas must come to terms with a popular proof-text (II Maccabees 12.40–46) that seems to imply that prayers can benefit even the damned.[25] Judas Maccabeus offered intercession for those who died in mortal sin (having violated the prohibition against taking things that have been consecrated to idols). Because they died in a state of mortal sin, they were already in hell, but Judas seems to assume that they are not immune to the benefit of his prayers. Biel refutes this argument by pointing to Thomas's exegesis of the text. The gifts were taken not in reverence of idols but merely as spoils of war. The greed of the victors was not a mortal but a venial sin: thus their souls were not in hell but in purgatory, where they were still within the scope of intercession by the living. Even if the victors sinned in taking what was offered to idols, moreover, it is likely that they would have repented when they saw themselves in danger of being killed in the ensuing battle. In that case, again, they would not have died, as the objection presupposes, in a state of mortal sin.[26] So the text from II Maccabees must be understood as referring to intercession for souls in purgatory, not for the damned.

IN PATRIA: THE LOVE AND KNOWLEDGE OF THE BLESSED

In two lengthy citations, Biel provides considerable insight into Thomas's analysis of the condition of the blessed in heaven. The twin foci of that analysis are the will and the intellect in their glorified state.

The Order of Charity in Heaven

When Biel asks about the appropriate objects of the saints' charity, and the relative magnitude and intensity of the love due to each, he turns to Thomas's account of the *ordo caritatis* in heaven.[27] The order of charity that is now in force will persist in heaven, according to both Thomas and Biel, as far as the love of God *super omnia* is concerned. Then as now, the order of charity will require that God be loved more than anything else, both by himself and by all others. This requirement will include both the magnitude of the good that is desired for him and the intensity of the act of loving him. For in heaven the command to love God above all things will be fulfilled in the most perfect way possible, with respect to every dimension or qualification of the *actus diligendi.*

Each of the blessed will love himself more than any of his fellow saints as far as the intensity of the act is concerned. By the gift of charity, he directs his mind absolutely to God as his End, which pertains, therefore, to the ordinate love of himself. In charity he wishes all things to be directed toward God, and thus he wills his own beatitude, by which he is united to God, more intensely than any other created good, including the blessedness of anyone else; the intensity of love is determined by reference to the lover rather than the beloved. But with respect to the relative share of glory that the blessed wills, in charity, for each of his neighbors, he will have a greater love for those who are more worthy (hence more blessed) than himself. His will, after all, will be in perfect harmony with God's, which ordains that each should have what is due him, according to divine justice, in view of the degree of his own merit. Accordingly, each will desire a greater good for those who are better than himself. In this sense, each saint will love his neighbors strictly in proportion to their nearness to God. The whole of life for the *beatus* will consist in an ordering of the mind toward God, which means that the order of love will be defined with reference to him. *In via,* the necessities of life require one to provide for his own family before turning to assist his neighbor with any resources that may be left over; *in patria,* neither children nor neighbors will require such help. It will still be possible, however, to have a special affection for those to whom one had special attachments or responsibilities in this life. The causes of virtuous love (such as the special nearness of family members) will not come to an end in heaven. But these causes will pale into insignificance when compared to the greater nearness of another *beatus* not to oneself but to God.[28]

The Knowledge of the Saints

Biel's treatment of the *scientia beatorum* gives him an opportunity to discuss one important element in Thomas's epistemology in order to express Thomas's view of the contrast between the knowledge that we may have *in via* and that which will be enjoyed *in patria.*[29] Paul's statement that knowledge is ephemeral (I Corinthians 13.8) prompts Biel to ask, with Thomas, whether human knowledge is consistent with the glorified state (*utrum scientia evacuetur in patria*). He reports that, according to Thomas, the habit of knowledge (as a perfection of the soul) will not be done away with, whereas the mode of all human knowledge *in via*—that is, by means of phantasms arising through the senses—will be replaced by an immediate cognition of the intelligible object *in patria.* In heaven as on earth, things will be known in their proper genus, but the mode of this knowledge will no longer be bound to the senses.[30] Biel finds no fault with Thomas's presentation up to this point, but he proceeds to set himself in opposition to Thomas with respect to the *actus scientiae:* he argues that Paul's language excludes the act (though not the habit) of knowledge in heaven, whereas Thomas contends that "to say the habit remains but not the act seems absurd, since a habit is nothing but the capacity for an act."[31] Thomas insists, therefore, that the *actus* is changed (*mutabitur*) but not abolished (*evacuatur*). Biel seeks to treat knowledge as he does faith and hope in relation to the *beati,* whereas Thomas draws a sharp distinction: faith and hope are entirely done away with,[32] but knowledge continues, in a modified way, among the blessed. Biel does not make this conflict explicit; he simply registers his own opinion without acknowledging that it is refuted by Thomas in the texts that he has just cited.

CONCLUSIONS

A close reading of Biel's citations will provide a reliable account of Thomas's perspective on numerous issues involving the state of the soul after death. Thomas is cited less frequently here than in many other areas, but Biel's interpretations prove to be almost uniformly accurate and sympathetic.

This discussion provides the context for Biel's presentation of Thomas's insistence on the crucial role of sense-based phantasms in the processes of human knowledge. Although the depth and complexity of Thomas's arguments are not adequately reflected, still the fundamental tendency of his epistemology is clearly suggested in Biel's citation. Thomas's Aristotelian emphasis on the priority of sense-experience as the ground of all our knowledge is made perfectly clear, even though the logic of that position is not expressed in Thomas's terms.

In relation to theological discussions concerning "soul-sleep,"[33] Biel's painstaking account of Thomas's argument against the doctrine that reward and punishment are postponed until the eschaton must be recognized as the refutation of a view very similar to one that Luther sometimes seems to have entertained.[34]

Perhaps the most important of the texts reviewed in this chapter are those delineating Thomas's view of the ways in which the

Church's intercession may—or may not—be of benefit to the dead. Although Thomas sanctions the sale of indulgences to raise funds for the construction of a church, Biel also reports that Thomas (1) binds the merit of an indulgence to the charity and intention of the one who secures it and (2) restricts the benefit of an indulgence to the reduction of temporal penalties (i.e., in purgatory). From Thomas (through Biel) Luther could have learned that an eternal reward cannot be obtained through the purchase of indulgences (for oneself or for others). Tetzel's alleged overstatement of their efficacy is less compatible with Thomas's teaching than is Luther's critique.[35]

TEN

POST THOMAM

Perhaps the most obvious of our conclusions is that Thomas is indeed a major source for Biel's theological enterprise. We have noted 421 texts in which Biel puts himself in dialogue with Thomas. The preceding eight chapters have made it clear that in reading the *Collectorium* and *Expositio* one encounters a great deal of information—along with some misinformation—about Thomas's positions on a wide range of philosophical and theological issues.

The areas in which Biel proves most prone to cite Thomas's opinions are sacramental theology and ethics (especially social ethics). The heavy concentration of Biel's references to Aquinas in these two areas suggests that he finds Thomas most helpful in dealing with concrete-practical rather than with abstract-speculative matters. The contrast is not, of course, absolute or exclusive. Yet it is undeniable that Thomas helps Biel to understand not the ontology of the God-Man so much as the concrete saving work of the incarnate Christ. Biel sometimes refers to Thomas in connection with questions of value theory, but he more frequently appeals to Thomas for guidance concerning what ought to be done (*agenda*) in particular cases. Similarly, Thomas helps Biel to explain what a sacrament is and how Christ's presence in the eucharist is to be understood, but it is clear that Biel is even more receptive to Thomas's suggestions for dealing with concrete liturgical questions: how, for instance, should a celebrant priest deal with the discovery that poison or a spider has somehow been placed in the consecrated chalice?

In sharp contrast to some of his fellow nominalists, Biel is generally quite sympathetic in his handling of St. Thomas's theology.[1] He speaks of Thomas in tones of reverence (*sanctus Thomas, beatus Thomas*); even in the relatively rare instances in which Biel rejects Thomas's opinion, it is clear that he does so cautiously and reluctantly. Biel's instinct is that of a synthesist. He has a keen sense of Thomas's authority, and he makes a sustained (if not always successful) attempt to bridge the gap between the *viae*. It would be the grossest of caricatures to portray Biel as systematically hostile to the Thomistic point of view. Explicitly or implicitly, entirely or (more rarely) in part, Biel associates himself with Thomas's position in more than 95 percent of the citations. Even when Biel is convinced that Thomas is fundamentally in error, he acknowledges that Thomas's opinion is a matter to be reckoned with. Ordinarily he will seek to resolve a conflict between Thomas and Occam into a deeper harmony that will allow him to stop short of turning his back on Thomas altogether. And when Biel knows that he simply must draw a sharp contrast between his own position and Thomas's, quite frequently the disagreement will be at the level of *ratio* rather than *opinio*. In many instances, that is, Biel affirms on the basis of faith what Thomas believes he can prove on the basis of reason; what Biel rejects is not Thomas's opinion but the methodology by which Thomas seeks to establish a conclusion that Biel, in fact, shares with him.

In 1927, Carl Feckes took note of the generous, moderate thrust of Biel's Occamism. Biel, he argued, was anything but a narrow sectarian in his allegiance to Occam's system.[2] Feckes pointed to the friendly reception accorded the Gabrielist point of view at the Council of Trent as an indication of the Catholic breadth of Biel's theology.[3] Perhaps it is not too much to suggest that Biel's profound, empathic engagement with Thomistic thought is part of what underlies this perception of Biel as a resource for theological breadth and moderation.

The single most frequent source of Biel's substantive disagreement with Thomas is the voluntarism that underlies Biel's doctrine of God. Biel fears that Thomas's theological method—and above all the way in which Thomas uses reason for dogmatic purposes—will jeopardize the ultimacy of God's freedom and power. Frequently an urgent sense of the absolute priority of the divine will in relation to every conception of what is just or appropriate makes Biel uneasy with Thomas's attempt to show why God acts as he does or to posit a significant continuity between the natural and the supernatural. (Biel's critique of Thomas's doctrine of divine ideas is a vivid illustration of this tendency.) God's acts, Biel will insist, are subject to no external norms of what is good or true or just. His will, rather, is constitutive of whatever goodness or truth or justice there may be. Biel attempts—though not always successfully—to observe this principle as the first criterion of responsible language about God. And he fears that this whole enterprise is threatened by Thomas's manner of using reason to extrapolate from human ideas of justice to some view (however remote) of certain ways in which God simply *must* act because he is just. Thomas's God, he senses, is just too predictable, bound to the norms of reason and justice rather than sovereign over them. For Biel, on the contrary, "it is just because God wills it" (*iustum est quia Deus vult*), not the other way around: here Biel draws the line sharply and without his customary attempt to find the *via media* in which, by temperament, he feels most at home. One result of Biel's unwillingness to compromise at this point is a serious lacuna in his presentation of St. Thomas's point of view: nowhere in the *Collectorium* or *Expositio* does Biel offer a thorough exposition of the Thomistic view of the coherence of faith and reason, or Aquinas's doctrine of divine ideas, or his way of conceiving the analogy between God and the cosmos.

On the whole, Biel is quite careful and accurate in his presentation of St. Thomas's thought. Often he sees fit to cite long passages from Thomas's works almost verbatim. Statistically speaking, it is exceedingly rare for Biel to lay himself open to the charge of infidelity to Thomas's intention. Indeed, Biel's integrity as an interpreter of Thomas's thought is most clearly established when he deftly summarizes an opinion or an argument to which he then registers a pointed dissent. Heiko Oberman's claim that Biel is, for the most part, a competent expositor of the medieval tradition[4] finds ample confirmation in our survey of the ways in which Biel appropriates elements of Thomas's theology.

Yet it is arguable that the one area in which Biel is most prone to misrepresent Thomas's opinion involves precisely the complex of issues that proved central to the crisis from which the Protestant Reformation was born. When Biel begins to talk about contrition, grace, and merit, his customary skill as a guide to Aquinas's thought often deserts him. On the crucial point of the sinner's ability to set himself in motion toward God (by disposing himself for grace *ex suis naturalibus,* thus meriting grace *de congruo*), Biel falls into a pattern that is all too clear: St. Thomas would not recognize as his own the doctrine of justification that Biel attributes to him. A diligent reading of the *Expositio* and *Collectorium* provides a wealth of information about Thomas's opinions on a wide range of issues, but one whose primary access to the Thomist perspective is by way of Biel's interpretations will remain uninformed or misinformed about Thomas's doctrines of sin, grace, and justification. How can the sinner be turned toward God and disposed to receive the infusion of justifying grace? The answer that Biel places on the lips of Thomas reflects Biel's own semi-Pelagian optimism about the inner resources available even to fallen, unengraced humanity. Especially intriguing is the fact that Biel's error at this point occurs in the context of a larger fidelity to Thomas's teaching on such related topics as the need for explicit faith and the sinner's inability to love God above all things apart from grace. Biel is so correct elsewhere that one is left puzzled about how he could be so consistently wrong here. The total effect, in any case, is to make it all too easy for an unsuspecting reader to assume that, here as elsewhere, Biel's accuracy equals his reverence for Thomas. In fact, as we have seen, Biel is clearly wrong about Thomas's conception of the sinner's involvement in the earliest stages of the process of justification. The hands may be the hands of St. Thomas, but the voice is the voice of Gabriel Biel.

Heiko Oberman rightly cautions against a too-hasty censure of Biel's interpretation of Thomas's teaching concerning the basis on which the sinner must be disposed for grace. In light of the *Summa theologiae,* Biel is clearly mistaken in his claim that, according to

Thomas, no special help beyond God's *influentia generalis* is required in order for the sinner to prepare himself for grace. But Oberman observes that Biel's interpretation was not so unacceptable by fifteenth-century standards as it seems today.[5] As Otto Scheel reminded Denifle, it is unhistorical to hold Biel to the same standards by which we judge the work of a modern historian of dogma.[6] And we have already noted that the specific text on which Biel bases what seems to be an erroneous interpretation is not so explicit as to leave no room at all for Biel's interpretation. The cautious way in which Biel expresses himself and the minimal claim he makes for Thomas are not suggestive of a clumsy or thoughtless procedure.

We may grant that Biel's interpretation of Thomas is incorrect without becoming insensitive to the real ambiguity of the evidence in which it is grounded. Indeed, it would be remarkable to find unanimity at this point among Thomas's interpreters in the fifteenth century (or in the twentieth). Our point is surely not that Biel was an incompetent interpreter of Thomas, even though others in the fifteenth and early sixteenth centuries may be deemed, by contemporary standards, to have made a more faithful presentation of Thomas's position regarding the preparation for grace.[7] But if Biel were one's primary source for a knowledge of Thomas's doctrine of grace, the pattern of misinterpretations that we have identified would certainly have the effect of associating Thomas with certain semi-Pelagian tendencies in Biel's soteriology. Indeed, Biel's frequent and largely sympathetic references to Thomas create the impression that, unless otherwise noted, Biel intends to maintain a basic continuity between his own position and that of St. Thomas. One who knows Thomas only—or mainly—on the basis of Biel's summaries will hardly be in a position to distinguish Thomas's perspective from Biel's. For nothing in Biel's descriptions of Thomas's point of view gives any hint that there are resources in Thomas's soteriology for correcting the semi-Pelagian thrust of Biel's teaching about the sinner's preparation for grace.

More positively, Biel finds in Thomas important resources for his own perspective in the areas of social ethics and sacraments. Biel's critique of usury, for instance, leans heavily on a careful and sympathetic analysis of the precapitalist economic theory articulated by Thomas. Similarly, Biel appropriates Thomas's doctrine of the sword in such a way as to leave no opening for the possibility of a morally justified revolution. Finally, in his presentation of elements of Thomas's sacramental theology, Biel provides extended summaries of Thomistic teachings on a wide range of issues. By and large, Biel is a faithful expositor of Thomas's teachings about the sacraments. Here as elsewhere, however, the one area in which Biel consistently misrepresents Thomas's position involves the questions of grace, merit, free will, and justification. The single theme emerging most emphatically in Biel's treatment of Thomas's doctrine of the Lord's Supper is a strong affirmation of the real presence of the body and blood of Christ in the consecrated elements. Thus one whose primary access to the thought of St. Thomas Aquinas is by way of Biel's summaries and interpretations will find abundant resources for a medieval social theory and a thoroughly Catholic view of the eucharist.

What is beginning to emerge is a picture of the religious situation in early sixteenth-century Europe in which the importance of Thomistic perspectives is clearly both profound and far-reaching. Not only in the late medieval Thomist school as such but in Biel's strand of the *via moderna* as well, Thomistic thought remained surprisingly vital and influential. Not only in Tridentine Catholicism but in several varieties of Protestant theology as well,[8] Thomism continued to be an important element in the ongoing theological conversation. Not only Luther's relation to St. Thomas but also the fate of Thomism at the hands of such figures as Pierrre d'Ailly, John Staupitz, Henry of Gorkum, Martin Bucer, Peter Martyr Vermigli, and Jerome Zanchi merits careful consideration by those who are interested in developing a comprehensive account of the intellectual roots of Protestantism.

NOTES

ABBREVIATIONS

De pot.	Thomas Aquinas, *De potentia Dei*
De reg. Iud.	Thomas Aquinas, *De regimine Iudaeorum*
De reg. princ.	Thomas Aquinas, *De regno (De regimine principum), ad regem Cypri*
Eth. Nicom.	Aristotle, *Nicomachean Ethics*
Exp.	Gabriel Biel, *Expositio canonis missae*
Inst.	John Calvin, *Institutio Christianae Religionis*
In x lib. Eth.	Thomas Aquinas, *In decem libros Ethicorum expositio*
PL	Migne, *Patrologiae cursus completus . . . series Latina*
Polit.	Aristotle, *Politics*
Quaest. quodlib.	Thomas Aquinas, *Quaestiones quodlibetales*
Sent.	General reference to *Scripta super libros Sententiarum* by Gabriel Biel (i.e., the *Epithoma pariter et collectorium circa quattuor Sententiarum libros*), Thomas Aquinas, Johannes Capreolus, Alexander of Hales, John Duns Scotus, and William of Occam
S.T.	Thomas Aquinas, *Summa theologiae,* or Alexander of Hales, *Summa theologica*
WA	Martin Luther, *D. Martin Luthers Werke: Kritische Gesamtausgabe* (Weimar)

PREFACE

1. Professor Denis R. Janz of Loyola University in New Orleans is currently engaged in important research designed to address the question of Luther's knowledge

of St. Thomas's theology (along with the related questions of Luther's attitude toward the person and authority of the *Doctor Angelicus*). A preliminary report on his analysis of references to Aquinas in the Weimar edition of Luther's works was presented at a colloquy held in connection with the December 1985 meeting of the American Society of Church History in New York. Those who are concerned about the interface between Medieval and Reformation studies await the publication of the results of Janz's research with keen interest.

THOMAS AQUINAS AND THE *VIA MODERNA*

1. Heinrich Hermelink, *Geschichte der theologischen Fakultät in Tübingen vor der Reformation* (Tübingen: J. C. B. Mohr, 1906), p. 133: "Es sind nur Andeutungen, die über das theologische System Ockams und über das *Collectorium* Biels gemacht werden konnten. Allein sie ermöglichen ein deutliches Bild über die Bedeutung und historische Stellung der via moderna an der Hochschule zu Tübingen. Ihre Bedeutung besteht nicht in der Ueberwindung der scholastischen Spitzfindigkeiten und nicht in der Herbeiführung einer Aera der realen Wissenschaften; sondern diese scholastische Schule hat deshalb eine grosse Wirkung hinterlassen, weil sie zum erstenmal deutlich die beiden Gebeite des Wissens und Glaubens getrennt und weil sie sowohl positive, als noch mehr negative die reformatorische Entwicklung Luthers vorbereitet hat. Sind alle Vermutungen richtig, die über die Vorgeschichte der via moderna ausgesprochen wurden, dann wäre merkwürdig, dass durch ein neues Hereinfluten greichisch-stoischen Geistes (in der terministischen Logik und Ethik) die deutsche Tat der Reformation veranlasst worden wäre. Doch sei dem wie ihm wolle, zum Verständnis der Theologie Luthers muss eine Geschichte dieser scholastischen Richtung eschrieben werden, von dem venerabilis inceptor und seinen Vorlaufern an bis zum 'letzten Scholastiker' und bis zum Erfurter Lehrer Trutfetter."

2. Important studies include Bengt Hägglund, *Theologie und Philosophie bei Luther und in der occamistischen Tradition* (Lund: C. W. K. Gleerup, 1955); Paul Vignaux, "Luther: lecteur de Gabriel Biel" (*Eglise et Théologie* 22, 1959), pp. 33–52; Irwin Iserloh, *Gnade und Eucharistie in der philosophischen Theologie des Wilhelm von Ockham: Ihre Bedeutung für der Reformation* (Wiesbaden: Franz Steiner, 1956); Steve Ozment, "Homo Viator: Luther and Late Medieval Theology," in Steve Ozment, ed., *The Reformation in Medieval Perspective* (Chicago: Quadrangle Books, 1971), pp. 142–54; Heiko A. Oberman, *The Harvest of Medieval Theology: Gabriel Biel and Late Medieval Nominalism*, 3rd ed. (Durham, N.C.: The Labyrinth Press,

1983); Charles Trinkhaus and Heiko A. Oberman, eds., *The Pursuit of Holiness in Late Medieval and Renaissance Religion* (Leiden: E. J. Brill, 1974).

3. David C. Steinmetz, *Misericordia Dei: The Theology of Johannes von Staupitz in Its Late Medieval Setting* (Leiden: E. J. Brill, 1968); idem, *Luther and Staupitz: An Essay in the Intellectual Origins of the Protestant Reformation* (Durham, N.C.: Duke University Press, 1980).

4. Heinrich Denifle, *Luther und Luthertum in der ersten Entwickelung* I, 2 (Mainz: F. Kirchheim and Co., 1906), pp. 523, 574.

5. Joseph Lortz, *Die Reformation in Deutschland I,* 3rd ed. (Freiburg: Herder, 1948), pp. 170, 396. Lortz's view of the critical importance of Luther's inability to draw on Thomistic resources finds emphatic expression in his *Wie kam es zur Reformation?* (Einsiedeln: Johannes Verlag, 1950), p. 20: "Luther ausserhalb des Klosters, ausserhalb der Theologie, Luther erfullt von der Theologie des heiligen Thomas oder des römischen Messbuchs statt von der Theologie ockhamistischer Prägung—: seine reformatorische Wendung hätte sich nie vollziehen können; jene innere Reibung, die zur Entzündung und dann zur durchreissenden Krisis führte, bliebe vollkommen unerklarlich . . ." Completely overlooked in Lortz's argument is the fact that a number of figures with a thorough training in Thomism—Martin Bucer, Peter Martyr Vermigli, and Jerome Zanchi, for instance—did in fact become articulate champions of the Protestant cause. If in these cases a thoroughly Thomistic education was not enough to prevent conversion to Protestantism, there is no convincing reason to believe that exposure to the theology of St. Thomas would have immunized Luther against what Lortz regards as a lapse into heresy.

6. Otto Pesch, "Existential and Sapiential Theology: The Theological Confrontation between Luther and Thomas Aquinas," *Catholic Scholars Dialogue with Luther,* ed. Jared Wicks (Chicago: Loyola University Press), pp. 61–62.

7. Denis R. Janz, *Luther and Late Medieval Thomism: A Study in Theological Anthropology* (Waterloo, Ontario: Wilfrid Laurier University Press, 1983), p. 8.

8. Ibid., p. 5.

9. Friedrich Benary, *Zur Geschichte der Stadt und der Universität Erfurt am Ausgang des Mittelalters* III (Gotha: Friedrich Andreas Perthes, A.-G., 1919), pp. 34–35, 48, 55. We shall see shortly that Biel is himself precisely such a mediating theologian, although his allegiance to the *via moderna* is clear. Cf. below, pp. 5–6.

10. Gerhard Ritter, "Romantische und revolutionäre Elemente in der deutschen Theologie am Vorabend der Reformation," *Deutsche Vierteljahrschrift für Literaturwissenschaft und Geistesgeschichte* 5 (1937), p. 359.

11. According to a comment attributed to Luther in the *Tischreden,* the reading of Biel's theology was a profoundly moving experience for the young divinity student: "Gabriel scribens librum super canonem missae, qui liber meo iudicio tum optimus fuerat; wenn ich darinnen las, da blutte mein herz. Bibliae auctoritas nulla

fuit erga Gabrielem." *WATR*, 3, 3722. The historical value of A. Lauterbach's *Tagebuch* (in which these comments are recorded) is frequently open to question, but in this instance we have corroborating evidence from Melanchthon. Even as an old man, says Melanchthon, Luther was still able to recall passages from Biel (and Pierre d'Ailly) "pene ad verbum memoriter." *Corp. Ref.* IV, p. 159.

12. Heiko Oberman, *The Harvest of Medieval Theology*, op. cit., pp. 17–20. Among those who were influenced directly by Biel's theology were Wendelin Steinbach, one of the teachers of Johann Eck, Henry Bebel, a humanist teacher of rhetoric and poetics at Tübingen, Johannes Altenstaig, the author of the *Vocabularius theologiae*, and Johann Brassican, a student of Bebel and a friend of Altenstaig who became the mentor of Philip Melanchthon.

13. Cf. Pesch, "Existential and Sapiential Theology," op. cit., p. 184, n. 3.

14. Wilhelm Ernst, *Gott und Mensch am Vorabend der Reformation, Erfurter Theologische Studien*, vol. 29 (Leipzig: St. Benno, 1972), pp. 92–93.

15. Cf. David C. Steinmetz, *Luther in Context*, pp. 47–58.

16. Cf. Carl Feckes, "Gabriel Biel, der erste grosse Dogmatiker der Universität Tübingen in seiner wissenschaftlichen Bedeutung," *Theologische Quartalschrift* 108 (1927), pp. 55, 75.

GOD AND CREATURES

1. Heiko A. Oberman, *The Harvest of Medieval Theology*, op. cit., p. 99.

2. Cf. Leif Grane, "Gabriel Biels Lehre von der Allmacht Gottes," *Zeitschrift für Theologie und Kirche* 53 (1956), pp. 53–75.

3. For a fuller discussion of Aquinas's doctrine of God, see Etienne Gilson, *The Christian Philosophy of St. Thomas Aquinas* (New York: Random House, 1956), pt. 1, pp. 29–143. Cf. Hampus Lyttkins, *The Analogy between God and the World: An Investigation of its Background and an Interpretation of its Use by Thomas of Aquino* (Uppsala: Almqvist and Wiksells, 1952); Henry Chavannes, *L'Analogie entre Dieu et le monde selon saint Thomas et selon Karl Barth* (Paris: Les Éditions du Cerf, 1969); Thomas Gornall, *A Philosophy of God: The Elements of Thomist Natural Theology* (New York: Sheed and Ward, 1963); Otto H. Pesch, *The God Question in Thomas Aquinas and Martin Luther*, trans. Gottfried G. Krodel (Philadelphia: Fortress Press, 1972).

4. Aquinas, *Summa theologiae* (hereafter *S.T.*) I q. 1 a. 3 *corp.*; cf. q. 14 a. 8 ad 3.

5. Aquinas *S.T.* I q. 21 a. 1 ad 2.

6. Aquinas *S.T.* I q. 8 aa. 1–4.

7. Cf. Gilson, *The Christian Philosophy of St. Thomas Aquinas*, pp. 107ff.
8. Aquinas *S.T.* I q. 3 aa. 2, 6, 7.
9. Aquinas *S.T.* I q. 19 aa. 3, 5; q. 46 a. 1; q. 7 aa. 1, 2; q. 9 a. 2; q. 10 a. 3.
10. Aquinas *S.T.* I q. 19 a. 1 *corp.* (translation mine).
11. Aquinas *S.T.* I q. 21 a. 1 ad 2 (translation mine).
12. Aquinas *S.T.* I q. 3.
13. Aquinas *S.T.* I q. 13 a. 4 *corp.*
14. Aquinas *S.T.* I q. 18 a. 3 *corp.*
15. Thomas believes that God's creative activity is patterned after ideas (exemplars and archetypes) in the divine intellect. Cf. *S.T.* I q. 15 and *De veritate* q. 3. For a fuller discussion of Thomas's doctrine of divine ideas, see L. B. Geiger, "Les idées divines dans l'oeuvre de S. Thomas," *St. Thomas Aquinas, 1274–1974: Commemorative Studies* 1, ed. Armand A. Maurer, et al. (Toronto: Pontifical Institute of Medieval Studies, 1974), pp. 175–209, and John L. Farthing, "The Problem of Divine Exemplarity in St. Thomas," *The Thomist* 49, 2 (April, 1985), pp. 183–222. Cf. Mark D. Jordan, "The Intelligibility of the World and the Divine Ideas in Aquinas," *Review of Metaphysics* 38 (September, 1984), pp. 17–32.
16. Aquinas *S.T.* I q. 4 a. 2 *corp.*
17. Biel I *Sent.* d. 24 q. 1 (A); Aquinas, *S.T.* I q. 11 a. 1 ad 1, a. 3 ad 2.
18. Biel I *Sent.* d. 2 q. 11 a. 1 n. 2 (A); Aquinas I *Sent.* d. 2 q. 1 a. 4 ad 2, a. 5 *resp.*
19. Occam I *Sent.* d. 2 q. 11 (B).
20. Aquinas *S.T.* I q. 30 a. 1 ad 1.
21. Aquinas I *Sent.* d. 2 q. un. a. 4 ad 2: "Ad secundum dicendum, quod essentia et suppositum sunt in Deo idem re, nihilominus tamen differunt ratione, sicut de attributis dictum est supra, art. praeced."
22. Aquinas I *Sent.* d. 2 a. 4 *resp.*: "Respondeo: concedendum est absque ulla ambiguitate, esse in Deo pluralitatem suppositorum vel personarum in unitate essentiae . . ."
23. Aquinas I *Sent.* d. 2 q. un. a. 5 *resp.*: "Sciendum est igitur quod proprietas personalis, scilicet relatio distinguens, est idem re quod divina essentia, sed differens ratione, sicut et de attributis dictum est."
24. Biel I *Sent.* d. 26 q. 2 a. 1 n. 1 (A): "Quoad articulum primum considerandum quod Doctor in hac quaestione primum recitat et impugnat opinionem beati Thomae I q. 40 art. 2 tenentis quod in divinis sunt origines et relationes ratione distinctae, non re, et personae constituuntur et distinguuntur non per origines, sed per relationes non ut relationes, sed ut proprietates." Aquinas *S.T.* I q. 40 a. 2 *corp.*: "Inveniuntur autem in divinis personis duo secundum quae differunt, scilicet origo et relatio. Quae quidem quamvis in re non differant, differunt tamen secundum modum significandi; nam origo significatur per modum actus, ut generatio; relatio vero per modum formae, ut paternitatis. . . . Unde melius dicitur quod per-

sonae seu hypostases distinguuntur relationibus quam per originem. Licet enim distinguantur utroque modo, tamen primo et principalius per relationes secundum modum intelligendi: Unde hoc nomen, pater, non solum significat proprietatem, sed etiam hypostasim; sed hoc nomen, genitor vel generans, significat tantum proprietatem."

25. Aquinas *S.T.* I q. 40 a. 2 *corp.* (translation mine).

26. Biel I *Sent.* d. 12 q. 1 a. 2 (B): "Consequenter videndum est de secundo, an scilicet illae concedendae: 'Pater et Filius sunt unus spirator et unum principium spirans.'

"De illo Doctor primum recitat et impugnat opinionem sancti Thomae prima secundae q. 36 art. 4 in solutione ultimae rationis, qui dismissis variis opinionibus tandem concludit: 'Quia *spirans* est adiectivus, *spirator* vero substantivam, possumus dicere quod Pater et Filius sunt dou spirantes propter pluralitatem suppositorum, non autem duo spiratores propter unam spirationem. Nam adiectiva nomina habent numerum secundum supposita, substantiva vero a seipsis secundum formam significatam.'" Cf. Aquinas *S.T.* I q. 36 a. 4 ad 7. See Roberto Busa, "De voce *Spiritus* in operibus S. Thomae," *Spiritus* IV (Rome: Edizioni dell'Ateneo, 1984), pp. 191–222.

27. Biel I *Sent.* d. 12 q. 1 a. 2 (B): "Et ad Hilarium dicentem 'quod Spiritus Sanctus est a Patre et Filio auctoribus,' dicit: 'Exponendum est quod ponitur substantivum pro adiectivo.'" Cf. Aquinas *S.T.* I q. 36 a. 4 ad 7.

28. Aquinas *S.T.* I q. 36 a. 4 ad 4.

29. Biel I *Sent.* d. 12 a. 1 a. 2 op. Gab. (H): "Quoad affirmativas est haec conclusio: Pater et Filius sunt unus spirator Spiritus Sancti. Item: Sunt unum principium spirans."

30. Occam I *Sent.* d. 12 q. 1: "quia si praedictum hic, quia est masculini generis ex usu loquentium, non possit supponere nisi pro persona, sic est haec neganda; quia Pater et Filius non sunt una persona spirans. Si autem praedictum de virtute semonis posset supponere pro omni illo quod spirat, sive sit persona formaliter sive non sit formaliter persona, cuiusmodi est tale constitutum ex essentia et spiratione actione circumscribendo, tam paternitatem quam filiationem; et simpliciter est concedendum."

31. Biel I *Sent.* d. 12 q. 1 a. 2 op. Gab. (H).

32. Biel I *Sent.* d. 11 q. 1 c. (A); Aquinas *S.T.* I q. 36 a. 2 *corp.*

33. Biel I *Sent.* d. 11 q. 1 ob. (D); Aquinas *S.T.* I q. 36 a. 2 arg. 2 ad 2.

34. Biel I *Sent.* d. 16 q. un. a. 3 dub. 1 (F); Aquinas *S.T.* I q. 43 a. 7 ad 4.

35. Biel I *Sent.* d. 35 q. 2 a. 2 c. 2 (C); Aquinas *S.T.* I q. 14 a. 5 *corp.*

36. Biel I *Sent.* d. 35 q. 1 a. 2 n. 1 (A); Aquinas *S.T.* I q. 14 a. 1 *corp.*

37. Biel I *Sent.* d. 35 q. 6 a. 3 dub. 4 (X); Aquinas *De pot.* q. 1 a. 5 ad 11.

38. Geiger, "Les idées divines," op. cit. and Farthing, "The Problem of Divine Exemplarity," op. cit.

39. Helpful discussions of Aquinas's cosmology and doctrine of creation include

Thomas Litt, *Les corps célestes dans l'univers de saint Thomas d'Aquin* (Paris: Beatrice Nauwerlaerts, 1963); Gilson, *The Christian Philosophy of St. Thomas Aquinas*, op. cit., pt. 1, chs. 1, 3; idem, *History of Christian Philosophy in the Middle Ages* (New York: Random House, 1955), pp. 368–75; idem, *The Spirit of Thomism* (New York: P. J. Kennedy and Sons, 1964), pp. 61–83.

40. Biel I *Sent.* d. 8 q. 1 (A); Aquinas *S.T.* I q. 3 a. 5 *corp.*

41. Biel I *Sent.* d. 8 q. 1 op. Gab. (D): "Alio modo aliquid dicitur esse in genere vel praedicamento, quia de eo genus aliquod quidditative praedicatur. Et illo modo nulla res, quae non est signum vel terminus, est in genere vel in praedicamento, quia res ut sic non praedicatur nec subiicitur, cum non sit par propositionis etc."

42. See Lyttkins, *The Analogy between God and the World*, op. cit.; Gerald B. Phelan, *St. Thomas and Analogy* (Milwaukee, Wisc.: Marquette University Press, 1941); and George P. Klubertanz, *St. Thomas Aquinas on Analogy* (Chicago: Loyola University Press, 1960). Cf. Norbert W. Mtega, *Analogy and Theological Language in the Summa Contra Gentiles: A Textual Survey of the Concept of Analogy and its Theological Application by St. Thomas Aquinas* (New York: Lang, 1984).

43. Biel I *Sent.* d. 43 q. 1 a. 2 (A), II d. 1 q. 2 a. 3 dub. 1 (H); Aquinas *De pot.* q. 1 a. 5 *resp.*; *S.T.* I q. 19 a. 1 ad 3, a. 2 ad 2, a. 3 *corp.*, ad 2, 5, 6.

44. Aquinas *S.T.* I q. 19 a. 1 ad 3, a. 2 ad 2, a. 3 *corp.*, ad 2, 5, 6.

45. Aquinas *S.T.* I q. 19 a. 3 *corp.*, q. 25 a. 5 *corp.*

46. Biel I *Sent.* d. 42 q. un. a. 1 n. 1 (A): "Notandum pro articulo primo, quod 'omnipotens' dupliciter accipitur: Uno modo, quia est 'agens, quod potest in omne possibile, mediate vel immediate.'

"Alio modo accipitur 'proprie theologice' pro illo 'qui potest in omnem effectum' immediate et in 'quodcumque possibile,' 'quod non est ex se necessarium nec includit contradictionem; ita inquam immediate, quod sine omni cooperatione cuiuscumque alterius causae agentis potest in quemlibet effectum."

47. Aquinas *S.T.* I q. 25 a. 6 *corp.* "Respondeo dicendum quod bonitas alicujus rei est duplex: una quidem, quae est de essentia rei, sicut esse rationale est de essentia hominis. Et quantum ad hoc bonum, Deus non potest facere aliquam rem meliorem quam ipsa sit, licet possit facere aliquam aliam ea meliorem. Sicut etiam non potest facere quaternarium majorem; quia si esset major, jam non esset quaternarius, sed alius numerus."

48. Biel I *Sent.* d. 37 q. un. a. 3 dub. 1 (E): "Prima, an ex hoc, quod Deus est in omnibus rebus per potentiam, ita scilicet quod est causa immediata omnium rerum, sequitur ipsum esse ubique per essentiam.

"Et dicunt aliqui quod sic, ut habet sanctus Thomas parte I q. 9 art. 3 qui inter cetera ait quod 'est in omnibus per essentiam, inquantum adest omnibus ut causa essendi.'

"Quod probant auctoritate Philosophi, quia opportet movens et motum esse simul, VII Physicorum." Cf. Aquinas *S.T.* I q. 8 a. 3 *corp.*

49. Biel I *Sent.* d. 37 q. un. a. 3 dub. 1 (E): "Sed illum non videtur verum. Nam

non oportet universaliter omne movens esse simul cum motu, nec in agentibus corporalibus nec agentibus per intellectum et voluntatem."

50. Biel I *Sent.* d. 37 q. un. a. 3 dub. 2 (F); Aquinas *S.T.* I q. 8 a. 4 *corp.*

51. A similar issue arises in Biel's discussion of sacramental causality. Biel rejects Aquinas's attempt to show that to create is incompatible with creatureliness. Biel argues that since it involves no logical contradiction to speak of God as sharing his creative power with some creature, the possibility of his doing so falls within the scope of the *potentia Dei absoluta.* Cf. Biel IV *Sent.* d. 1 q. 1 a. 3 dub. 2 (K); Aquinas *S.T.* I q. 45 a. 5 *s.c.*, *corp.* Biel puts the matter as follows: "Potest Deus novam creaturam corporalem vel spiritualem producere et velle creaturam sibi cooperari ad producendum talem effectum totum secundum se et quodlibet sui, cum hoc nullam includat contradictionem; quod si faceret creatura, crearet."

52. Biel II *Sent.* d. 11 q. 2 a. 3 dub. 2 (H); Aquinas *S.T.* I q. 66 a. 1.

53. The argument might run as follows. The *nihil* out of which God is supposed to have created would have been infinitely formless. As such it would have been the subject of all contradictory privations. Hence there must never have been a *nihil.* So God must have created out of something. But this "something" is precisely what we mean by "matter." And if matter preceded creation, it is uncreated; if uncreated, then eternal.

54. Biel II *Sent.* d. 11 q. 2 a. 3 dub. 2 (H): "licet per naturalem potentiam materia non potest stare nuda, tamen per potentiam divinam potest ab omni forma tam substantiali quam accedentali separari et conservari. Ratio fundamentalis est, quia nihil negandum est a potentia Dei quod non implicat contradictionem. Materiam stare nuda nullam contradictionem implicat. Ergo etc."

55. Ibid.: "Sic enim capiendo actum, actus non distinguitur a re existente; sic nec esse vel existentia distinguitur a re existente."

56. Biel II *Sent.* d. 14 q. un. a. 2 n. 1 (E); Aquinas *S.T.* I q. 68 a. 4 *corp.*

57. Biel II *Sent.* d. 12 q. 2 a. 1 n. 1 (B); Aquinas II *Sent.* d. 12 q. 1 a. 1 *resp.*; *S.T.* I q. 66 a. 2 *corp.*

58. Biel II *Sent.* d. 12 q. 2 (H): "Tertia opinio ponens materiam eiusdem rationis in caelo cum materia inferiorum magis videtur concordare litterae." (I) "Opinio vero media minus videtur probabilis quae tenet materiam esse in caelo sed alterius rationis: quia minus servit intellectui scripturae, et minus habet rationis simul et auctoritatis."

59. Ibid. (F).

60. Biel II *Sent.* d. 14 q. un. a. 1 n. 1 (A); Aquinas *S.T.* I q. 68 a. 2 *corp.*

61. Biel II *Sent.* d. 14 q. un. a. 1 n. 3 (C); Aquinas *S.T.* I q. 68 a. 2 ad 3. An almost astrological assumption is involved here. The approach and recession of the stars are thought to account for the diversities of generation and corruption, while the uniformity of the heaven itself is viewed as somehow effecting a certain continuity of generation.

62. Biel II *Sent.* d. 13 q. 1 a. 1 n. 2 (B); Aquinas *S.T.* I q. 67 aa. 2, 3.

63. Aquinas *S.T.* I q. 67 a. 3 *corp.*

64. Biel II *Sent.* d. 13 q. 1 a. 2 c. 1 (E).

65. Biel II *Sent.* d. 8 q. 1 a. 1 c. un. (B); Aquinas *S.T.* I q. 51 a. 1 ad 1, q. 50 aa. 1, 2, I–II q. 5 a. 4 *corp.*; II *Sent.* d. 3 q. 1 a. 1 *s.c.*, *resp.*

66. Aquinas *S.T.* I q. 51 a. 2 *corp.*

67. Biel II *Sent.* d. 8 q. 1 a. 2 (C); Aquinas *S.T.* I q. 51 a. 2 ad 2.

68. Biel II *Sent.* d. 9 q. 1 a. 1 n. 2 (C): "Ex quo posset probabiliter sustineri contra beatum Thomam quod omnes angeli eiusdem ordinis essent eiusdem speciei eo quod omnes conveniunt in naturalibus, quod non potest intelligi de convenientia secundum numerum, quia illa non est plurium eo quod nihil idem numero est in pluribus; ergo de specivoca." Cf. Aquinas *S.T.* I q. 50 a. 4 *corp.*

69. Biel II *Sent.* d. 9 q. 1 a. 3 dub. 2 (I): "Beatus Thomas parte I q. 48 a. 4 recitat plures opiniones . . . Sed omnes eas reputat falsas.

"Tenet quod impossibile est duos angelos esse eiusdem speciei, quia secundum eum quae conveniunt specie et differunt numero conveniunt formaliter et differunt materialiter. Angeli non habent materiam; ergo." Cf. Aquinas *S.T.* I q. 50 a. 4 *corp.*

70. Biel II *Sent.* d. 9 q. 1 a. 3 dub. 2 (I): "Ad dubium igitur potest cautius dubitari quam determinate responderi. Si autem urget improbus exactor, una ex duabus opinionibus recitatis acceptari potest, quoniam responsio sive opinio sancti Thomae omnino videtur improbabilis et nulla ratione fundata."

71. Biel II *Sent.* d. 9 q. 1 a. 3 dub. 1 (H): "Ideo respondetur ad dubium quod maxima est multitudo angelorum, licet eius numerus nobis est incertus. Utrumque probatur auctoritate Scripturae." Cf. Aquinas *S.T.* I q. 50 a. 3 *corp.*

72. Biel II *Sent.* d. 8 q. 1 a. 3 c. 4 (H): "Quarta conclusio: Omnes cognitiones quas angelus habere videtur per membra seu partes assumpti corporis non sunt nisi cognitiones intellectivae, quas habere posset corpore non assumpto. Patet, quia movendo linguam verba format quibus loqui videtur, et per haec verba conceptus suos aliis exprimere. Percipit etiam voces loquentium et intellegit sermones eorum quae sine cognitione fieri non possunt. Haec autem cognitiones in angelo non sunt sensitivae; ergo sunt intellectivae. Tenet consequentia a sufficienti divisione. Et antecedens patet per conclusionem praecedentem. Haec sunt de intentione doctorum communiter (Alexandri, Thomae, Scoti, Bonaventurae, etc.)" Cf. Aquinas *S.T.* I q. 62 a. 3 *corp.*

73. Biel II *Sent.* d. 4 q. un. a. 2 op. 1 (C): "Sunt autem duae extremae. Una quod omnes angeli creati sunt in gratia gratum faciente. Alia quod sunt creati in puris naturalibus, et quod non habuerunt gratiam ab instanti creationis. Primae favet beatus Thomas parte I q. 62 art. 3." Cf. Aquinas *S.T.* I q. 62 a. 3 *corp.*

74. Biel II *Sent.* d. 4 q. un. a. 2 n. 2 (F): "Proprissime . . . pro illo quod est his virtutibus superadditum complens et elevans ac acceptum faciens Deo. Et haec dicitur gratia gratum faciens."

75. Biel II *Sent.* d. 4 q. un. a. 2 n. 2 *resp. ad rationes* (F–G).

76. Biel I *Sent.* d. 43 q. 1 a. 2 (A); II *Sent.* d. 11 q. 2 a. 3 dub. 2 (H).

CHRIST AND MARY

1. On Thomas's Christology, see Othmar Schweizer, *Person und hypostatische Union bei Thomas von Aquin* (Freiburg: Universitätsverlag Freiburg Schweiz, 1957); Thomas R. Potvin, *The Theology of the Primacy of Christ according to St. Thomas and its Scriptural Foundations* (Fribourg: University Press, 1973); A. Patfoort, *L'Unité d'être dans le Christ d'après s. Thomas: à la croisée de l'ontologie et de la christologie* (Paris: Desclée, 1964); William D. Lynn, *Christ's Redemptive Merit: The Nature of its Causality according to St. Thomas* (Rome: Gregorian University, 1962); Bernard Catão, *Salut et rédemption chez s. Thomas d'Aquin* (Paris: Aubier, 1965).

2. Biel III *Sent.* d. 6 q. 1 a. 1 (A); Aquinas III *Sent.* d. 6 *div. text.*

3. Biel III *Sent.* d. 6 q. 2 a. 3 dub. 2 (I): "Ad secundum de Isidoro dicitur quod exponendum est; nam quia suppositum divinae naturae non est aliud a supposito humanae naturae, nec divina natura quae de Christo praedicatur est aliud a supposito eius, nec per consequens a supposito humanae naturae; ideo Christus non proprie dicitur aliud et aliud. Sed verba Isidori referenda sunt ad naturam, id est, alterius et alterius naturae. Vel (et est idem) Christus est aliud a patre, id est aliam naturam accepit a patre, et aliud, id est aliam naturam assumpsit a virgine. Ita exponit beatus Thomas in tertio scripto distinctione 6 q. 4." Cf. Aquinas III *Sent.* d. 6 q. 2 a. 1 ad 1.

4. Cf. *S.T.* III q. 17 a. 1 *corp.*, ad 2.

5. Biel III *Sent.* d. 4 q. un. a. 3 dub. 2 (L): "Secundo dubitatur utrum Spiritus Sanctus vere et proprie posset dici pater Christi et Christus filius Spiritus Sancti. . . . Unde secundum sanctum Thomam Spiritus Sanctus fecit illas actiones non mediante semine ex se deciso quod ad patrem patet, sed quasi artifex operando in materiam exteriorem." Cf. Aquinas III *Sent.* d. 4 q. 1 a. 2 qla. 1 ad 2.

6. Biel III *Sent.* d. 7 q. 3 a. 1 (A): "Recitatur et impugnatur a Doctore opinio sancti Thomae prima secundae q. 41 art. 6 et in disputatis De potentiis art. 4 tenentis quod potentia generandi non potest communicari Filio, ita quod Filius generet alium Filium, quia impossibile est in divinis esse plures filios."

7. Aquinas *De potentia Dei* q. 2 a. 4 *s.c.*: "Praeterea, Augustinus dicit . . . quod si Pater posset generare et non generaret, invidus esset. Sed Filius non est invidus. Ergo cum non generet, generare non potest. Et sic non possunt esse plures Filii in divinis."

8. Cf. *S.T.* I q. 25 a. 5 *corp.*

9. Biel I *Sent.* d. 7 q. 3 a. 2 c. *resp.* (C): "Conclusio responsialis secundum Doctorem est: Potentia generandi non potest communicari Filio, ita ut Filius generet.

"Ista conclusio magis auctoritate Scripturae conceditur quam ratione manifesta probatur. Unde solvit rationes Thomae ad id probandum per eum inductas."

10. Ibid., a. 1 n. (B).

11. Biel III *Sent.* d. 2 q. un. a. 3 dub. 2 (H); Aquinas *S.T.* III q. 1 a. 1 *s.c.*

12. Biel III *Sent.* d. 2 q. un. a. 3 dub. 3 (I): "Tertio dubitatur: Utrum si homo non pecasset, nihilominus Deus incarnatus fuisset.

"Respondet sanctus Thomas distinctione 1 tertii q. 1 quod huius quaestionis veritatem solus iste scire potest qui natus et oblatus est, quia voluit. . . . Beatus Thomas in III parte q. 1 a. 3 et in tertio scripto distinctione 1, licet ambas opiniones tangat, magis tamen declinat ad oppositum prioris, scilicet si homo non peccasset, Deus incarnatus non fuisset; cuius motivum est quia ea quae ex sola Dei voluntate proveniunt supra omne debitum creaturae nobis innotescere non possunt, nisi quatenus in sacra Scriptura traduntur per quam voluntas divina nobis innotescit. Unde cum in sacra Scriptura ubique incarnationis ratio ex primi hominis peccato assignatur, convenientius dicitur incarnationis opus ordinatum a Deo in remedium peccati, ita quod peccato non existente incarnatio non fuisset, quamvis potentia Dei ad hoc non limitatur. Potuisset enim peccato non existente incarnari. Haec ille part III." Cf. Aquinas *S.T.* III q. 1 a. 3 *corp.*, and III *Sent.* d. 1 q. 1 a. 3 *resp.*

13. Scotus III *Sent.* d. 7 q. 3 n. 3, d. 19 n. 6; Alexander of Hales III *Sent.* q. 2 m. 13 n. 23.

14. Biel III *Sent.* d. 14 q. un. a. 1 n. 1 op. 1 (B); Aquinas III *Sent.* d. 14 a. 2 qla. 1 *resp.* and *S.T.* III q. 10 a. 1 *corp.*

15. Cf. Biel I *Sent.* d. 35 q. 2 a. 2 c. 2 (C) and q. 6 a. 3 dub. 4 (X); Aquinas *S.T.* I q. 14 a. 5 *corp.* and *De pot.* q. 1 a. 5 ad 11.

16. Aquinas III *Sent.* d. 14 q. 1 a. 2 qla. 2 ad 2: "Et quia ratio virtutis determinatur ad obiectum, ideo contingit aliquam virtutem finitam quantum ad essentiam posse in infinita obiecta; sed non operari modo infinito: quia efficacia infinita in agendo non potest esse nisi ab essentia infinita; cum unumquodque agat secundum quod est ens actu . . . Ita etiam anima Christi, quamvis finita sit in essentia non tamen prohibetur quin infinita cognoscere possit, sed quod non possit cognoscere ea limpiditate infinita."

17. Aquinas *S.T.* III q. 10 a. 2 ad 2.

18. Ibid., *corp.*: "Horum autem quaedam sunt solum in potentia divina. Et huiusmodi non omnia cognoscit in Verbo anima Christi. Hoc enim esset comprehendere omnia quae Deus potest facere: quod esset comprehendere divinam virtutem, et per consequens divinam essentiam. . . ."

19. Biel III *Sent.* d. 14 q. un. n. 3 op. 1 (B): "Sed contra istam opinionem arguitur.

"Contra rationem suam in qua fundatur: Ex hoc quod intellectus videt omnia, quae videt Verbum, non sequitur quod comprehendit Verbum. Probatur: Quia si sic, hoc esset ex eo, quia videns omnia in Verbo, quae Verbum videt, videret eius infinitatem, et ita comprehenderet. Sed propter videre infinitatem Verbi non sequitur comprehensio Verbi. Nam anima Christi et cuiuslibet beati videt infinitatem intensivam, quod magis est quam videre infinitatem extensivam, et tamen propter hoc non comprehendit Verbum."

20. Ibid: "Praeterea: Exemplum de principio non procedit. Nam videns conclusionem aliquam ut effectum principii non ideo perfectius videt principium ut causam. Nam causa naturaliter est prior effectu, et ideo cognitio principii non augetur nec perficitur ex cognitione conclusionum ex ipso deductorum . . . Nihil perfectionis accepit causa ab effectu, et ita nec principium ex conclusionibus, sed econverso; alioquin esset circulus inter illa. Unde, licet perfectius cognoscens causam repraesentantem effectum perfectius vel etiam plures cognoscat effectus, non tamen econverso."

21. Ibid.: "Verbum aeque clare videt intuitive possibilia quae numquam fuerunt nec erunt sicut quae aliquando existunt; alioquin quomodo vocaret 'ea quae non sunt, sicut ea quae sunt,' ad Rom. 4. . . . Et ita distincte cognoscit omnia possibilia et singula eorum sicut quandoque existentia."

22. Ibid.: "Nihil enim accipit intellectus divinus a rebus, sed sua essentia est omnium cognitio."

23. Thus Biel proposes to treat the difference between past, present, and future as a model for understanding the importance of the difference between possibles and actuals for the doctrine of God's knowledge of things external to himself. The contrast between a temporal and a logical distinction seems to give him no pause. On Thomistic assumptions, the notion of God's knowing in an eternal present can account for his knowledge of a future event: past, present, and future are equally present—indeed, simultaneous—to the divine intellect. Cf. *S.T.* I q. 14 a. 13 *corp.*, ad 3. The distinction between actuals and possibles, on the other hand, is a far more complex matter. Cf. *S.T.* I q. 14 a. 9 *corp.* Biel's discussion fails to do justice to Thomas's careful treatment of the "actual/possible" dimension of the question as distinct from the issue of God's knowledge of future contingents.

24. Biel III *Sent.* d. 14 q. un. n. 3 op. 1 (B): "Praeterea: Anima Christi potest cognoscere in Verbo aliquod possibile nunquam factum. Ideo non est ponendus terminus cognitionis animae Christae in cognitione eorum, quae Verbum novit scientia visionis. Veresimile est enim non solam animam Christi, sed et aliorum beatorum; videre in Verbo ipsum posse creare aliquid, quod non creabit, etiam distincte, et ita videre aliquod possibile in Verbo; et qua ratione unum, et aliud, et ita de omnibus."

25. Biel IV *Sent.* d. 1 q. 4 a. 4 dub. 4 prop. 2, 3 (Q); Aquinas IV *Sent.* d. 1 q. 2 a. 5 qla. 2 *sol.*, ad 1.

26. Biel IV *Sent.* d. 5 q. un. a. 3 dub. 3 (K); Aquinas IV *Sent.* d. 5 q. 1 a. 1 *resp.*

Aquinas argues that Christ possesses the power of authority insofar as he is divine but not by virtue of his humanity (*secundum quod homo*). Biel ignores the former clause and focuses upon the latter. In that way Biel simplifies Aquinas's comment but not in such a way as to do violence to the point Aquinas wants to make.

27. Biel III *Sent.* d. 17 q. un a. 2 c. 5 (E): "Quinta conclusio: Quantum ad volendi actum quaelibet voluntas in Christo homine perfecte conformabatur voluntati divinae. Probatur: quaelibet voluntas in Christo sic voluit quomodo eam velle divinae voluntati complacuit . . . Antecedens probatur, quia quamvis Deus non vellet hoc quod sensualitas vel voluntas ut natura sensui coniuncta volebat, volebat tamen illum actum utriusque voluntatis, inquantum secundum Damascenum permittebat unicuique partium agere et pati quod sibi erat naturale et proprium, quantum expediebat ad finem redemptionis humanae generis et ostensionem veritatis naturae, ut dicit sanctus Thomas distinctione praesenti q. 2." Cf. Aquinas III *Sent.* d. 17 a. 2 qla. 1 *sol.*

28. Biel III *Sent.* d. 17 q. un. a. 3 dub. 1 (F): "Etiam ut dicit Thomas: Numquam motus sensualitatis in aliquid ferebatur nisi praeordinaretur a ratione. Et sic quamvis voluntas rationis non vellet illud volitum in quod sensualitas tendebat, voluit tamen quod sensualitas in illud tenderet. Similiter sicut dictum est de voluntate divina et humana supra, conclusione quinta, sic etiam motus sensualitatis non impediebat motum rationis, quia non erat violenta redundantia potentiae in potentiam in Christo." Cf. Aquinas III *Sent.* d. 17 a. 2 qla. 2 *sol.*, ad 1, 2, a. 3 qla. 1–4.

29. Biel III *Sent.* d. 20 q. un. a. 2 c. 2 (D); Aquinas *S.T.* III q. 46 a. 2 *corp.*, a. 3 *corp.*

30. Biel III *Sent.* d. 20 q. un. a. 2 c. 2 (D): "Probatur: Quia ille modus praevisus est et praeordinatus ab infinita sapientia trinitatis et ex nimia dilectione hominis . . ."

31. Biel III *Sent.* d. 17 q. un. a. 3 dub. 2 (G): Aquinas III *Sent.* d. 17 a. 3 qla. 1 *sol.*, qla. 2 *sol.*, ad 3, qla. 4 *sol.*, and *S.T.* III q. 21 a. 4 *corp.*

32. Biel III *Sent.* d. 17 q. un. a. 3 dub. 3 (I); Aquinas III *Sent.* d. 17 a. 4 *resp.*, ad 1.

33. Biel III *Sent.* d. 15 q. un. a. 2 c. 3 (G): "Tertia conclusio secundum primam viam opinionem scilicet Scoti, cui satis consentire videtur Alexander de Hales et sanctus Bonaventura ac Thomas: Voluntas Christi ut natura, similiter ut sensui coniuncta, de eisdem tristabatur, de quibus dolebat potentia sensitiva." Cf. Aquinas III *Sent.* d. 15 q. 2 a. 1 qla. 1, qla. 2, and *S.T.* III q. 15 a. 6 *corp.*

34. Note Biel's cautious way of expressing himself: ". . . cui satis consentire videtur . . . Thomas." Ibid.

35. Aquinas *S.T.* III q. 18 a. 1 *corp.*, a. 2 *corp.*

36. Aquinas *S.T.* III q. 15 a. 5 *corp.*, a. 6 *corp.*

37. Aquinas *S.T.* III q. 15 a. 4 ad 1, and III *Sent.* d. 15 q. 2 a. 2 qla. 1 *resp.*

38. Biel III *Sent.* d. 15 q. un. a. 2 c. 2 (M); Aquinas *S.T.* III q. 46 a. 6 *corp.*, ad 2, ad 6.

39. Biel III *Sent.* d. 15 q. un. a. 2 c. 1 (L): "Minor fuit Christi nostri redemptoris passio quam animae separatae in inferno aut purgatorio.

"Haec conclusio est sancti Thomae III q. 46 art. 6 in solutione tertiae rationis. Et probatur: Quia passio animae separatae excedit omne malum huius vitae, sicut gloria sanctorum excedit omne bonum huius vitae." Cf. Aquinas *S.T.* III q. 46 a. 6 ad 3.

40. Biel III *Sent.* d. 22 q. un. a. 3 dub. 3 (I); Aquinas III *Sent.* d. 22 q. 2 a. 1 qla. 2 *sol.*

41. Biel III *Sent.* d. 18 q. un. a. 2 c. 3 (H): "Et beatus Thomas q. 4 a. 4 huius distinctionis dicit: 'Unio, quae est in persona, quae est ultima et completissima, praesupponit omnem aliam unionem ad Deum. Unde ex hoc ipso, quod anima Christi erat Deo in persona coniuncta, debebatur sibi fruitionis unio, et non per operationem aliquam ei facta est debita. Et ideo Christus fruitionem non meruit.' Haec Thomas." Cf. Aquinas III *Sent.* d. 18 q. 1 a. 4 qla. 4 *sol.*

42. Biel III *Sent.* d. 18 q. un. a. 3 dub. 3 (N); Aquinas III *Sent.* d. 18 q. 1 a. 5 *resp.*, and *S.T.* III q. 34 a. 3 *s.c.*, a. 4 *corp.*

43. Heiko Oberman, for instance, notes that Gregory of Rimini shares with Augustine, Bernard, and Thomas a rejection of the doctrine of Mary's immaculate conception; then he charts the contrast between Biel and Gregory. Cf. *The Harvest of Medieval Theology*, pp. 286, 296–98. Much earlier, F. X. Linsenmann argued that Biel's divergence from Thomas on the question of original sin reflected a prior Mariological disagreement. Cf. his article, "Gabriel Biel, der letzte Scholastiker, und der Nominalismus," *Theologische Quartalschrift* 47 (1865), p. 662. For a discussion of medieval developments in Mariology, with numerous references to Thomas's position, see E. Dublanchy, "Marie," *Dictionaire de la théologie catholique* 9, II (Paris: Librairie Létouzey et Ané, 1927), cols. 2339–2474. Cf. also Hilda Graef, *Mary, A History of Doctrine and Devotion. I: From the Beginnings to the Eve of the Reformation* (New York: Sheed and Ward, 1963), esp. pp. 279–81; Maria Elizabeth Gossmann, *Die Verkündigung an Maria im dogmatischen Verständnis des Mittelalters* (Munich: Max Hueber, 1957), pp. 162–70; Gabriele M. Roschini, *La Mariologia di San Tomasso* (Rome: Angelo Belardetti Editore, 1950); Walter Delius, *Geschichte der Marienverehrung* (Munich: Ernst Reinhardt, 1963); and Franz Morgott, *Die Mariologie des heiligen Thomas von Aquin* (Freiburg: Herder, 1878).

44. Biel III *Sent.* d. 4 q. un. a. 3 dub. 1 n. 2 ad rationes pro resp. neg. (K). Cf. Aquinas III *Sent.* d. 4 q. 2 a. 1 ad 5: "Quamvis . . . hypostasis Filii Dei secundum generationem eius aeternam non sit a Virgine, tamen secundum generationem temporalem ex ea est."

45. Biel III *Sent.* d. 4 q. un. a. 3 dub. 1 n. 2 ad rationes pro resp. neg. (K): "Ad primam conceditur quod filiatio sit hypostasis ex not. 2, et secundum illam aeternam hypostasim est a Virgine temporaliter genitus homo in mundum, id est haec aeterna hypostasis facta est homo, ut habet sanctus Thomas."

46. Aquinas *S.T.* III q. 16 a. 2 *corp.*

47. Biel III *Sent.* d. 3 q. 1 a. 2 c. un. (G): "His praemissis, respondetur ad quaestionem per unicam conclusionem: Beatissima genitrix Dei Virgo Maria ab omni originalis peccati contagio fuit penitus praeservata. . . .

"Tertio probatur idem auctoritate ecclesiae, quae maior est auctoritate cuiuscumque sancti, saltem post canonicos scriptores: Nam ecclesia statuit festum conceptionis generaliter per universum celebrandum; ergo eius conceptio fuit sancta et per consequens peccato immaculata; ergo sine originali, cum conceptio passiva non potuit peccato actuali maculari.

"Consequentia prima probatur per beatum Bernardum ad canonicos Lugdunenses, qui per hoc probat eam in utero sancitificatum antequam natam . . .

"Antecedens probatur: Quia et in urbe Romana sollemniter celebratur et in ceteris ecclesiis fidelium. Hanc rationem beatus Thomas, sanctus Bonaventura, Alexander et ceteri eorum opinionem sequaces faciunt, imitantes in hoc Bernardum." Cf. Aquinas *S.T.* III q. 27 a. 1 *s.c.*, a. 2 ad 3.

48. Aquinas *S.T.* III q. 27 a. 1 *corp.*, ad 1; a. 2 *corp.*, ad 2.

49. Biel III *Sent.* d. 3 q. 1 a. 2 c. un. (G): "Nec propter hoc culpandus est beatus Bernardus, sed nec sanctus Thomas, sanctus Bonaventura ceterique doctores cum magno moderamine oppositum opinantes, quoniam eorum tempore hoc licuit, quoniam nulla determinatio vel concilii vel apostolicae sedis facta fuit, nec festivitas illa generaliter tunc fuit per orbem celebrata. Quae si praecessissent, haud dubium, quin promptissimae suae opinioni cessissent et apostolico magisterio consensissent."

50. Biel III *Sent.* d. 3 q. 1 a. 1 n. 4 (B); Aquinas *S.T.* III q. 27 a. 2 *corp.*, ad 2, ad 4, and III *Sent.* d. 3 q. 1 a. 1 qla. 1 *sol.* Cf. Scotus III *Sent.* d. 3 q. 1.

51. Biel III *Sent.* d. 3 q. 2 a. 3 dub. 1 (D); Aquinas III *Sent.* d. 3 q. 1 a. 2 qla. 1 *sol.*, qla. 3 *sol.*, and *S.T.* III q. 27 a. 3.

52. Aristotle *Eth. Nicom.* VII c. 5 (c. 3) (1147a, 10–14).

THE HUMAN CONDITION

1. On Aquinas's anthropology, see Robert Edward Brennan, *Thomistic Psychology: A Philosophical Analysis of the Nature of Man* (New York: Macmillan, 1941); N. A. Luyten, ed., *L'Anthropologie de saint Thomas* (Fribourg: Editions Universitaires, 1974); Etienne Gilson, *History of Christian Philosophy in the Middle Ages* (New York: Random House, 1955), pp. 375–81; idem, *The Christian Philosophy of St. Thomas Aquinas* (New York: Random House, 1956), pp. 187–248; idem, *The Spirit of Thomism* (New York: P. J. Kennedy & Sons, 1964), pp. 33–60; Ian Hislop, *The Anthropology of St. Thomas* (Oxford: Blackfriars, 1950); M. C. D'Arcy, *St.*

Thomas Aquinas (London: Burnes, Oates, & Washbourne, 1953), pp. 142–68; George P. Klubertanz, *The Discursive Power Sources and the Doctrine of the Vis Cognitiva According to St. Thomas Aquinas* (St. Louis: Modern Schoolman, 1952); François Marty, *La perfection de l'homme selon saint Thomas d'Aquin: ses fondements ontologiques et leur vérification dans l'ordre actuel* (Rome: Gregorian University, 1962); A. C. Pegis, *At the Origin of the Thomistic Notion of Man* (New York: Macmillan, 1963); Karl Rahner, *Geist in Welt: Zur Metaphysik der endlichen Erkenntnis bei Thomas von Aquin* (Munich: Kösel-Verlag, 3rd ed., 1964); Marcos F. Manzanedo, "La anthropologia filosófica en el commentario tomista al libro de Job," *Angelicum* 62 (1985), pp. 419–71.

2. Cf. infra, ch. 8.

3. Biel I *Sent.* d. 3 q. 10 a. 2 c. 3 (C): "Tertia conclusio: imaginis ratio consistit radicaliter et originaliter in animae substantia, sed perfecte et completive in substantia animae et duobus actibus ab ea productis. . . . Secunda pars patet et est contra sanctum Thomam, qui ponit quod imago Dei consistit in potentiis animae et non in actibus, quia sine actibus anima non est perfecta imago Dei." Cf. Aquinas *S.T.* I q. 93 a. 7 *corp.*: "Et ideo primo et principaliter attenditur imago Trinitatis in mente secundum actus . . . Sed quia principia actuum sunt habitus et potentiae, unumquodque autem virtualiter est in suo principio, secundario et quasi ex consequendi imago Trinitatis potest attendi in anima secundum potentias, et praecipue secundum habitus, prout in eis scilicet actus virtualiter existunt."

4. Biel II *Sent.* d. 20 q. un. a. 3 dub. 1 (I); Aquinas *S.T.* I q. 99 a. 2 ad 3.

5. Biel II *Sent.* d. 20 q. un. a. 3 dub. 2 (K); Aquinas *S.T.* I q. 98 a. 1 ad 1, 3, a. 2 ad 3.

6. Biel II *Sent.* d. 30 q. 2 a. 1 n. 1 (A–C); Aquinas *S.T.* I–II q. 82 a. 3 *corp.*

7. Heinrich Denifle, *Luther und Luthertum in der ersten Entwickelung* I, 2 (Mainz: F. Kirchheim, 1906), p. 532.

8. Biel II *Sent.* d. 30 q. 2 a. 3 dub. 1 (H): "Quantum ad tertium articulum est dubium primum, quae illarum opinionum sit probabilior. Responditur quod omnes sunt probabiles, nec aliqua earum potest evidenter improbari."

9. Ibid.: "Tertia opinio videtur magis tolerabilis ad hominem, quae medians inter primas duas facile solvit auctoritates utriusque opinionis, quia quomodo amplectitur ambas."

10. Biel II *Sent.* d. 30 q. 2 a. 2 c. 5 (G): "Est igitur conclusio quinta: utrumque et fomitem includi in ratione peccati originalis tanquam materiale et ipsum non includi sed esse annexum de facto est probabile. Patet conclusio, quia utramque partem tenent viri sancti et doctores famosissimi. Neutraque pars est ab ecclesia reprobata . . ."

11. Cf. Oberman, *The Harvest of Medieval Theology*, op. cit., pp. 121–23.

12. Biel III *Sent.* d. 16 q. un. a. 1 n. 3 (B); Aquinas III *Sent.* d. 16 q. 1 a. 1 *resp.*

13. Biel III *Sent.* d. 16 q. un. a. 1 n. 3 (B): "Tamen in statu innocentiae per donum a Deo gratis datum (sive id fuerit lignum vitae sive originalis iustitia sive

utrumque simul) largita est homini immortalitas. Nam per hoc donum potuit caveri omnis corruptio et per consequens mors. Sed propter peccatum donum illud perdidit, et ideo relicta est humana natura (ut dicit Dionysius De ecclesiastica hierarchia) in statu, qui debetur ei ex natura suorum principiorum, secundum quod dictum est, Gen. 3: 'Terra es, et in terram reverteris.'"

14. Biel II *Sent.* d. 16 q. 1 a. 1 n. (B); Aquinas *S.T.* I q. 76 a. 3 *corp.*, a. 4 *corp.*

15. Biel II *Sent.* d. 16 q. 1 a. 1 n. (C).

16. Biel II *Sent.* d. 16 q. un. a. 2 c. 2 (L–M); Aquinas *S.T.* I q. 77 a. 1 *corp.*, ad 3, 5, a. 2 *corp.*, ad 3, a. 3 *corp.*, I–II q. 110 a. 4 ad 1.

17. Biel II *Sent.* d. 16 q. un. a. 2 c. 2 (M): "Quod anima, cum sit potentia et principium multarum operationum et actuum in homine, diversa sortitur vocabula, quorum aliquod significat ipsam essentiam simpliciter et absolute non connotando aliquod distinctum ab anima, ut 'essentia' vel 'substantia' animae vel 'anima' si capitur absolute. Aliquod significat eandem animae essentiam et connotat certam eius operationem, ut 'intellectus' significat essentiam animae connotando noticiam sive actum intelligendi."

18. Ibid.: "Nam uno modo accipitur pro tota descriptione exprimente quid nominis 'potentia.' Alio modo tantum pro illo quod denominatur ab illo nomine vel conceptu."

19. Ibid., c. 1 (N): "His praemissis est conclusio prima ad illud articulum. Potentiae animae (intellectus, memoria, voluntas) accepiendo primo modo distinguuntur inter se et ab ipsa anima."

20. Ibid. "Secundo conclusio: Potentiae animae intellectivae, scilicet intellectus, memoria, voluntas, accepiendo secundo modo non distinguitur ab anima neque inter se neque re neque ratione."

21. Biel I *Sent.* d. 1 q. 3 a. 1 (A); Aquinas *S.T.* I–II q. 31 a. 1.

22. Biel II *Sent.* d. 24 q. un. a. 2 c. 2 (D); Aquinas *S.T.* I q. 79 a. 9 *corp.*, ad 1, ad 4, and II *Sent.* d. 24 q. 2 a. 2 *resp.*

23. Biel III *Sent.* d. 26 q. un. a. 3 dub. 1 (K); Aquinas *S.T.* I q. 81 a. 2 *corp.*, ad 1.

24. Biel III *Sent.* d. 26 q. un. a. 3 dub. 1 (K): "Ex illo sequitur quod illa distinctio, qua plerique, scilicet Henricus de Gandavo, sanctus Thomas, Bonaventura, distinguunt concupiscibilem et irascibilem penes obiecta, dicentes obiectum concupiscibilis esse bonum delectabile et obiectum irascibilis esse bonum arduum, non est bona nec propria. Nam bonum arduum proprie loquendo vel dicitur bonum absens vel bonum excedens facultatem potentiae, cui dicitur arduum, aut bonum appretiabile et amabile ut excedens omnia alia sibi contraria. Sed omnibus his modis concupiscibilis est respectu ardui."

25. Biel II *Sent.* d. 39 q. un. a. 1 n. 2 (B); Aquinas *S.T.* I q. 79 aa. 12, 13, and *In x lib. Eth.* II, 5.

26. Biel II *Sent.* d. 39 q. un. a. 1 n. 3 (D); Aquinas *S.T.* I q. 79 a. 13 *corp.*

27. Biel I *Sent.* d. 3 q. 6 (A); Aquinas *S.T.* I q. 86 a. 1 *corp.*

28. Biel I *Sent.* d. 3 q. 6 a. 2 c. 3 (E); Aquinas *S.T.* I q. 86 a. 1 ad 4.

29. Biel I *Sent.* d. 3 q. 8 a. 1 n. (A); Aquinas *S.T.* I q. 85 a. 1 *corp.*

30. Biel I *Sent.* d. 1 q. 6 a. 1 (A); Aquinas *S.T.* I q. 82 a. 1 *corp.*, a. 2 *corp.*

31. Biel III *Sent.* d. 23 q. 1 a. 3 dub. 1 prop. 4 (T–U); Aquinas *In x lib. Eth.* I, 20.

ETHICS

1. On St. Thomas's ethics, see Etienne Gilson, *Moral Values and the Moral Life: The System of St. Thomas Aquinas,* trans. Leo Richard Ward (St. Louis: B. Herder, 1931); idem, *The Christian Philosophy of St. Thomas Aquinas,* trans. L. K. Shook (New York: Random House, 1956), pt. 3, pp. 251–378; Michael Wittman, *Die Ethik des Hl. Thomas von Aquin in ihrem systematischen Aufbau dargestellt und in ihren geschichtlichen, besonders in dem antiken Quellen erforscht* (Münich: Max Hueber, 1933); A. D. Sertillanges, *La philosophie morale de St. Thomas d'Aquin* (Paris: Aubier, 1942); Vernon J. Bourke, *Ethics* (New York: Macmillan, 1951); idem, *History of Ethics* (Garden City, N.Y.: Doubleday, 1968), pt. 2, ch. 6, esp. pp. 97–99; M. C. D'Arcy, *St. Thomas Aquinas* (London: Burns, Oates, & Washbourne, 1953), pp. 169–84; Ralph McInerny, *Ethica Thomistica: The Moral Philosophy of Thomas Aquinas* (Washington, D.C.: Catholic University Press, 1982). See also the important collection of essays that were brought together in L. Elders and K. Hedwig, eds., *The Ethics of Thomas Aquinas* (Vatican City: Libreria Editrice Vaticana, 1984); J. I. Omoregbe, "The Moral Philosophy of St. Thomas Aquinas: A Critical Look," *Nigerian Journal of Philosophy* 2 (1982), n. 1, pp. 20–28; and Guido Soaje Ramos, "Ensayo de una interpretación de la doctrina moral tomista en terminos de participación," *Ethos* 10–11 (1982–83), pp. 271–94. Aquinas's contributions to social, political, and economic theory are discussed in Otto Schilling, *Die Staats- und Soziallehre des heiligen Thomas von Aquin* (Munich: Max Hueber, 1930); F. C. Copleston, *Aquinas* (Baltimore: Penquin Books, 1955), pp. 192–234; Thomas Gilby, *Principality and Polity: Aquinas and the Rise of State Theory in the West* (New York: Longmans, Green, & Co., 1958); idem, *The Political Thought of Thomas Aquinas* (Chicago: University of Chicago Press, 1958); Walter Friedberger, *Der Reichtumserwerb in Urteil des Hl. Thomas von Aquin und der Theologen im Zeitalter des Frühkapitalismus* (Passau: Passavia, 1967); Angelo Scola, *La fondazione teologica della legge naturale nello Scriptum super Sententiis di San Tommaso d'Aquino* (Freiburg/Schweiz: Universitätsverlag, 1982); Philippe Veysset, *Situation de la politique dans la pensée de S. Thomas d'Aquin* (Paris: Le Cèdre, 1981); Richard J. Regan, "Aquinas on Political Obedience and Disobedience," *Thought* 56 (1981), no. 220, pp. 77–88.

2. Biel III *Sent.* d. 33 q. un. a. 2 c. 2 (E); Aquinas III *Sent.* d. 33 q. 3 a. 1 qla. 1 *sol.*, and *S.T.* II–II q. 48 *corp.*

3. Biel III *Sent.* d. 34 q. un. a. 2 c. 3 (K); Aquinas III *Sent.* d. 34 q. 1 a. 1 *sol.*, and *S.T.* I–II q. 68 a. 1 *corp.*

4. Biel III *Sent.* d. 23 q. 1 a. 3 dub. 1 prop. 4 (T); Aquinas *S.T.* I–II q. 56 a. 4 *corp.*, ad 1.

5. Biel III *Sent.* d. 33 q. un. a. 3 dub. 1 (G).

6. Biel III *Sent.* d. 27 q. un. a. 1 n. 3 (F); Aquinas *S.T.* I–II q. 26 a. 3 *corp.*

7. Biel III *Sent.* d. 27 q. un. a. 1 n. 5 (H); Aquinas *S.T.* II–II q. 44 a. 5 *corp.*

8. Biel III *Sent.* d. 29 q. un. a. 2 c. 6 (G); Aquinas *S.T.* II–II q. 26 a. 7 *corp.*

9. Biel *Exp. Lect.* 76 (C); Aquinas *S.T.* II–II q. 25 a. 8 *corp.*, a. 9 *corp.*

10. Biel III *Sent.* d. 28 q. un. a. 3 dub. 2 (H); Aquinas *S.T.* II–II q. 25 aa. 2, 3, 11.

11. Biel IV *Sent.* d. 15 q. 8 a. 1 n. 3 (N); Aquinas *Quaest. quodlib.* IX q. 7 a. 2.

12. Biel IV *Sent.* d. 16 q. 3 a. 1 n. 4 (F); Aquinas IV *Sent.* d. 15 q. 3 a. 1 qla. 2 ad 2, qla. 4 ad 1.

13. Biel III *Sent.* d. 23 q. 1 a. 1 n. 4 (P); Aquinas III *Sent.* d. 23 q. 1 a. 4 qla. 1 *sol.*

14. Aquinas *S.T.* I–II q. 55 a. 1 *corp.*, ad 1, ad 2, a. 3 *corp.*

15. Biel II *Sent.* d. 21 q. un. a. 1 n. 1 (A); Aquinas *In orat. dom.*, 6.

16. Biel IV *Sent.* d. 16 q. 3 a. 3 dub. 6 (GG); Aquinas *S.T.* II–II q. 43 a. 7 *corp.*

17. Biel II *Sent.* d. 41 q. un. a. 3 dub. 3 (R); Aquinas II *Sent.* d. 24 q. 1 a. 4 *s.c.*, d. 41 q. 2 a. 1 ad 3.

18. Biel II *Sent.* d. 22 q. 2 a. 1 n. 1 (C–D); Aquinas *S.T.* I–II q. 6 a. 8 *corp.*

19. Biel II *Sent.* d. 21 q. un. a. 1 n. 1 (A); Aquinas *In orat. dom.*, 6.

20. Biel *Exp.* Lect. 77 (B); Aquinas *S.T.* I q. 114 a. 2 *corp.*, ad 3.

21. Biel II *Sent.* d. 8 q. 2 a. 3 c. (F); Aquinas *De pot.* q. 6 a. 5 *resp.*, ad 1, 3, 4, 6, 8.

22. Biel II *Sent.* d. 41 q. un. a. 3 dub. 3 (O); Aquinas *S.T.* I–II q. 71 a. 5 *corp.*, and II *Sent.* d. 41 q. 2 a. 1 ad 3, 4.

23. Biel II *Sent.* d. 41 q. un. a. 3 dub. 3 (O): "Alia opinio dicentium quod licet in peccato omissionis frequenter concurrat talis actus positivus, non tamen oportet nec requiritur ad peccatum omissionis aliquis actus positivus. Ipsum enim non facere quod praeceptum est est peccatum omissionis, secluso omni actu positivo. Huic opinioni favet sanctus Thomas."

24. In a pre-Freudian era, obviously, it did not seem necessary to take into account the possibility of subconscious processes and motivations.

25. Biel II *Sent.* d. 41 q. un. a. 3 dub. 3 (R): "Propter hanc rationem videtur opinio Occam . . . et sancti Thomae verior, licet raro contingat obiectum aliquid apprehendere et voluntatem nullum actum circa ipsum elicere. Et ideo vix aut raro contingit cogitare quod nunc audienda est missa et stante cogitatione nec velle nec nolle audire missam. Et tamen possibile est; potest enim voluntas fluctuare circa hanc cogitationem donec tempus audiendi missam transiit."

26. Biel IV *Sent.* d. 15 q. 3 a. 1 n. 1 (A); Aquinas *S.T.* II–II q. 66 a. 3 *corp.*

27. Biel IV *Sent.* d. 15 q. 3 a. 1 n. 1 (A): "Verum quia haec descriptio est nimis generalis, accipiendo furtum proprie (convenit enim simoniae, usurae, dolosae, seu iniquae mercantiae), et est nimis restricta accipiendo furtum comuniter pro qualibet iniusta contractione rei alienae, quo modo accipitur in septimo praecepto, 'Non furtum facies': unde Augustinus in libro q. Exodi dicit: 'Furti nomine bene intelligitur omnis illicita usurpatio rei alienae. Non enim rapinam permisit qui furtum prohibuit.'"

28. Biel IV *Sent.* d. 15 q. 3 a. 1 n. 5 (E); Aquinas *S.T.* II–II q. 66 aa. 6, 8, 9.

29. Biel IV *Sent.* d. 18 q. 2 a. 1 n. 1 (A); Aquinas IV *Sent.* d. 18 q. 2 a. 1 qla. 1 *sol.*

30. Biel IV *Sent.* d. 18 q. 2 a. 1 n. 3 cor. 5 (F); Aquinas IV *Sent.* d. 18 q. 2 a. 1 qla. 2 ad 1, 2.

31. Biel IV *Sent.* d. 18 q. 3 a. 1 n. 5 (K); Aquinas IV *Sent.* d. 18 q. 2 a. 4 qla. 3 *sol.* Cf. Biel IV *Sent.* d. 18 q. 3 a. 1 n. 5 (L); Aquinas IV *Sent.* d. 18 q. 2 a. 4 qla. 3 *sol.* See also Biel IV *Sent.* d. 18 q. 3 a. 2 c. 5 (P); Aquinas IV *Sent.* d. 18 q. 2 a. 4 qla. 3 ad 2.

32. Biel IV *Sent.* d. 16 q. 4 a. 2 c. 2 (F); Aquinas IV *Sent.* d. 15 q. 2 a. 4 qla. 1 *sol.*, and *S.T.* II–II q. 32 a. 6 *corp.* Biel notes Thomas's distinction between two kinds of necessities—those that are required in order to maintain life itself and those that are required in order to maintain a certain lifestyle. Biel correctly notes that Thomas shares his own view that one is not obligated to give alms of goods that are necessary to him or to his family in the first sense. Cf. Walter Friedberger, *Der Reichtumserwerb in Urteil des Hl. Thomas von Aquin und der Theologen in Zeitalters des Frühkapitalismus*, pp. 99–100.

33. Biel IV *Sent.* d. 16 q. 4 a. 2 c. 1 (E); Aquinas *S.T.* II–II q. 32 a. 6 *corp.*

34. Biel IV *Sent.* d. 16 q. 4 a. 2 c. 5 (H); Aquinas IV *Sent.* d. 15 q. 2 a. 6 qla. 2 *sol.*, and *S.T.* II–II q. 32 a. 5 *corp.*

35. Biel IV *Sent.* d. 16 q. 4 a. 2 c. 5 (I); Aquinas IV *Sent.* d. 15 q. 2 a. 1 qla. 4 *sol.*, and *S.T.* II–II q. 32 a. 5 *corp.*

36. Biel IV *Sent.* d. 16 q. 4 a. 3 dub. 4 (X); Aquinas *S.T.* II–II d. 32 a. 3 *corp.*; cf. a. 4 *corp.*

37. Biel IV *Sent.* d. 16 q. 4 a. 2 c. 8 (M); Aquinas IV *Sent.* d. 15 q. 2 a. 6 qla. 3 *sol.*; cf. *S.T.* II–II q. 32 a. 9 ad 2.

38. Biel IV *Sent.* d. 16 q. 3 a. 3 dub. 2 (R); Aquinas IV *Sent.* d. 15 q. 3 a. 1 qla. 1 *sol.*, qla. 2 *sol.*, and *S.T.* II–II q. 147 a. 1 *corp.*

39. Biel IV *Sent.* d. 16 q. 3 a. 2 c. un. (N); Aquinas *S.T.* II–II q. 147 a. 3 ad 2, and IV *Sent.* d. 15 q. 3 a. 1 qla. 4 ad 3; a. 2 qla. 2 *sol.*

40. Biel IV *Sent.* d. 16 q. 3 a. 1 n. 4 (D); Aquinas IV *Sent.* d. 15 q. 3 a. 2 qla. 3 *sol.*, and *S.T.* II–II q. 147 a. 4 ad 2.

41. Biel IV *Sent.* d. 16 q. 3 a. 1 n. 4 (F); Aquinas IV *Sent.* d. 15 q. 3 a. 1 qla. 2 ad 2, qla. 4 ad 1.

42. Biel IV *Sent.* d. 16 q. 3 a. 3 dub. 1 (O); Aquinas *S.T.* II–II q. 147 a. 6 ad 3, and IV *Sent.* d. 15 q. 3 a. 4 qla. 1 *resp.*, ad 3.

43. Biel IV *Sent.* d. 16 q. 3 a. 1 n. 4 (F); Aquinas IV *Sent.* d. 15 q. 3 a. 2 qla. 1 *sol.*

44. Biel *Exp.* Lect. 84 (B); Aquinas *S.T.* II–II q. 33 a. 2 *corp.*, a. 3 ad 1.

45. Biel *Exp.* Lect. 74 (K); Aquinas *S.T.* II–II q. 33 a. 2 ad 4.

46. Biel *Exp.* Lect. 78 (O); Aquinas *S.T.* II–II q. 33 a. 6 *corp.*, ad 2, 3.

47. Biel *Exp.* Lect. 74 (U); Aquinas *Quaest. quodlib.* XI a. 13.

48. Biel *Exp.* Lect. 74 (F); Aquinas *S.T.* II–II q. 33 a. 2 ad 3.

49. Biel *Exp.* Lect. 74 (N); Aquinas *S.T.* II–II q. 33 a. 8 ad 1. Cf. Biel *Exp.* Lect. 74 (Q); Aquinas *S.T.* II–II q. 33 a. 7 *corp.*

50. Biel *Exp.* Lect. 27 (T); Aquinas *In x. lib. Eth.* I, 2.

51. Cf. Aquinas's "fourth way" (*S.T.* I q. 2 a. 3 *corp.*). Biel's *bonum universale* recalls St. Thomas's notion of God as the maximal goodness by comparison to which anything else that is good may be called good.

52. Biel IV *Sent.* d. 15 q. 5. a. 1 n. 1 (A); Aquinas *De reg. Iud.*, 6, and *S.T.* II–II q. 66 a. 8 *corp.*

53. Biel III *Sent.* d. 37 q. un. a. 1 n. 5 (I); Aquinas *S.T.* I–II q. 100 a. 5 *corp.*

54. Ibid.

55. Biel IV *Sent.* d. 16 q. 3 a. 1 n. 6 cor. 1 (H); Aquinas *S.T.* I–II q. 96 a. 4 *corp.*

56. The importance of will, motivation, and intention in determining the moral quality of an act (or of an omission) becomes clear at various points in Thomas's treatment of ethical questions, especially when he is dealing with the specific issue of the sinfulness of some act: cf. *S.T.* I–II q. 74, aa. 1, 2, q. 75 a. 2, and q. 76 a. 4. As we have already noted, an emphasis on the importance of the agent's intention is integral to Thomas's way of dealing with the issues involved in the duty to exercise fraternal correction; cf. *S.T.* II–II q. 33 a. 2 ad 3. Similarly, as Biel correctly observes in IV *Sent.* d. 15 q. 3 a. 1 n. 5 (E), the question of motivation is crucial for Thomas in assessing the gravity of a sinful act: "Sed si pergis quaerere an omnis rapina et furtum sint peccatum mortale, respondetur quod sic de genere. Patet, quia est contra expressum praeceptum negativum Decalogi, 'Non furtum facies,' ubi 'furtum' accipitur communiter pro omni iniusta ablatione sive per fraudem occulte sive per violentiam manifeste, ut dictum est. Et ita illo praecepto prohibetur omne furtum et omnis rapina, et per consequens est mortale, per diffinitionem mortalis peccati beati Augustini . . . Si tamen aliquid minimum contracteretur ex surreptione non ex malitia, excusaretur a mortali, ut dicit sanctus Thomas." Cf. Aquinas *S.T.* II–II q. 66 a. 7 ad 3.

57. Biel IV *Sent.* d. 16 q. 3 a. 1 n. 6 (K–L); Aquinas *S.T.* I–II q. 96 a. 4 *corp.*

58. Biel IV *Sent.* d. 16 q. 3 a. 1 n. 1 (C); Aquinas IV *Sent.* d. 15 q. 3 a. 1 qla. 4 ad 3.

59. Biel IV *Sent.* d. 15 q. 13 a. 1 n. 4 (D); Aquinas IV *Sent.* d. 15 q. 2 a. 4 qla. 3 ad 2, and *S.T.* II–II q. 32 a. 7 ad 2.

60. Biel IV *Sent.* d. 15 q. 13 a. 1 n. 4 (E).

61. Biel IV *Sent.* d. 15 q. 3 a. 1 n. 5 (E): "Unde ut dicit beatus Thomas secunda secundae q. 66 art. 8: 'Rapina dicit quandam violentiam et coactionem per quam contra iusticiam auferetur alicui quod suum est. Coactionem autem iustam in humana societate nemo habet nisi publica potestas. Idcirco privata persona non utens publica potestate si quid per coactionem aut violentiam aufert, iniuste agit et rapinam comittit. Principibus vero ac rectoribus comunitatum publica potestas ad hoc commititur, ut sint iusticiae custodes. Et ideo non licet eis violentia et coactione uti nisi secundum iusticiae tenorem et hoc vel contra hostes pugnando vel contra cives malefactores puniendo. Et quod per talem violentiam aufertur non habet rationem rapinae, cum non sit contra iusticiam. Si vero contra iusticiam aliqui auferunt per publicam potestatem violenter res aliorum, illicite agunt et rapinam comittunt.'" Cf. Aquinas *S.T.* II–II q. 66 a. 8 *corp.*, ad 3.

62. Biel IV *Sent.* d. 16 q. 3 a. 1 n. 6 (K–L); Aquinas *S.T.* I–II q. 96 a. 4 *corp.*

63. Biel IV *Sent.* d. 15 q. 5 a. 3 dub. 1 (S); Aquinas *S.T.* II–II q. 104 a. 6 ad 3.

64. Biel IV *Sent.* d. 15 q. 4 a. 1 (A–B); Aquinas *S.T.* II–II q. 40 a. 1 *corp.* On the development of the Just War tradition in early Catholic thought, see Sydney D. Bailey, *Prohibitions and Restraints in War* (London: Oxford University Press, 1972); Roland H. Bainton, *Christian Attitudes toward War and Peace: A Historical Survey and Critical Re-evaluation* (Nashville: Abingdon Press, 1960), ch. 6, pp. 85–100; Yves de la Brière, *Le droit de juste guerre* (Paris: Pedone, 1933); Richard Shelly Hartigan, "Noncombatant Immunity: Reflections on its Origins and Present Status," *Review of Politics* 29 (1966), pp. 204–20; J. Bryan Hehir, "The Just-War Ethic and Catholic Theology: Dynamics of Change and Continuity," in *War or Peace: The Search for New Answers*, ed. Thomas A. Shannon, pp. 15–39; James T. Johnson, *Ideology, Reason and the Limitation of War* (Princeton, N.J.: Princeton University Press, 1975); idem, *Just War Tradition and the Restraint of War: A Moral and Historical Inquiry* (Princeton, N.J.: Princeton University Press, 1981); Paul Ramsey, *The Just War: Force and Political Responsibility* (New York: Charles Scribners' Sons, 1968); Robert Regout, *La doctrine de la guerre juste de saint Augustin à nos jours d'après les théologiens et les juristes canoniques* (Paris: Pedone, 1935); Alfred Vanderpol, *La doctrine scolastique du droit de guerre* (Paris: Pedone, 1919).

65. Biel IV *Sent.* d. 15 q. 5 a. 2 c. 3 (K); Aquinas *De reg. Iud.* 7.

66. Aquinas *S.T.* II–II q. 42 a. 2 ad 3 and *De reg. princ.* I, 6. Cf. Richard J. Regan, "Aquinas on Political Obedience and Disobedience," *Thought* 56 (1981), no. 220, pp. 77–88; Gilby, *The Political Thought of Thomas Aquinas* (Chicago: University of Chicago Press, 1958), pp. 156–57, 289, 301. See also Heinrich A. Rommen, *The State in Catholic Thought* (St. Louis: Herder, 1945), pp. 473–76, and Johannes Messner, *Social Ethics*, trans. J. J. Doherty, rev. ed. (St. Louis: Herder, 1965), pp. 723–24.

67. Biel IV *Sent.* d. 15 q. 3 a. 3 dub. 2 prop. 2 (I); Aquinas *S.T.* II–II q. 32 a. 8 *corp.*, ad 2.

68. Biel IV *Sent.* d. 15 q. 3 a. 3 dub. 3 (M); Aquinas *S.T.* II–II q. 66 a. 5 ad 3.

69. Biel IV *Sent.* q. 3 a. 3 dub. 7 (T); Aquinas *S.T.* II–II q. 66 a. 5 ad 2. Cf. Biel IV *Sent.* d. 15 q. 3 a. 3 dub. 7 (S); Aquinas *S.T.* II–II q. 62 a. 2 *corp.*

70. Biel IV *Sent.* d. 15 q. 10 a. 2 c. 2 (N); Aquinas *S.T.* II–II q. 77 a. 1 ad 1. On scholastic economic theory, see Bernard W. Dempsey, *Interest and Usury* (Washington, D.C.: American Council on Public Affairs, 1943), ch. 6, "Late Medieval Usury Analysts"; J. T. Noonan, *The Scholastic Analysis of Usury* (Cambridge, Mass.: Harvard University Press, 1957); R. de Roover, "The Concept of the Just Price: Theory and Economic Policy," *Journal of Economic History* 18 (1958), pp. 418–34; Joseph Alois Schumpeter, *History of Economic Analysis* (New York: Oxford University Press, 1954), pp. 73–107. On the relation between the *via moderna* and the early development of European capitalism, with special reference to the economic thought of Gabriel Biel, see Oberman, *Werden und Wertung der Reformation: Vom Wegestreit zum Glaubenskampf* (Tübingen: J. C. B. Mohr, 1977), ch. 8, "*Oeconomia moderna,*" pp. 161–200.

71. Aristotle *Polit.* I c. 9 (c. 6) (1257a 19 ss.).

72. Biel IV *Sent.* d. 15 q. 10 a. 1 n. 3 (D); Aquinas *S.T.* II–II q. 77 a. 1 *corp.*

73. Biel IV *Sent.* d. 15 q. 10 a. 1 n. 3 reg. 3 (F); Aquinas *S.T.* II–II q. 77 a. 1 *corp.* Cf. Biel IV *Sent.* d. 15 q. 10 a. 3 dub. 3 (Q); Aquinas *S.T.* II–II q. 77 a. 3 ad 4.

74. Biel IV *Sent.* d. 15 q. 11 a. 1 n. 2 (F); Aquinas *S.T.* II–II q. 78 a. 2 ad 1. Cf. a. 1 *corp.*

75. Biel IV *Sent.* d. 15 q. 10 a. 3 dub. 1 (O); Aquinas *S.T.* II–II q. 77 a. 3 *corp.*

76. Biel IV *Sent.* d. 15 q. 11 a. 1 n. 1 (A); Aquinas *S.T.* II–II q. 78 a. 2 *corp.*

77. Biel IV *Sent.* d. 15 q. 11 a. 1 n. 1 (C); Aquinas *S.T.* II–II q. 78 a. 2 ad 2, 4.

78. Biel IV *Sent.* d. 15 q. 10 a. 1 n. 3 (D); Aquinas *S.T.* II–II q. 77 a. 1 *corp.*

79. Aristotle *Eth. Nicom.* V, 5 (1133a 18 s.); *Polit.* I, 9 (1257a 35 s.).

80. Biel IV *Sent.* d. 15 q. 11 a. 1 n. 2 (D); Aquinas *S.T.* II–II q. 78 a. 1 *corp.* Cf. Oberman, *Werden und Wertung der Reformation*, pp. 169–70. In spite of the tension between the economic thought of a late medieval nominalist, such as Biel, and the presuppositions of finance capitalism, Oberman rightly notes the critical importance of nominalist value theory (especially the notion of *divina acceptatio*) in clearing the way for the use of script as legal tender in the early stages of European captialism. Ibid., pp. 168–69: "Der Nominalismus erwies sich auch darin als 'modern,' dass er den Begriffsapparat bereitstellen konnte, der die monetären Entwicklungen durchsichtig macht. In seinem Geldtraktat argumentiert Biel keineswegs als radikaler Neuerer. Er wirkt eher konservativ, wenn er den inhärenten und externen Wert, das im Geld enthaltene Edelmetall und seinen äusseren Kurs oder Nennwert, soweit wie möglich einander angeglichen sehen möchte. Wiederum greifen Wirtschaftstheorie und Theologie ineinander; denn auch in seiner Rechfertigungslehre hat der Gedanke der göttlichen Akzeptation ihn nicht davon zurückgehalten, im Interesse eines komplementären Verhältnisses von gutem Werk und göttlicher Annahme das optimale Wachstum der menschlichen Ge-

rechtigkeit zu fordern. Es wird etwas sichtbar vom Profil des Altmeisters der ersten Tübinger Schule, wenn Biel die Konsequenzen zieht und die in der kanonistischen Tradition gebotenen Möglichkeiten verwendet, um mit grosser Umsicht jene Entwicklung zu fördern, die für die Expansion des Frühkapitalismus notwendig war: vom Münzverkehr zur finanziellen Transaktion auf der Basis von Wertpapieren."

81. Biel IV *Sent.* d. 15 q. 11 a. 1 n. 2 ad 6 (M–N); Aquinas *S.T.* II–II q. 78 a. 1 ad 2, 3, 4.

82. Deut. 23.19 s.; 15.6.

83. Biel IV *Sent.* d. 15 q. 11 a. 1 n. 2 (M–N); Aquinas *S.T.* II–II q. 78 a. 1 ad 2, 3, 4.

84. Biel IV *Sent.* d. 15 q. 11 a. 3 dub. 14 (OO); Aquinas *S.T.* II–II q. 78 a. 4 *corp.*

85. Biel IV *Sent.* d. 15 q. 11 a. 2 c. 5 (X); Aquinas *S.T.* II–II q. 78 a. 3 *s.c.*, *corp.*, ad 2, 3.

86. Ibid.

87. Biel IV *Sent.* d. 15 q. 11 a. 3 dub. 16 (SS); Aquinas *De reg. Iud.* 2. Thomas puts the matter thus: "respondendum videtur secundum praedicta, quod expedit eum pecuniaria poena puniri, ne ex sua iniquitate commodum reportet . . ."

88. Biel III *Sent.* d. 38 q. un. a. 1 n. 4 (E); Aquinas *S.T.* II–II q. 110 a. 3 *corp.*

89. Biel III *Sent.* d. 38 q. un. a. 2 c. 1 (F): "Quantum ad articulum secundum est conclusio prima: Accipiendo 'mendacium' primo modo, nullum mendacium fieri potest sine peccato in sensu composito; secus in sensu diviso. Hoc est, quod non potest actus aliquis simul esse mendacium et non esse peccatum; sed eo ipso quod est mendacium, est peccatum. Potest tamen actus idem, qui nunc est mendacium, esse et non esse peccatum. Sed tunc, cum non est peccatum, non est neque dicitur mendacium." Ibid., c. 2 (G): "Secunda conclusio: De potentia Dei absoluta cuiuslibet generis mendacium acceptum secundo modo fieri potest sine peccato. . . .

"Item: Deus potest alicui praecipere, ut per mendacium alium decipiat; ergo sic per mendacium decipiens non peccat. Consequentia nota. Antecedens probatur: Quia nullam includit contradictionem; ergo Deus potest. . . .

"Item: Potest tollere praeceptum de mendacio, et tunc mentiens non peccat. Siquidem nemo peccat, qui non agit contra legem."

90. Biel III *Sent.* d. 39 q. 2 a. 1 n. 1 (B); Aquinas *S.T.* II–II q. 98 a. 1 ad 1, q. 110 a. 2 *corp.*, and III *Sent.* d. 39 a. 4.

91. Biel III *Sent.* d. 38 q. un. a. 1 n. 1 (B); Aquinas III *Sent.* d. 38 a. 1 ad 2.

92. Biel IV *Sent.* d. 15 q. 6 a. 2 c. 6 (I); Aquinas *S.T.* II–II q. 69 a. 1 *corp.*, ad 2.

93. Biel IV *Sent.* d. 15 q. 6 a. 2 c. 6 (K); Aquinas *S.T.* II–II q. 69 a. 4 *corp.*, ad 2.

94. Biel IV *Sent.* d. 15 q. 4 a. 1 n. 1 (A–B); Aquinas *S.T.* II–II q. 40 *corp.*

95. Biel III *Sent.* d. 39 q. 1 a. 1 n. 3 (D); Aquinas III *Sent.* d. 39 a. 2 qla. 3 *sol.*

96. Biel III *Sent.* d. 39 q. 1 a. 2 c. 6 (K); Aquinas III *Sent.* d. 39 a. 3 qla. 1 ad 1.

97. Biel III *Sent.* d. 39 q. 2 a. 2 c. 7 (K); Aquinas *S.T.* II–II q. 98 a. 3 ad 2.

98. Biel III *Sent.* d. 39 q. 2 a. 3 dub. 4 op. 1 (O); Aquinas *Quaest. quodlib.* I q. 9 a. 2.

99. Biel III *Sent.* d. 39 q. 2 a. 3 dub. 2 (M); Aquinas *S.T.* II–II q. 98 a. 4 *corp.*, ad 3, 4.

100. Biel IV *Sent.* d. 15 q. 6 a. 2 c. 6 (I); Aquinas *S.T.* II–II q. 69 a. 3 *corp.*

101. Aquinas *S.T.* II–II q. 62 a. 2 ad 2.

102. Biel IV *Sent.* d. 15 q. 6 a. 2 c. 9 (N); Aquinas *S.T.* II–II q. 71 a. 3 *corp.*

103. Biel IV *Sent.* d. 15 q. 6 a. 2 c. 9 (N); Aquinas *S.T.* II–II q. 71 a. 3 ad 3.

104. Biel IV *Sent.* d. 15 q. 6 a. 2 c. 5 (H); Aquinas *S.T.* II–II q. 68 a. 3 *corp.*, ad 2.

105. Biel IV *Sent.* d. 15 q. 7 a. 3 dub. 1 (K); Aquinas *Quaest. quodlib.* IV q. 5 a. 3.

106. Aquinas *Quaest. quodlib.* VIII q. 4 a. 1 *corp.*: "Si autem eligat quis eum quem reputat minus idoneum ad tale officium, peccat."

107. Biel IV *Sent.* d. 15 q. 15 q. 7 a. 3 dub. 1 n. 2 (G–H); Aquinas *Quaest. quodlib.* VIII q. 4 a. 1.

108. Cf. Biel *Exp.* Lect. 2 (D); Aquinas IV *Sent.* d. 24 q. 1 a. 3 qla. 1 *sol.*, ad 2.

109. Ibid.

110. Aquinas *Quaest. quodlib.* VIII q. 4 a. 1 *s.c.*: "sufficit eligere bonum, nec requiritur quod melior eligatur."

111. Biel IV *Sent.* d. 15 q. 7 a. 3 dub. 1 (F); Aquinas *Quaest. quodlib.* VI q. 6 a. 3, VIII q. 4 a. 1. Cf. Biel IV *Sent.* d. 15 q. 7 a. 3 dub. 1 (K); Aquinas *Quaest. quodlib.* VI q. 5 a. 3.

112. Biel IV *Sent.* d. 15 q. 7 a. 3 dub. 1 (M); Aquinas *Quaest. quodlib.* VIII q. 4 a. 1 ad ob., and *S.T.* II–II q. 63 a. 2 *corp.*, ad 3.

113. Biel *Exp.* Lect. 28 (A); Aquinas IV *Sent.* d. 25 q. 3 a. 1 qla. 1 ad 5. Cf. Biel IV *Sent.* d. 15 q. 6 a. 3 dub. 4 (X); Aquinas *De reg. Iud.* 5.

114. Biel IV *Sent.* d. 15 q. 7 a. 3 dub. 3 (O); Aquinas *S.T.* II–II q. 63 a. 3 *corp.*

115. Biel IV *Sent.* d. 15 q. 7 a. 3 dub. 3 (O): "'Eadem ratione parentes et domini honorandi sunt propter participationem divinae dignitatis, qui est omnium Pater et Dominus.'"

116. Biel IV *Sent.* d. 15 q. 7 a. 2 c. 1 (D); Aquinas *S.T.* II–II q. 63 a. 1 *s.c.*, *corp.*

117. Biel IV *Sent.* d. 13 q. 1 a. 3 dub. 5 (S); Aquinas IV *Sent.* d. 9 a. 5 qla. 1 *resp.*

118. Biel *Exp.* Lect. 87 (U); Aquinas *S.T.* III q. 82 a. 10 *corp.*, and IV *Sent.* d. 13 q. 1 a. 2 qla. 1 *sol.*

119. Biel IV *Sent.* d. 9 q. 2 a. 3 dub. 1 (G); Aquinas IV *Sent.* d. 9 a. 5 qla. 1 *resp.*

120. Biel IV *Sent.* d. 9 q. 2 a. 3 dub. 4 (K); Aquinas *S.T.* III q. 80 a. 9 *corp.*

121. Biel IV *Sent.* d. 21 q. un. a. 3 dub. 1 (H); Aquinas IV *Sent.* d. 21 q. 3 a. 1 qla. 1 ad 2. Cf. Biel IV *Sent.* d. 21 q. un. a. 3 dub. 1 ad 3 (K); Aquinas IV *Sent.* d. 21 q. 3 a. 1 qla. 1 *resp.*, ad 3.

122. Biel IV *Sent.* d. 21 q. un. a. 3 dub. 1 ad 3 (K): "Dicendum ergo quod confessor quae audit et dicit, puta absolvit, facit in persona sua, sed ut minister Dei, sicut omnia sacramenta ministrantur ex persona ministri, sed auctoritate Dei."

123. Biel IV *Sent.* d. 21 q. un. a. 3 dub. 1 (L): "Ideo ad rationem aliter re-

spondetur quod in casu quo confessor producitur in testem et iurat respondere veritatem de interrogatis, si quaeritur de aliquo, quod non novit nisi ex confessione, non debet respondere, nec 'Scio' nec 'Nescio.' Nec non respondendo est transgressor iuramenti, quia iuramentum intellegi debet de interrogatis, ad quae potest licite respondere, licet sonat generaliter; alioquin si generaliter intelligeretur, esset iuramentum temerarium et illicitum et per consequens non obligaret."

124. Biel IV *Sent.* d. 21 q. un. a. 3 dub. 4 (Q); Aquinas IV *Sent.* d. 21 q. 3 a. 2 *resp.*

125. Biel IV *Sent.* d. 21 q. un. a. 3 dub. 3 (P); Aquinas IV *Sent.* d. 21 q. 3 a. 3 *resp.*

126. Biel *Exp.* Lect. 2 (D); Aquinas IV *Sent.* d. 24 q. 1 a. 3 qla. 5 ad 2.

127. Biel *Exp.* Lect. 2 (E); Aquinas IV *Sent.* d. 24 q. 1 a. 3 qla. 5 *sol.* Cf. Biel *Exp.* Lect. 50 (P); Aquinas IV *Sent.* d. 24 q. 1 a. 3 qla. 5 *sol.*, and *S.T.* III q. 64 a. 6 *corp.*

128. Biel *Exp.* Lect. 7 (C); Aquinas IV *Sent.* d. 9 a. 3 qla. 1 *sol.* Cf. Biel *Exp.* Lect. 10 (H); Aquinas IV *Sent.* d. 9 q. 1 a. 4 qla. 2 *sol.*

129. Biel *Exp.* Lect. 10 (F–G); Aquinas IV *Sent.* d. 9 a. 4 qla. 2 *sol.*, qla. 3 *sol.*

130. Biel *Exp.* Lect. 10 (H); Aquinas IV *Sent.* d. 9 a. 4 qla. 2 *resp.*

131. Ibid.

132. Biel *Exp.* Lect 10 (K); Aquinas IV *Sent.* d. 9 a. 4 qla. 1 *sol.*

133. Biel IV *Sent.* d. 15 q. 4 a. 1 n. 1 (C); Aquinas *S.T.* II–II q. 40 a. 2 ad 2.

134. Biel IV *Sent.* d. 15 q. 8 a. 1 n. 2 (P); Aquinas *Quaest. quodlib.* IX q. 7 a. 2.

135. Biel IV *Sent.* d. 15 q. 8 a. 2 c. 4 (E); Aquinas *S.T.* II–II q. 185 a. 7 *corp.*

136. Ibid.

137. Biel IV *Sent.* d. 15 q. 8 a. 2 c. 5 op. 2 (G); Aquinas *S.T.* II–II q. 185 a. 7 *corp.*

CHURCH, MINISTRY, AND WORSHIP

1. St. Thomas's ecclesiology is intertwined with his sacramental theology. The present chapter, therefore, should be read in close connection with Chapter 7, "Sacraments." For secondary literature on Aquinas's doctrine of the Church, see 224.

2. Biel *Exp.* Lect. 22 (M); Aquinas *Com. in Matt.* 24.33.

3. Ibid.

4. Biel III *Sent.* d. 37 q. un. a. 1 n. 4 (H); *S.T.* I–II q. 99 a. 3 *corp.*

5. Biel III *Sent.* d. 40 q. ult. a. 2 c. resp. (C); Aquinas III *Sent.* d. 40 a. 4 qla. 1 *sol.*, ad 1.

6. Biel III *Sent.* d. 40 q. ult. a. 3 dub. 3 (F): "Respondetur quod ideo lex vetus lex timoris est et nova amoris secundum beatum Thomam distinctione praesenti q. 4 art. 2, quia 'lex nova ex ostensione divinae caritatis initium sumpsit, quia in effusione sanguinis Iesu Christi, quae fuit perfectissimae caritatis signum.' In eo etiam novum testamentum confirmatum est. 'Lex autem vetus in ostensione divinae potestatis (quae timorem incutit) initium sumpsit. Unde et in ipsa legislatione propter fulgura, voces et tonitrua terror audientes invasit, ut dicerent: "Non loquatur nobis Dominus, ne forte moriamur," Ex. 20.' Sic et lex vetus ad sui observantiam homines 'inducebat per comminationem poenarum, nova vero lex per beneficia exhibita et speranda.'" Cf. Aquinas III *Sent.* d. 40 a. 4 qla. 2 *sol.*

7. Biel III *Sent.* d. 40 q. ult. a. 3 dub. 3 (F): "'Et hoc satis competebat statui humani generis, ut prius quasi rudis populus per timorem poenae cogeretur, postmodum vero per amorem in bono proficeret. Sicut enim timor est via ad amorem, ita lex vetus ad novam.'" Cf. Aquinas III *Sent.* d. 40 a. 4 qla. 2 *sol.*

8. Biels IV *Sent.* d. 19 q. un. a. 2 c. 2 (D); Aquinas IV *Sent.* d. 19 q. 1 a. 1 qla. 1 *resp.*

9. Biel *Exp.* Lect. 35 (H); Aquinas *S.T.* III q. 74 a. 2 ad 2.

10. Ibid.

11. Biel *Exp.* Lect. 5 (A); Aquinas IV *Sent.* d. 13 q. 1 a. 1 qla. 2 *sol.*, ad 2, 3. Cf. Lécuyer, "Aux origines de la théologie thomiste de l'épiscopat," *Gregorianum* 35 (1954), pp. 56–89.

12. Biel *Exp.* Lect. 61 (H); Aquinas *S.T.* II–II q. 83 a. 1 *corp.*

13. Biel *Exp.* Lect. 61 (O, T); Aquinas *S.T.* II–II q. 83 a. 1 *corp.*, a. 10 *corp.*

14. Aquinas IV *Sent.* d. 15 q. 4 a. 6 qla. 3 *sol.*: "Ad tertiam quaestionem dicendum, quod brutis nullo modo competit orare: tum quia non sunt participes beatae vitae, quae principaliter in oratione petitur."

15. Aquinas *S.T.* I q. 64 a. 2 *s.c.*, *corp.*

16. Biel *Exp.* Lect 61 (M); Aquinas IV *Sent.* d. 15 q. 4 a. 3 qla. 1 *sol.*, and *S.T.* II–II q. 83 a. 17.

17. Biel *Exp.* Lect. 62 (C); Aquinas *S.T.* II–II q. 83 a. 12 *corp.*, ad 1, 2, 3, and IV *Sent.* d. 15 q. 4 a. 2 qla. 1 *sol.*

18. Biel *Exp.* Lect. 63 (A); Aquinas IV *Sent.* d. 15 q. 4 a. 7 qla. 3 *sol.*

19. Biel *Exp.* Lect. 62 (I); Aquinas *S.T.* II–II q. 83 a. 13 *corp.*

20. Biel *Exp.* Lect. 62 (L); Aquinas IV *Sent.* d. 15 q. 4 a. 2 qla. 4 ad 2, and *S.T.* q. 83 a. 13 *corp.*, ad 3.

21. Biel *Exp.* Lect. 62 (N); Aquinas *S.T.* II–II q. 83 a. 13 *corp.*, and IV *Sent.* d. 15 q. 4 a. 2 qla. 4, 5.

22. Biel *Exp.* Lect. 62 (G); Aquinas *S.T.* II–II q. 83 a. 14 *corp.*

23. Biel *Exp.* Lect. 66 (B–C); Aquinas *S.T.* II–II q. 83 a. 9 *corp.*

24. Biel *Exp.* Lect. 69 (I); Aquinas *S.T.* II–II q. 83 a. 9 ad 1, and *In Matt. Evan.* c. 6 n. 6.

25. Biel *Exp.* Lect. 71 (P); Aquinas *S.T.* II–II q. 83 a. 9 *corp.*

26. Biel *Exp.* Lect. 31 (R); Aquinas IV *Sent.* d. 45 q. 3 a. 1 *resp.*

27. Biel *Exp.* Lect. 49 (H): "De hac duplici adoratione loquitur beatus Johannes Damascenus in suo quarto: 'Quia,' inquit, 'ex duplici natura compositi sumus, intelligibili, scilicet, et sensibili, duplicem adorationem deo offerimus, scilicet spiritualem que consistit in interiori mentis devotione et corporalem que consistit in exteriori corporis humiliatione. Et quia in omnibus actibus latrie, id quod est exterius refertur ad id quod est interius sicut ad principalius, ideo ipsa exterior adoratio fit propter interiorem, ut scilicet per signa humilitatis quae corporaliter exhibemus, excitetur noster affectus ad subiiciendum se deo, quia connaturale est nobis ut per sensibilia ad intelligibilia procedamus.' Hec Thomas secunda secundae, quest. lxxxiiii, art. 2." Cf. Aquinas *S.T.* II–II q. 84 a. 2 *corp.*

28. Biel *Exp.* Lect. 50 (C); Aquinas III *Sent.* d. 9 q. 1 a. 2 qla. 4 *sol.*

29. Biel *Exp.* Lect. 50 (R); Aquinas III *Sent.* d. 9 q. 1 a. 2 qla. 6 ad 2.

30. Biel *Exp.* Lect 16 (G); Aquinas *S.T.* II–II q. 86 a. 4 *corp.*, ad 3.

31. Biel *Exp.* Lect. 16 (I); Aquinas *S.T.* II–II q. 86 a. 3 ad 1.

32. Biel *Exp.* Lect. 16 (K); Aquinas *S.T.* III q. 74 a. 3 ad 4, q. 83 a. 6 ad 7.

33. Cf. Oberman's discussion of Biel's place in the Scripture/Tradition debate: *The Harvest of Medieval Theology*, 3rd ed., pp. 361–422, 468.

SACRAMENTS

1. Ernst, *Gott und Mensch am Vorabend der Reformation*, pp. 92–93.

2. For analysis of S. Thomas's doctrines of church and sacrament, see M. Grabmann, *Die Lehre des heiligen Thomas von Aquin von der Kirche als Gotteswerk: Ihre Stellung in der thomistischen System und in der Geschichte der mittelalterlichen Theologie* (Regensburg: G. J. Manz, 1903); Manuel Useros Carretero, *"Statuta ecclesiae" y "sacramenta ecclesiae" en la eclesiología de st. Thomas de Aquino* (Rome: Università Gregoriana Editrice, 1962); Francesco Marinelli, *Segno e realtà: studi di sacramentaria tomista* (Lateranum, n.s., XLIII, no. 2, 1977).

3. Biel IV *Sent.* d. 1 q. 1 a. 1 n. 1 (B); Aquinas IV *Sent.* d. 1 q. 1 a. 1 qla. 5 ad 3.

4. Biel IV *Sent.* d. 1 q. 1 a. 1 n. 1 (B): "Nam ad hoc quod aliquid sit sacramentum, tria requiruntur: Primum quod sit res sensibilis habens naturalem similitudinem ad gratiam sive effectum Dei gratuitum quam vel quem representat. 'Naturalem similitudinem' dico non per participationem eiusdem qualitatis—sic enim corporalia seu sensibilia non sunt similia spiritualibus, cum nulla eadem qualitas secundum speciem insit utrisque—sed similitudinem per proportionabilitatem, quae est similitudo proportionatorum, ut sicut se habet hoc ad illud, ita hoc ad istud."

5. Ibid.: "Exempli causa: Sicut se habet aqua ad diluendas maculas corporales, ita se habet gratia ad abluendas maculas spirituales."

6. Biel is extremely conscientious in his use of St. Thomas's language to describe the proportional similarity between *res* and *signum*, but he does not pursue the question in terms of the way in which Aquinas finds in analogy a basis for responsible discourse about God. The germ of the Thomistic view of the possibility and scope of "natural theology"—and of the relationship between the creation and the Creator—is certainly present in Biel's discussion, but the epistemological and metaphysical significance of the notion of proper proportionality in Thomism is left undeveloped and, for the most part, unacknowledged. The crucial position of the doctrine of analogy in the perspective of St. Thomas is outlined clearly and systematically in Klubertanz, *St. Thomas Aquinas on Analogy: A Textual Analysis and Systematic Synthesis* (Chicago: Loyola University Press, 1960). Cf. J. Habbel, *Die Analogie zwischen Gott und Welt nach Thomas von Aquin* (Regensburg: J. Habbel, 1928); Gerald B. Phelan, *St. Thomas and Analogy* (Milwaukee: Marquette University Press, 1941); Lyttkins, *The Analogy between God and the World: An Investigation of its Background and an Interpretation of its Use by Thomas of Aquino;* O. A. Varangot, "Analogía de atribución intrínseca en Santo Tomas," *Ciencia y Fe* 13 (1957), pp. 293–319; idem, "Analogía de atribución intrínseca y analogía del ente según Santo Tomás," *Ciencia y Fe* 13 (1957), pp. 467–85; idem, "El analogado principal," *Ciencia y Fe* 14 (1958), pp. 237–53.

7. Biel IV *Sent.* d. 1 q. 1 a. 1 n. 1 (B); Aquinas IV *Sent.* d. 1 q. 1 a. 1 qla. 1 ad 4. Cf. *S.T.* III q. 60 a. 3 *corp.*

8. Ibid.

9. Biel IV *Sent.* d. 1 q. 1 a. 2 c. 4 (H); Aquinas IV *Sent.* d. 1 q. 1 a. 4 qla. 3 *sol.*

10. Biel IV *Sent.* d. 1 q. 1 a. 3 dub. 2 (K); Aquinas *S.T.* I q. 45 a. 5 *s.c.*, *corp.* Biel rejects Thomas's proofs in order to safeguard the freedom of God (in light of the nominalist doctrine of the *potentia Dei absoluta*). For God to communicate this power to a creature implies no contradiction; thus it is a possibility that the omnipotent God is free to actualize. That he does not, in fact, choose to do so results not from a metaphysical or logical necessity but simply from a contingent ordinance of the divine will.

11. Biel IV *Sent.* d. 1 q. 1 a. 1 n. 1 (A); Aquinas IV *Sent.* d. 1 q. 1 a. 1 qla. 5 *resp.* Aquinas observes that ". . . sacramentum secundum proprietatem vocabuli videtur importare sanctitatem active, ut dicatur sacramentum quo aliquid sacratur, sicut ornamentum quo aliquid ornatur."

12. Biel IV *Sent.* d. 1 q. 1 a. 1 n. 2 op. 1 (D); Aquinas IV *Sent.* d. 1 q. 1 a. 4 qla. 1 *sol.*, ad 2, 5, qla. 2 *sol.*, ad 1–5.

13. Aquinas IV *Sent.* d. 1 q. 1 a. 4 qla. 1 *sol.*, qla. 2 *sol.*, ad 1–5.

14. Biel IV *Sent.* d. 1 q. 1 a. 1 n. 2 op. 2 (D): "Alia est opinio cui consentit Sanctus Bonaventura, Richardus de Mediavilla, Scotus, Occam, Thomas de Argentina, et eorum sequaces, quae tenet quod Deus constituit sacramenta sensibilia

tanquam signa certa gratiae, quam ipse creando producit in anima suscipientis sacramentum aut in ipso sacramento effectum gratuitum ad hominum salutem ordinatum, quod additur propter sacramentum eucharistiae. Statuit enim quod, adhibito tali signo secundum modum et formam suae institutionis, infallibiliter vult assistere suo signo, producendo gratiam, si non ponatur obex in suscipiente sacramentum; quam gratiam alias non produceret, si sacramentum illud non exhiberetur. Et de hoc fecit ecclesiam suam certam. Et ista ordinatio sive institutio divina vocatur pactum initum cum ecclesia."

15. Biel IV *Sent.* d. 1 q. 1 a. 1 n. 2 (D): "Probatio unius opinionis est improbatio alterius."

16. Biel IV *Sent.* d. 1 q. 1 a. 2 c. 1 (G): "Quantum ad articulum secundum est conclusio prima: Sacramenta novae legis effectum sacramentalem causant, quem ex institutione divina certitudinaliter significant." Ibid., c. 2 (G): "Secunda conclusio: Novae legis sacramenta non sunt causa gratiae ex natura propria eis in prima rerum conditione tradita."

17. Biel IV *Sent.* d. 1 q. 1 a. 2 c. 3 (G); Aquinas IV *Sent.* d. 1 q. 1 a. 4 qla. 1 *sol.*

18. Biel IV *Sent.* d. 1 q. 1 a. 2 c. 3 (G): "Secunda conclusio est quod sacramenta attingunt ad productionem dispositionis ad gratiam, quae est character vel ornatus, et pari ratione ad gratiam sacramentalem si differat ab alia gratia. Et secundum eius dictum supra recitatum probatur conclusio: Quia illa dispositio secundum eum esset character in sacramentis initerabilibus et in aliis ornatus quidam characteri similis. . . . Sed character ille non est dispositio ad effectum sacramentalem. . . . Dispositio, quae potest stare sine gratia sacramentali et sine qua potest infundi et stare gratia sacramentalis vel eiusdem speciei, non est dispositio necessitans ad gratiam sacramentalem; sed talis est character; ergo . . . Quia character manet in recidivantibus, immo in damnatis, in quibus non est gratia . . . Secunda pars minoris, quod sine charactere datur gratia, patet in circumcisione, quae non imprimit characterem secundum eum et tamen confert gratiam."

19. Biel IV *Sent.* d. 1 q. 1 a. 2 c. 4 (H): "Conclusio quarta: In sacramenta novae legis non est ponenda virtus supernaturalis, per quam respectu sacramentalis effectus eis conveniat ratio causalis.

"Haec conclusio ponitur contra tertium dictum sancti Thomae, qui ponit virtutem quandam spiritualem in sacramentis, per quam concurrunt active instrumentaliter ad dispositionem et dispositive ad gratiam." Cf. Aquinas IV *Sent.* d. 1 q. 1 a. 4 qla. 1 *sol.*

20. Biel IV *Sent.* d. 1 q. 1 a. 2 c. 4 (H): "Et si dicis (sicut ipse dicit) quod virtus datur sacramentis inchoative, dum instituuntur in specie sacramenti, sed completive in usu sacramenti;—contra primum: Illa institutio facta est a Christo, dum adhuc ageret vitam mortalem in terris, saltem ante ascensionem, ut infra dicetur. Tunc autem sacramenta, quibus nunc utimur, non fuerunt. Quod vero non fuit, nihil recipere potuit, nec inchoative nec completive, tunc quando non fuit."

21. Ibid.: "Contra secundum: Quod non recipiunt hanc virtutem completive, dum sunt in usu, probatur: Quia ex quo sacramenta consistunt in certa verborum forma, quae sunt de sacramentorum essentia, quaero, quando ipsam virtutem recipiunt: an existente prima syllaba, media vel ultima. Et non potest dici nisi existente ultima, quia illa deficiente ceterae non constituunt sacramentum, nec sequitur effectus sacramentalis deficiente aliquo substantiali in forma. Ultima autem syllaba, quae est de necessitate sacramenti, quando est perfecta, desinit. Desinit autem per primum instans non esse. Et sic recipiet virtutem, quando non est; quod est impossibile."

22. Aquinas *S.T.* I q. 14 a. 13 *corp.*, ad 3.

23. Biel IV *Sent.* d. 5 q. un. a. 3 dub. 3 (K); Aquinas IV *Sent.* d. 5 q. 1 a. 1 *resp.* Cf. Biel IV *Sent.* d. 7 q. un. a. 1 n. (D), and a. 2 c. 3 (H); Aquinas IV *Sent.* d. 7 q. 1 a. 1 qla. 1 ad 1.

24. Biel IV *Sent.* d. 1 q. 3 a. 1 n. 1 (B); Aquinas IV *Sent.* d. 1 q. 1 a. 5 qla. 1 *sol.*

25. Scotus IV *Sent.* d. 1 q. 6 n. 10: "Sacramentum enim ex virtute operis operati confert gratiam, ita quod non requiritur ibi bonus motus interiori, qui mereatur gratiam: sed sufficit, quod suscipiens non ponat obicem."

26. Aquinas IV *Sent.* d. 45 q. 2 a. 1 qla. 3 *sol.*: "in suffragiis quae fiunt per malos duo possunt considerari. Primo ipsum opus operatum . . . et quia nostra sacramenta ex seipsis efficaciam habent absque opere operantis, quam aequaliter explent per quoscumque fiant; quantum ad hoc suffragia per malos facta defunctis prosunt."

27. Biel IV *Sent.* d. 2 q. 1 a. 1 n. 1 (A); Aquinas IV *Sent.* d. 2 q. 1 a. 2 *resp.*

28. Biel IV *Sent.* d. 1 q. 2 a. 3 dub. 1 (F); Aquinas IV *Sent.* d. 1 q. 2 a. 6 qla. 2 *sol.*

29. Biel IV *Sent.* d. 14 q. 2 a. 1 n. 1 (B); Aquinas IV *Sent.* d. 14 q. 1 a. 1 qla. 1 ad 1, and *S.T.* III q. 84 a. 1 ad 1.

30. Biel IV *Sent.* d. 2 q. 1 a. 3 dub. 2 (G); Aquinas IV *Sent.* d. 1 q. 1 a. 4 qla. 5 *sol.*, and II *Sent.* d. 26 q. 1 aa. 3, 4, 6.

31. Biel IV *Sent.* d. 2 q. 1 a. 3 dub. 2 (G): "Nam Thomas tenet quod gratia distinguatur a caritate re et subiecto. Nam gratia secundum eum inhaeret essentiae animae et caritas potentiae affectivae, quae realiter distinguitur ab essentia animae. Consequenter dicit: 'Sicut potentiae fluunt ab essentia, ita a gratia, quae est in essentia animae, fluunt virtutes, quae sunt in potentia, et distinguuntur secundum actus diversos perficientes potentias.' Consequenter dicit quod a gratia illa, quae est in essentia animae, fluunt aliquae ad temperandum defectus ex peccato accidentes, et haec dicuntur gratiae sacramentales, quia ad has sacramenta directe ordinantur. Et quoniam gratia, quae respicit essentiam animae, non potest esse sine virtutibus, potest autem esse sine gratia sacramentali, ideo gratia, quam sacramentum continet, differt a gratia, quae est in virtutibus et donis. Haec Thomas . . ."

32. Ibid. "Sed ut clarior sit responsio, notandum: Cum quaeritur, utrum gratia sacramentorum sit eadem cum gratia virtutum, per gratia sacramentorum intel-

ligitur gratia gratum faciens, quam conferunt sacramenta et quae est res sacramenti, sed per gratiam virtutum intelligitur gratia, quae est virtus vel causa virtutis aut forma virtutis.

"Consequenter supponitur ex dictis in II dist. 26 et in I dist. 17, quod gratia identificatur caritati sicut et potentiae animae ipsi eius essentiae."

33. Biel IV *Sent.* d. 6 q. 2 a. 1 n. 4 (D); Aquinas IV *Sent.* d. 4 q. 1 a. 1 *resp.*, ad 1, 2, 3.

34. Biel IV *Sent.* d. 6 q. 2 a. 1 n. 4 (D): "Quamvis autem conclusio sit vera illius opinionis ponendo characterem esse entitatem positivam . . . tamen rationes praedictae hoc non probant . . ."

35. Biel IV *Sent.* d. 7 q. un. a. 2 c. 3 (H); Aquinas IV *Sent.* d. 7 q. 1 a. 1 qla. 1 ad 1. Cf. Biel IV *Sent.* d. 7 q. un. a. 1 n. (D); Aquinas IV *Sent.* d. 7 q. 1 a. 1 qla. 1 ad 1.

36. Biel IV *Sent.* d. 2 q. 1 a. 1 n. 2 (B); Aquinas IV *Sent.* d. 2 q. 1 a. 4 qla. 4 *sol.*, ad 1.

37. Biel IV *Sent.* d. 8 q. 1 a. 3 dub. 1 (E); Aquinas IV *Sent.* d. 8 q. 1 a. 1 qla. 3 *sol.*

38. Aquinas *S.T.* III q. 76 a. 2 *corp.*

39. Biel *Exp.* Lect. 85 (E); Aquinas *S.T.* III q. 22 a. 2 *corp.*

40. Biel IV *Sent.* d. 8 q. 1 a. 3 dub. 3 (I): "Principalis tamen ratio est divina voluntas, cui placuit tunc instituere. Et quia sic placuit, bene et congrue institutum fuit. Voluntatis enim divinae prior causa quaerenda non est."

41. Biel *Exp.* Lect. 85 (E); Aquinas *S.T.* III q. 22 a. 2 *corp.*

42. Biel *Exp.* Lect. 38 (K); Aquinas *S.T.* III q. 82 a. 1 *corp.*, q. 74 a. 1 *corp.*, q. 78 a. 1 *corp.*, ad 1, 2, 4.

43. Biel IV *Sent.* d. 13 q. 1 a. 2 c. 3 (D); Aquinas IV *Sent.* d. 13 q. 1 a. 1 qla. 3 *sol.*, ad 1.

44. Biel *Exp.* Lect. 38 (K): "Et addit sanctus Thomas: 'Unde dicendum est, quod si sacerdos sola praedicta verba proferret, cum intentione conficiendi hoc sacramentum, perficeretur hoc sacramentum; quia intentio faceret ut hec verba intelligerentur quasi ex persona christi prolata, etiam si verba precedentia non recitarentur; gravitur tamen peccaret sacerdos sic conficiens, utpote ritum ecclesie non servans.'" Cf. Aquinas *S.T.* III q. 78 a. 1 ad 4.

45. Biel *Exp.* Lect. 47 (N); Aquinas *S.T.* III q. 78 a. 4 *corp.* The power that is under discussion here is the power of the formula to consecrate the sacrament, which in turn possesses an instrumental, dispositive power of bringing about an infusion of grace.

46. Biel *Exp.* Lect. 47 (O); Aquinas *S.T.* III q. 78 a. 4 *corp.*, q. 62 a. 4 ad 3, q. 64 a. 4 *corp.* Cf. IV *Sent.* d. 1 q. 1 a. 4 qla. 1 *resp.*

47. Cf Biel IV *Sent.* d. 1 q. 1 a. 2 c. 4 (H).

48. Biel *Exp.* Lect. 47 (P): "Propter hec et multa alia est alia opinio quam multi tanquam magis probabilem amplectuntur, negantes omnem virtutem instrumen-

talem, concurrentem effective ad transsubstantionem, inexistere verbis consecrationis. Unde dicunt quod sola divina potentia et virtute panis in corpus christi convertatur, quia panis in hac conversione desinit esse . . . tam secundum materiam quam secundum formam. Ad hanc desitionem substantie composite non potest agere virtus creata, sicut nec ad annihilationem et ad creationem."

49. Biel *Exp.* Lect. 38 (H); Aquinas *S.T.* III q. 78 a. 1 *corp.*, ad 1, 2.

50. Biel *Exp.* Lect. 38 (H): "Cuius ratio est, quia per formam exprimi debet aliquod perfectum vel faciendum circa materiam consecrandam vel transsubstantiandam in corpus christi, per ista autem verba: *accipite et comedite* non exprimitur aliquod pertinens ad consecrandum, nec ad consecrationem ipsam ut perfectam, sed respiciunt usum sacramenti qui non est de necessitate sacramenti, et sequitur perfectionem seu conversionem." Cf. Aquinas *S.T.* III q. 78 a. 1 *corp.* ad 1, 2.

51. Biel *Exp.* Lect. 53 (B); Aquinas *S.T.* III q. 78 a. 3 *corp.*

52. Biel *Exp.* Lect. 53 (O); Aquinas *S.T.* q. 78 a. 3 ad 4.

53. Biel *Exp.* Lect. 13 (I); Aquinas IV *Sent.* d. 13 q. 1 a. 2 qla. 5 *sol.*

54. Biel *Exp.* Lect. 6 (B); Aquinas IV *Sent.* d. 6 q. 2 a. 1 qla. 1 ad 1.

55. Biel *Exp.* Lect. 10 (E); Aquinas *S.T.* III q. 83 a. 6 *corp.*, ad 4; Biel *Exp.* Lect. 88 (B); Aquinas *S.T.* III q. 83 a. 6 ad 4, q. 74 a. 7 ad 3; Biel *Exp.* Lect. 88 (H); Aquinas *S.T.* III q. 83 a. 6 ad 3. Biel *Exp.* Lect. 88 (C); Aquinas *S.T.* III q. 83 a. 6 ad 1.

56. Biel *Exp.* Lect. 38 (K); Aquinas *S.T.* III q. 82 q. 74 a. 1 *corp.*, q. 78 a. 1 *corp.*, ad 1, 2, 4, q. 82 a. 1 *corp.*

57. Biel *Exp.* Lect. 35 (C); Aquinas *S.T.* III q. 74 a. 3 *s.c.*, *corp.*, ad 2. Biel IV *Sent.* d. 11 q. 2 a. 1 n. 2 (A); Aquinas *S.T.* III q. 74 a. 3 *corp.*, ad 2, 3.

58. Biel IV *Sent.* d. 11 q. 2 a. 2 c. 2 (B): "Secunda conclusio: Non sufficienter probatur quod in solo pane triticeo fiat sacramenti eucharistiae consecratio.

"Probatur, quia ad hoc neque est auctoritas sacrae Scripturae neque determinatio ecclesiae neque revelatio neque experientia vel ratio."

59. Biel IV *Sent.* d. 11 q. 2 a. 2 c. 3 (B): "Tertia conclusio: Non excusatur a peccato, qui in pane nontriticeo scienter celebrat, nisi usus ecclesiae, in qua sacramentum conficit, oppositum teneat."

60. Biel *Exp.* Lect. 35 (S); Aquinas *S.T.* III q. 74 a. 7 ad 3. Biel's argument in favor of using natural water is that it is the kind of water thought to have been used by Christ at the Last Supper. This line of reasoning differs from the argument offered by St. Thomas, who points instead to the water that flowed, mixed with blood, from Christ's side. Thomas's sense of the intrinsic appropriateness of wine mixed with water, as a symbol of the blood of Christ mingled with water, drops out in favor of an appeal to divine ordinance (revealed by way of Christ's own practice at the Last Supper).

61. Biel *Exp.* Lect. 48 (C); Aquinas *S.T.* III q. 78 a. 5 *corp.*

62. Biel *Exp.* Lect. 52 (Q); Aquinas *S.T.* III q. 78 a. 3 ad 1, a. 5 *corp.*, ad 3.

63. Biel *Exp.* Lect. 48 (K); Aquinas *S.T.* III q. 78 a. 5 *corp.*

64. Biel *Exp.* Lect. 48 (K): "Beatus Thomas, par. iii, quest, lxxviii, art. v, et redit in idem. Dicit quod hec locutio: *hoc est corpus meum,* resolvitur in illam, id est contentum sub *hoc est corpus meum.* Contentum dicit indeterminate, non determinando ad panem. Quia sic locutio esset falsa. Nec ad corpus christi, quia sic significaretur quod corpus christi esset corpus christi. Et hec dicit est ratio quare cum pronomine, 'hoc,' non ponitur nomen a parte subiecti, ne scilicet eius demonstratio ad aliquam certam speciem substantie determinetur, sed indeterminate demonstrat contentum sub speciebus, quod commune est et substantie panis et corpori christi, que ambo successive continentur sub speciebus panis."

65. Biel *Exp.* Lect. 41 (G); Aquinas IV *Sent.* d. 11 q. 1 a. 1 qla. 1 *sol.*

66. Biel *Exp.* Lect. 41 (G): "Item tollit significationem huius sacramenti, debet enim illud primum significare corpus christi ut primum signatum, sed si ibi maneret substantia panis, ipsa haberet rationem primi signati." Cf. Aquinas IV *Sent.* d. 11 q. 1 a. qla. 1 *resp.:* "Esset etiam contra significationem sacramenti: quia species non ducerent in verum corpus christi per modum signi, sed magis in substantiam panis."

67. Biel *Exp.* Lect. 41 (H): "Sed quod iste rationes non sint efficaces, ostendit Scotus . . ."

68. Ibid. (I): "Tenenda est ergo hec veritas quod panis substantia non manet, sed convertitur in corpus christi propter ecclesie determinationem, et auctoritatem sanctorum . . ."

69. Biel *Exp.* Lect. 80 (O–Q); Aquinas IV *Sent.* d. 10 a. 3 qla. 3 *sol.* Biel does not directly attribute this view to S. Thomas, but after following Aquinas's summary and critique of the opposite opinion (i.e., that the whole Christ is present in the host but not in each of its parts), Biel advances this interpretation as the "opinio . . . omnium." One can hardly escape the implication that Biel means to include Aquinas in this reference.

70. Biel *Exp.* Lect. 80 (S): "Ad primum respondet beatus Thomas . . . quod corpus christi, quamvis ante divisionem hostie sit totum sub qualibet parte hostie, non est tamen plures actu sub partibus illis, sed tantum potentia. Ad cuius intellectum pretendet quod unitas rei consequitur suum esse. Partes autem alicuius homogenei continui ante divisionem non habent esse actu, sed potentia tantum; et ideo nulla illarum habet unitatem propriam in actu. Unde actu non est accipere earum numerum, sed potentia tantum, sed post divisionem multiplicantur secundum actum." Cf. Aquinas IV *Sent.* d. 10 a. 3 qla. 1 ad 1.

71. Biel *Exp.* Lect. 80 (S): "Sed responsio hec videtur obscura, quia etsi unitas rei consequitur suum esse, verius est suum esse, tamen partes homogenii ita habent esse actu coniuncte in toto sicut ab invicem separate. Si enim coniuncte non essent actu (cum ex eis totum componitur), sequitur quod totum componitur ex non ente, quia quicquid est, actu est, et quod actu non est simpliciter non est."

72. Biel *Exp.* Lect. 80 (T).

73. Biel *Exp.* Lect. 42 (G); Aquinas *S.T.* III q. 75 a. 6 ad 2.

74. Biel *Exp.* Lect. 41 (H–I).

75. Biel *Exp.* Lect. 42 (G): "Sed hoc sustineri non potest, quia convertitur in illud corpus quod fuit idem in sepulchro, et in cena vel cruce, sed illud non includit animam, cum anima christi non fuit in sepulchro."

76. Biel *Exp.* Lect. 43 (E): "unde quidam dicunt quod sicut corpus christi realiter est in sacramento ita etiam eius quantitas qua extenditur in celo est realiter in sacramento. Asserunt enim quod ubicunque est substantia aliqua ibi etiam necessario sunt omnia accidentia absoluta sibi inherentia. Consequenter dicunt quod illa quantitate non extenditur corpus christi localiter, quia non est ibi quantitas christi modo suo, id est modo quanititativo, sed modo substantie."

77. Ibid.: "et ad hunc modum declinant beatus Thomas et Egidius."

78. Aquinas *S.T.* III q. 76 a. 4 *corp.*, a. 5 *corp.*

79. Biel *Exp.* Lect. 43 (O): "Dicitur ergo secundum hanc opinionem, quod corpus christi (ut in sacramento) non est quantum, quia ut ibi non habet partem extra partem, sed omnes partes coexistunt simul cuilibet puncto speciei sacramentalis . . ." Heiko A. Oberman concludes from Biel's language here that, when forced to choose, Biel "seems to incline to Occam's interpretation." Oberman, *The Harvest of Medieval Theology*, 3rd ed. (Durham, N.C.: Labyrinth, 1983), p. 275.

80. Biel *Exp.* Lect. 66 (Q); Aquinas *S.T.* III q. 75 a. 2 *corp.*, a. 4 *corp.*

81. Biel *Exp.* Lect. 46 (Q): "Sed hec opinio satis supra reprobatur, per hoc quod conversio non est ratio formalis corporis christi essendi sub speciebus panis, vide supra dicta." Cf. Scotus IV *Sent.* d. 10 q. 1.

82. Biel *Exp.* Lect. 88 (I); Aquinas *S.T.* III q. 77 a. 4 *corp.*, q. 83 a. 6 ad 7.

83. Biel *Exp.* Lect. 45 (A); Aquinas IV *Sent.* d. 12 q. 1 a. 2 qla. 2 *sol.*

84. Biel *Exp.* Lect. 45 (C): "Nec ratio Scoti aliquid probat, quia admisso quod causa totalis non sit imperfectior causato, non sequitur ideo quod causa partialis non possit esse imperfectior causato." Ibid. (D): "Per hoc ad propositum dicitur post Alexandrum de ales . . . quod species sacramentales habent eandem virtutem agendi in materiam exteriorem, quam haberent si essent coniuncte substantie panis et vini."

85. Biel *Exp.* Lect. 51 (C); Aquinas *S.T.* III q. 76 a. 8 *corp.*

86. Biel *Exp.* Lect. 51 (C): "Hoc autem sanctus Thomas reprobat, quia secundum eum corpus christi potest videri nisi in uno loco, in quo circumscriptive continetur. Unde cum in propria specie videatur in celis, non sic videtur in hoc sacramento sive in terris." Cf. Aquinas *S.T.* III q. 76 a. 8 *corp.*

87. Biel *Exp.* Lect. 51 (C): "Hoc autem quod sub specie carnis apparet, diu permanet, quinnimo quandoque legitur inclusum et multorum episcoporum consilio in pixide reservatum, quod nephas esset de christo sentire secundum propriam speciem."

88. Cf. Alexander *S.T.* IV q. 53 m. 4.

89. Biel *Exp.* Lect. 51 (F): ". . . huiusmodi revelationes fieri solent in miseri-

cordi condescensione defectu fidei alicuius, ut fides huius sacramenti roboretur. Si autem caro aut sanguis sic apparens esset caro vel sanguis alicuius animalis vel subito creata, nullum argumentum veritatis induceret ad fidem probandum vel roborandam, sed solummodo caro aut sanguis christi. Unde non videtur quod ob causam pretactam debeat apparere caro vel sanguis nisi ipsius domini. Quoniam licet virtute aliqua ostenderetur alicui hesitanti caro vel sanguis alienus (licet forte ex hac ostensione excitaretur ad credulitatem) non tamen hec fides proveneret ex signo vel ostensione veritatis, sed potius falsitatis."

90. Ibid.: "Et quicquid sit de corpore glorioso generaliter, hoc tamen esse in potestate christi, in cuius potestate sunt omnia corpora, et quantum ad esse et quantum ad sic vel sic esse seu apparere, nullus habet amgigere fidelis . . ."

91. Ibid. (G): "Nec hoc est impossibile deo, cum et angelus in corpore assumpto uni se ostendit et non alteri eque presenti, ut patet Dan. x ubi dicitur: 'Vidi ego Daniel solus visionem. Porro viri qui erant mecum non viderunt.' Loquitur autem de visione angeli apparentis in specie viri, lineis vestiti, et in alia forma uni quam alteri. Quod ergo potest angelus in corpore alieno, potest christus in corpore suo."

92. Biel *Exp.* Lect. 37 (H); Aquinas *S.T.* III q. 81 a. 3 *s.c.*, *corp.*, and III *Sent.* d. 11 q. 3 a. 3 *resp.*

93. Biel *Exp.* Lect. 37 (D); *S.T.* III q. 81 a. 2 *corp.*

94. Biel *Exp.* Lect. 88 (I); Aquinas *S.T.* III q. 77 a. 4 *corp.*, q. 83 a. 6 ad 7.

95. Biel *Exp.* Lect. 84 (D–G): "Prima opinio est, quod post consecrationem ubicunque manent species salva earum natura, id est, in tali dispositione in qua possent afficere panem, si non esset conversus, ibi manet et corpus christi, sive species intrent in ventrem animalis bruti sive hominis . . ." (F): "Huic opinioni prime, que est Alexandri, concordant sanctus Thomas et Richardus."

96. Biel *Exp.* Lect. 84 (B): "Virtus enim consecrationis respicit species illas; ideo non desinit illas quandiu sunt . . ." Cf. Aquinas *S.T.* III q. 76 a. 6 ad 3, q. 77 a. 8 *corp.*

97. Biel *Exp.* Lect. 84 (G).

98. Biel *Exp.* Lect. 84 (G); Aquinas IV *Sent.* d. 9 a. 2 qla. 3 *sol.*

99. Biel *Exp.* Lect. 84 (F).

100. Biel *Exp.* Lect. 84 (G): "Inter omnes has opiniones opinio Alexandri, Thome, Richardi videtur verior et communior. Et secundum illam respondetur ad rationes aliarum opinionum."

101. Biel *Exp.* Lect. 85 (O); Aquinas *S.T.* III q. 79 a. 1 *corp.* Biel substitutes *vitam animae* for Thomas's *vitam gratiae,* but the logical parallelism between the effects of Christ's advent in the flesh and his advent in the sacrament is by no means obscured in Biel's report. For Biel, no less than for Thomas, the life of the soul is effected by appropriation of the grace that entered the world when Christ came *in carne.*

102. Biel *Exp.* Lect. 85 (P); Aquinas *S.T.* III q. 79 a. 3 *corp.*

103. Biel IV *Sent.* d. 1 q. 3 a. 1 n. 1 (B); Aquinas IV *Sent.* d. 1 q. 1 a. 5 qla. 1 *sol.*

104. Biel *Exp.* Lect. 85 (P); Aquinas *S.T.* III q. 79 a. 3 *corp.*

105. Ibid.

106. Biel *Exp.* Lect. 85 (T); Aquinas IV *Sent.* d. 12 q. 2 a. 2 qla. 1 *sol.*, ad 1, and *S.T.* III q. 79 a. 4 *corp.*

107. Ibid.

108. Ibid.

109. Biel IV *Sent.* d. 12 q. 2 a. 2 c. 1 (C); Aquinas IV *Sent.* d. 12 q. 2 a. 2 qla. 2 ad 4.

110. Biel *Exp.* Lect. 85 (K–L); Aquinas *S.T.* III q. 79 a. 7 *corp.*, and IV *Sent.* d. 12 q. 2 a. 2 qla. 2 *resp.*

111. Biel *Exp.* Lect. 85 (L): "Non contra illud est, quod Augustinus *AD RENATUS* dicit: 'Quis offerat corpus christi, nisi pro his qui sunt membra christi?' Intelligitur enim pro membris christi offerri, quando offertur pro aliquibus, ut sint membra christi." The reference is to Augustine's *De anima et eius origine* I, 9 (PL 44, 480); cf. Aquinas IV *Sent.* d. 12 q. 2 a. 2 qla. 2 ad 3, 4.

112. Biel IV *Sent.* d. 9 q. 2 a. 1 n. 1 (A); Aquinas *S.T.* III q. 80 a. 4 ad 5.

113. Biel *Exp.* Lect. 85 (P); Aquinas *S.T.* III q. 79 a. 3 *corp.*

114. Biel *Exp.* Lect. 87 (H); Aquinas *S.T.* III q. 80 a. 5 *corp.*

115. Cf. supra, ch. 5, p. 63.

116. Biel *Exp.* Lect. 84 (O); Aquinas *S.T.* III q. 76 a. 2 *corp.*, q. 80 a. 12 *corp.*

117. Aquinas *S.T.* III q. 80 a. 12 ad 3.

118. Biel *Exp.* Lect. 80 (O–Q); Aquinas IV *Sent.* d. 10 a. 3 qla. 3 *sol.*

119. Biel IV *Sent.* d. 13 q. 1 a. 3 dub. 4 (N); Aquinas *Quaest. quodlib.* XI q. 8 a. 1 ad arg. Cf. Biel IV *Sent.* q. 1 a. 3 dub. 4 (K–L); Aquinas IV *Sent.* d. 13 q. 1 a. 3 qla. 3 *sol.*, *Quaest. quodlib.* XI q. 8 a. 1 *resp.*, and *S.T.* III q. 82 a. 9 *corp.*

120. Biel IV *Sent.* d. 13 q. 1 a. 2 c. 3 (D); Aquinas IV *Sent.* d. 13 q. 1 a. 1 qla. 3 ad 1.

121. Biel *Exp.* Lect. 57 (E); Aquinas IV *Sent.* d. 13 q. 1 a. 1 qla. 5 *sol.*, and *S.T.* III q. 82 aa. 5, 7, 9.

122. Biel IV *Sent.* d. 1 q. 3 a. 3 dub. 3 (G); Aquinas IV *Sent.* d. 1 q. 1 a. 5 qla. 3 *s.c.*, *sol.*, ad 1, 2, 3.

123. Biel IV *Sent.* d. 1 q. 3 a. 3 dub. 3 (G): "illa irregularitas inducta est propter tria, ut dicit sanctus Thomas: Primo, ut sacerdotes essent sub onere legis sicut ceteri; secundo ad tolendum superbiam de hoc quod alios sanctificabant; tertio ad significandum quod sacerdos novi Testamenti propter maximam sanctitatem sacrificii semper se debet inidoneum reputare." Cf. Aquinas IV *Sent.* d. 1 q. 1 a. 5 qla. 3 ad 2.

124. Biel IV *Sent.* d. 1 q. 3 a. 1 n. 3 (D); Aquinas IV *Sent.* d. 1 q. 1 a. 5 qla. 1 *sol.*, qla. 2 *sol.* Biel's *ex opere operante* seems to be intended in the sense of *ex opere operantis;* as such the phrase is a more general way of formulating Thomas's *ex caritate facta* in IV *Sent.* d. 1 q. 1 a. 5 qla. 2 *resp.*

125. Aquinas IV *Sent.* d. 1 q. 1 a. 5 qla. 1 *resp.* "Et ideo alii dicunt, et melius,

quod nullo modo sacramenta ipsa veteris legis, id est opus operatum in eis, gratiam conferebant, excepta circumcisione, de qua post dicitur." Cf. Aquinas IV *Sent.* d. 1 q. 1 a. 5 qla. 2 *sol.*, d. 1 q. 2 a. 4 qla. 3 *s.c.*, *sol.*

126. Biel IV *Sent.* d. 1 q. 4 q. 1 n. 1 (B); Aquinas IV *Sent.* d. 1 q. 2 a. 1 qla. 2 *sol.*

127. Aquinas IV *Sent.* d. 1 q. 2 a. 1 qla. 2 *resp.*: "Et ideo alii dicunt probabilius ut videtur, quod dabat gratiam quantum ad effectus privatos culpae et reatus, et quantum ad quosdam effectus positivos, sicut ordinare animam et facere dignam vita aeterna; non tamen quantum ad omnes quos habet gratia baptismalis; quia illa sufficit ad totaliter concupiscentiam reprimendam, et meritorie agendum, ad quod gratia in circumcisione data non valebat . . ."

128. Biel IV *Sent.* d. 1 q. 4 a. 2 c. 1, 2 (C).

129. Biel IV *Sent.* d. 6 q. 2 a. 3 dub. 5 (P); Aquinas IV *Sent.* d. 1 q. 2 a. 4 qla. 1 *sol.*, ad 1, 2, 3, and *S.T.* III q. 63 a. 1 ad 3, q. 72 a. 5 ad 3.

130. Biel IV *Sent.* d. 6 q. 2 a. 3 dub. 5 (P); Aquinas IV *Sent.* d. 1 q. 2 a. 4 qla. 1 *sol.*, ad 1, 2, 3, and *S.T.* III q. 63 a. 1 ad 3, q. 72 a. 5 ad 3. Biel adduces another reason, drawn from Bede and Scotus, which has no precise parallel in Aquinas: "Secunda: Tunc circumcisus non posset baptizari, quia, cum character baptismalis omnibus aliis praesupponitur, qui habet characterem iam non potest baptizari."

131. Biel IV *Sent.* d. 6 q. 2 a. 3 dub. 5 (Q): "Utrumque ergo dici potest. Pro nulla parte sunt rationes necessariae, sed tantum persuasivae et debiles sicut in tota ista materia de charactere."

132. Biel IV *Sent.* d. 1. q. 4 a. 3 n. 2 op. Thom. (I); Aquinas IV *Sent.* d. 1 q. 2 a. 5 qla. 3 *s.c.*, *sol.*

133. Biel IV *Sent.* d. 1 q. 4 a. 3 n. 2 op. Scot. (K): "Propter has rationes est alia opinio Scoti, quae videtur probabilior."

134. Biel IV *Sent.* d. 2 q. 2 a. 1 n. 1 (B); Aquinas IV *Sent.* d. 2 q. 2 a. 1 qla. 2 *s.c.*, *sol.*, ad 1. As Biel observes, Thomas holds that John baptized "in nomine venturi."

135. Biel IV *Sent.* d. 2 q. 2 a. 3 dub. 3 (H); Aquinas IV *Sent.* d. 2 q. 2 a. 3 qla. 1 *sol.*, ad 1, qla. 3 *sol.*, and *S.T.* III q. 38 a. 4 ad 3. John's baptism was appropriate to Jesus (who thus showed his humility, sanctioned John's ministry, and purified the water for use in Christian baptism). It was also appropriate for Jews who had reached the age of discretion (who were aroused to repentance and thus prepared to receive the baptism of Christ).

136. Biel IV *Sent.* d. 2 q. 2 a. 1 n. 1 (A); Aquinas IV *Sent.* d. 2 q. 2 a. 2 ad 1. Biel adheres to Thomas's interpretation of the way in which John's baptism was *in remissionem peccatorum:* in Mark 1.4, it was John's proclamation of the coming baptism of Christ, not his own baptizing, which was "for the remission of sins."

137. Biel IV *Sent.* d. 2 q. 2 a. 1 n. 2 (D); Aquinas IV *Sent.* d. 2 q. 2 a. 4 *sol.*, ad 2, and *S.T.* III q. 38 a. 6 *corp.*

138. Biel IV *Sent.* d. 2 q. 2 a. 2 c. un. (E).

139. Biel IV *Sent.* d. 3 q. un. a. 1 n. 1 (B); Aquinas IV *Sent.* d. 3 q. 1 a. 1 qla. 1 *sol.*, qla. 2 *sol.*, qla. 3 *sol.*, qla. 4 *sol.*; Biel IV *Sent.* d. 4 q. 1 a. 1 n. 2 (C); Aquinas IV *Sent.* d. 4 q. 2 a. 2 qla. 1 *sol.*

140. Biel IV *Sent.* d. 3 q. un. a. 2 c. 4 cor. 1, 2 (K–L); Aquinas IV *Sent.* d. 3 q. 1 a. 2 qla. 2 ad 3, 4, 5.

141. Biel IV *Sent.* d. 4 q. 2 a. 3 dub. 4 (P); Aquinas IV *Sent.* d. 3 q. 1 a. 4 qla. 3 *sol.*, ad 3.

142. Biel IV *Sent.* d. 4 q. 2 a. 3 dub. 2 (N); Aquinas IV *Sent.* d. 6 q. 1 a. 1 qla. 1 *sol.*, and *S.T.* III q. 68 a. 11 *corp.* Another reason, as Biel suggests, is Aquinas's conviction that the fetus is personally distinct from his mother: the baptism of one person cannot result in the salvation of another. The unborn infant cannot be treated merely as a part of his mother's body.

143. Biel IV *Sent.* d. 4 q. 2 a. 3 dub. 2 (N–O); Aquinas IV *Sent.* d. 6 q. 1 a. 1 qla. 1 ad 4.

144. Biel IV *Sent.* d. 5 q. un. a. 2 c. 2 (D); Aquinas IV *Sent.* d. 5 q. 2 a. 2 qla. 5 *sol.*, and *S.T.* III q. 67 a. 5 *s.c.*, *corp.* Biel IV *Sent.* d. 5 q. un. a. 2 c. 2 (E); Aquinas IV *Sent.* d. 5 q. 2 a. 2 qla. 5 ad 2. Biel IV *Sent.* d. 5 q. un. a. 3 dub. 2 (I); Aquinas IV *Sent.* d. 5 q. 2 a. 2 qla 4 *sol.*

145. Cf. Aquinas IV *Sent.* d. 5 q. 2 a. 3 qla. 1 *sol.*, qla. 2 *sol.*

146. Biel IV *Sent.* d. 6 q. 1 a. 2 c. 3 (F); Aquinas IV *Sent.* d. 6 q. 1 a. 2 qla. 1 *sol.*

147. Biel IV *Sent.* d. 6 q. 1 a. 3 dub. 2 (N); Aquinas IV *Sent.* d. 6 q. 1 a. 2 qla. 1 ad 2, and *S.T.* III q. 64 a. 8 ad 2.

148. Aquinas agrees that God cannot be a debtor in the absolute sense, but he recognizes that God may make freely himself a debtor by virtue of his own promises. Cf. II *Sent.* d. 27 q. 1 a. 3 ad 4, and *S.T.* I–II q. 114 a. 1 ad 3.

149. Biel's summary is based on Thomas's argument in IV *Sent.* d. 6 q. 1 a. 2 qla. 2 ad 2. By the time of the writing of the *Summa theologiae* (III q. 64 a. 8 ad 2), Thomas saw the need to qualify his earlier opinion: the baptism of fire, i.e., the ardor of one's devotion, can compensate for the lack of a proper intention as far as the forgiveness of sins is concerned, but not with respect to the sacramental character. Biel does not mention this refinement in Thomas's position, since he is concerned precisely with what remains constant in Thomas's perspective—i.e., a conviction that the salvation of the one being baptized is not jeopardized by the baptizer's failure to have the requisite intention.

150. Biel IV *Sent.* d. 6 q. 2 a. 3 dub. 6 (R); Aquinas IV *Sent.* d. 4 q. 1 a. 3 qla. 5 *s.c.*, *sol.* Biel appropriates Aquinas's statement that the character is only for those who receive something from being baptized. Then he applies this maxim not only to Christ (as is the case with Thomas) but also to Mary. Biel's inference seems fair enough: on Thomas's assumptions, Mary, like Christ, was already "full of grace" prior to her baptism.

151. Biel IV *Sent.* d. 4 q. 1 a. 2 c. 2 (G); Aquinas IV *Sent.* d. 4 q. 2 a. 1 qla. 2 *sol.*

152. Biel IV *Sent.* d. 4 q. 1 a. 2 c. 1 (F); Aquinas IV *Sent.* d. 4 q. 2 a. 1 qla. 1 ad 3.

153. A similar pattern will be noted in the way in which Thomas, according to Biel, handles the problem of insincere confession (Biel IV *Sent.* d. 16 q. 1 a. 3 dub. 2 [U]; Aquinas IV *Sent.* d. 17 q. 3 a. 1 qla. 2 *sol.*).

154. Biel IV *Sent.* d. 4 q. 1 a. 3 dub. 3 op. 2 (R); Aquinas IV *Sent.* d. 4 q. 3 a. 2 qla. 3 *sol.*, and *S.T.* III q. 69 a. 10 *corp.*

155. Biel IV *Sent.* d. 1 q. 1. a. 2 c. 3 (G), c. 4 (H).

156. Biel IV *Sent.* d. 14 q. 2 a. 3 dub. 2 (Q); Aquinas IV *Sent.* d. 14 q. 1 a. 2 qla. 3 *s.c.*, *sol.*

157. Aquinas IV *Sent.* d. 14 q. 1 a. 2 qla. 3 *sol.*: "Sed ratione sustentationis, in prosperis dicitur humilitas fundamentum, in adversis autem fortitudo. Poenitentiam autem et timor in recedendo a malo, diversimode sunt fundamenta: quia timor est primum in isto toto genere quod est recedere a malo; sed poenitentia quantum ad hanc speciem quae est recedere a malo commisso; et ideo etiam timor praecedit poenitentiam; sicut principia generis praecedunt principia speciei."

158. Biel IV *Sent.* d. 14 q. 1 a. 3 dub. 3 prop. 2 (Y); Aquinas IV *Sent.* d. 14 q. 1 a. 1 qla. 3 *sol.*, and *S.T.* III q. 85 a. 2 *corp.*

159. Biel IV *Sent.* d. 16 q. 1 a. 1 n. 3 (B); Aquinas IV *Sent.* d. 17 q. 2 a. 1 qla. 1 *sol.*

160. Aquinas IV *Sent.* d. 16 q. 1 a. 1 qla. 2 ad 2 (with regard to confession), ad 3 (with regard to satisfaction).

161. Aquinas IV *Sent.* d. 17 q. 2 a. 1 qla. 1 ad 6: "Ad sextum dicendum, quod contritio est a Deo solo quantum ad formam qua informatur; sed quantum ad substantiam actus est ex libero arbitrio, et a Deo, qui operatur in omnibus operibus et naturae et voluntatis."

162. Biel IV *Sent.* d. 14 q. 2 a. 1 n. 2 (D–G).

163. Biel IV *Sent.* d. 14 q. 2 a. 1 n. 2 op. med. (G); Aquinas IV *Sent.* d. 17 q. 1 a. 3 qla. 2, 5, a. 4 qla. 2, *sol.* Cf. a. 1 qla. 3 *sol.*

164. Aquinas IV *Sent.* d. 17 q. 2 a. 5 qla. 3 *s.c.*: "quaelibet gratia gratum faciens delet omnem culpam mortalem, quia simul cum ea stare non potest. Sed quaelibet contritio est gratia gratum faciente informata. Ergo quantumcumque sit parva, delet omnem culpam." Cf. qla. 1 *sol.*: "Contritio enim votum confessionis annexum habet; et satisfactio pro judicio sacerdotis cui fit confesio, taxatur." Aquinas claims that it is not only as a *pars sacramenti* but also as an *actus virtutis* that contrition effects the remission of sins. Cf. ibid. d. 17 q. 2 a. 5 qla. 1 *resp.*

165. Ibid., d. 17 q. 2 a. 5 qla. 2 *s.c.*: "Sed per exteriores actus absolvitur homo a poena et a culpa."

166. Ibid., d. 17 q. 2 a. 1 qla. 3 *s.c.*, *sol.* Biel's carelessness is all the more puzzling in view of the fact that in another context he correctly identifies Thomas's position on the possibility of attrition being transformed into contrition. Cf. Biel IV *Sent.* d. 16 q. 1 a. 3 dub. 1 (L); Aquinas IV *Sent.* d. 17 q. 2 a. 2 qla. 3 *sol.*

167. Biel IV *Sent.* d. 14 q. 2 a. 1 n. 2 (F); Aquinas IV *Sent.* d. 17 q. 3 a. 3 qla. 1 *sol.*

168. Biel IV *Sent.* d. 17 q. 1 a. 3 dub. 2 (U), and IV *Sent.* d. 1 q. 1 a. 2 c. 3 (G); Aquinas IV *Sent.* d. 17 q. 3 a. 4 qla. 1 *sol.*

169. Biel IV *Sent.* d. 17 q. 1 a. 3 dub. 2 (U); Aquinas IV *Sent.* d. 17 q. 3 a. 1 qla. 2 *sol.*

170. Biel IV *Sent.* d. 17 q. 1 a. 3 dub. 2 (U); Aquinas IV *Sent.* d. 17 q. 3 a. 4 qla. 1 *sol.*

171. Biel IV *Sent.* d. 17 q. 1 a. 3 dub. 2 (R); Aquinas IV *Sent.* d. 17 q. 3 a. 3 qla. 5 ad 4. Cf. Biel IV *Sent.* d. 17 q. 1 a. 3 dub. 2 (R); Aquinas IV *Sent.* d. 17 q. 3 a. 4 qla. 2 ad 4.

172. Biel IV *Sent.* d. 17 q. 1 a. 3 dub. 2 (X); Aquinas IV *Sent.* d. 17 q. 3 a. 4 qla. 2 ad 3.

173. Biel IV *Sent.* d. 17 q. 1 a. 3 dub. 2 (R); Aquinas IV *Sent.* d. 17 q. 3 a. 4 qla. 2 ad 4.

174. Biel IV *Sent.* d. 15 q. 2 a. 2 c. 3 (K); Aquinas IV *Sent.* d. 15 q. 1 a. 5 qla. 1 *sol.*

175. Biel IV *Sent.* d. 16 q. 2 a. 3 dub. 2 (N); Aquinas IV *Sent.* d. 15 q. 1 a. 3 qla. 4 *sol.*

176. Biel *Exp.* Lect. 57 (X); Aquinas IV *Sent.* d. 15 q. 1 a. 3 qla. 2 *sol.*

177. Biel IV *Sent.* d. 16 q. 2 a. 3 dub. 2 (N): "Et per satisfactionem intelligunt eam quae tollit omnem poenam, non eam, quae non sufficit ad totam tollendam, sed tantum partem."

178. See Aquinas IV *Sent.* d. 14 q. 2 a. 1 qla. 2 *sol.*, ad 2.

179. Biel IV *Sent.* d. 16 q. 2 a. 3 dub. 2 (N): "Haec opinio dura videtur et plena scrupulis, quia vix posset homo scire probabiliter, an satisfecerit vel non, licet omnia sibi (clave non errante) iniuncta expleverit."

180. Ibid. (P): "videtur opinio Scoti magis concordare misericordiae divinae . . ."

181. Biel *Exp.* Lect. 57 (X): "Et ista opinio est magis pia, licet prior sit securior et minus dubia. Satis enim certum est, quod suffragia, que impenduntur ab eo qui est in gratia, tanquam a principali agente valent. De aliis non ita certum."

182. Biel IV *Sent.* d. 18 q. 1 a. 1 n. 2 (B); Aquinas IV *Sent.* d. 18 q. 1 a. 1 qla. 1 *sol.*

183. Cf. supra pp. 139–41, and infra, pp. 153–66.

184. Biel IV *Sent.* d. 7 a. 1 n. (D), a. 2 c. 3 (H); Aquinas IV *Sent.* d. 7 q. 1 a. 1 qla. 1 ad 1.

185. Biel simply falls back on the familiar use of John 20.30 to show that the Scriptural record is not exhaustive. In IV *Sent.* d. 7 q. 1 a. 1 qla. 1 ad 1, Thomas claims that the silence of Scripture was designed to protect the sacrament from the derision of the heathen, while his argument in *S.T.* III q. 72 a. 1 ad 1 revolves around John 7.39 and 16.7.

186. Biel IV *Sent.* d. 7 q. un. a. 2 c. 3 (H); Aquinas IV *Sent.* d. 7 q. 1 a. 1 qla. 1 ad 1.

187. Biel IV *Sent.* d. 7 q. un. a. 1 n. (A); Aquinas IV *Sent.* d. 7 q. 2 a. 1 qla. 3 *sol.*

188. The striking instance of this tendency is Biel's inversion of Thomas's logic in relation to the appropriateness of the time for the institution of the eucharist. Cf. Biel IV *Sent.* d. 8 q. 1 a. 3 dub. 3 (I); Aquinas IV *Sent.* d. 8 q. 1 a. 3 qla. 3 *sol.*, ad 1, 4, and *S.T.* III q. 73 a. 5 ad 2.

189. E.g., God's power is not limited by his own sacraments. Cf. Biel IV *Sent.* d. 6 q. 1 a. 3 dub. 2 (N).

190. E.g., God would not be unjust even if he failed to provide extrasacramental means of salvation. Ibid.

191. As might have been anticipated, the *tertia pars* of Aquinas's *Summa theologiae* and his commentary on the fourth book of Lombard's *Sentences* provide the bulk of the sacramental materials that Biel borrows from Aquinas.

JUSTIFICATION

1. For an analysis of the extent to which Gabriel Biel should be regarded as a semi-Pelagian, see Harry J. McSorley, "Was Gabriel Biel a Semipelagian?" in Leo Scheffczyk et al., eds. *Wahrheit und Verkündigung* II, (Munich: Ferdinand Schöningh, 1967), pp. 1109–1120; J. E. Biechler, "Gabriel Biel on '*liberum arbitrium*': Prelude to Luther's *De servo arbitrio*," in *The Thomist* 34 (1970), pp. 114–27; Oberman, *The Harvest of Medieval Theology*, op. cit., pp. 131–41, 426–27. For a strong dissent to the Protestant accusation that nominalist theology tended toward a semi-Pelagian doctrine of justification, see Francis Clark, "A New Appraisal of Late Medieval Theology," in *Gregorianum* 46 (1965), pp. 733–65, and especially A. E. McGrath, "The Anti-Pelagian Structure of 'Nominalist' Doctrines of Justification," *Ephemerides Theologicae Lovaniensis* 57 (1981), pp. 107–19. McGrath argues that the accusations of semi-Pelagianism against Occam, Holcot, and Biel "result from a misunderstanding of the doctrines of justification associated with the 'nominalist' writers." Ibid., p. 107. In his *Iustitia Dei: A History of the Christian Doctrine of Justification. I: From the Beginnings to 1500* (Cambridge: Cambridge University Press, 1986), McGrath continues his attempt to refute the charge (by Oberman in particular) that Biel's doctrine of justification bears the taint of Pelagianism. We shall have occasion to consider the strength of McGrath's argument in the final section of this chapter. Cf. Denis Janz, "A Reinterpretation of Gabriel Biel on Nature and Grace," in *Sixteenth Century Journal* 8 (1977), pp. 104–108.

2. Helpful expositions of St. Thomas's doctrine of justification include Johann Stufler, *Divi Thomae Aquinatis doctrina de Deo operante in omni operatione naturae creatae praesertim liberi arbitrii* (Innsbruck: Buchdruckerie Tyrolia, 1923); Henri Bouillard, *Conversion et grâce chez S. Thomas d'Aquin* (Paris: Montaigne, 1944);

Stephanus Pfürtner, *Luther und Thomas im Gespräch: Unser Heil zwischen Gewissheit und Gefährdung* (Heidelberg: F. H. Kerle, 1961); Otto H. Pesch, *Theologie der Rechtfertigung bei Martin Luther und Thomas von Aquin: Versuch eines systematisch-theologischen Dialogs* (Mainz: Matthias-Grünewald, 1967); Horst Kasten, *Taufe und Rechtfertigung bei Thomas von Aquin und Martin Luther* (Munich: Chr. Kaiser, 1970); Bernard J. Lonergan, "St. Thomas' Thought on 'Gratia operans,'" *Theological Studies* 2 (1941), pp. 234–89, 3 (1942), pp. 69–88, 375–402, 532–78; idem, *Grace and Freedom: Operative Grace in the Thought of St. Thomas Aquinas* (New York: Herder & Herder, 1970). A. E. McGrath discusses St. Thomas's perspective on questions of sin and grace at several points in his *Iustitia Dei;* see especially pp. 44–47, 63–64, 81–82, 85–87, and 103–109.

3. Biel IV *Sent.* d. 14 q. 2 a. 1 n. 2 (E); Aquinas IV *Sent.* d. 17 q. 1 a. 3 qla. 2 *sol.*

4. Aquinas *S.T.* I–II q. 109 a. 2 *corp.*, cf. q. 108 a. 3 *corp.*

5. Biel III *Sent.* d. 35 q. un. a. 2 dub. 1 (I); Aquinas III *Sent.* d. 34 q. 1 a. 1, q. 2 a. 2 qla. 1 ad 1; cf. *S.T.* II–II q. 19 a. 4 *corp.*

6. Ibid. Cf. *S.T.* I–II q. 68 a. 2 *corp.*, a. 8 *corp.*

7. Biel II *Sent.* d. 28 q. un. (B); Aquinas *S.T.* I–II q. 109 aa. 1–9. Cf. Biel III *Sent.* d. 29 q. un. a. 1 n. 3 (B); Aquinas III *Sent.* d. 29 q. 1 a. 3 *resp.*, a. 7 *resp.*

8. Biel II *Sent.* d. 28 q. un. (B): "In utroque tamen statu ad quodcunque agendum requiritur auxilium primi moventis Dei. Sic ad praeparandum se ad bonum Dei suscipiendum, non indiget alio dono gratiae, sed Deo ipsum movente."

9. The correlative texts are as follows: (a): *S.T.* I–II q. 109 a. 1 *corp.* (b): Ibid. (c): Ibid., a. 2 *corp.* (d): Ibid., a. 2 *corp.*, a. 3 *corp.* (e) Ibid., a. 3 *corp.*, a. 4 *corp.*, ad 3.

10. Ibid., a. 6 ad 1.

11. Ibid., *corp.*

12. Ibid., a. 7 *corp.*

13. Ibid.

14. Ibid., a. 8 *corp.*; cf. a. 3 *corp.*, a. 4 ad 3.

15. Ibid., a. 8 *corp.*

16. The correlative texts are as follows: (1): *S.T.* I–II q. 109 a. 2 *corp.*, a. 5 *corp.* (2): Ibid., a. 2 *corp.* (3): Ibid. (4): Ibid., a. 6 *corp.* (5): Ibid., a. 7 *corp.*

17. Ibid., a. 7 *corp.*

18. Ibid., a. 4 *corp.*, a. 8 *corp.*

19. Ibid., a. 8 *corp.*

20. Ibid., a. 9 *corp.*

21. Ibid., a. 7 *corp.*

22. Biel II *Sent.* d. 28 q. un. (B): "Sed an illud, art. 9, speciali ratione homini impensum sit aliud ab influentia et cooperatione Dei generali, qua assistit omni agendi ipsum movendo, an sit idem, non determinat. Non enim dicit quod homo indiget speciali auxilio Dei, sed dicit, 'Indiget tali auxilio gratiae sub duplici ratione, scilicet generali et speciali, etc., art. 9 in corpore quaestionis."

23. Ibid.: "Dicit etiam art. 3 in fine in corpore quaestionis quod in statu naturae corruptae, licet non in statu naturae integrae, indiget homo auxilio Dei sive auxilio gratiae naturam sanantis ut Deum super omnia diligat. Tali vero dono non indigebat in statu naturae integrae ad diligendum Deum super omnia; nunc vero indiget et sine eo super omnia diligere Deum non potest."

24. Stufler, *Divi Thomae Aquinatis doctrina de Deo operante in omni operatione naturae creatae praesertim liberi arbitrii;* cf. Bouillard, *Conversion et grâce chez S. Thomas d'Aquin,* pp. 3–9.

25. Oberman, *The Harvest of Medieval Theology,* p. 145.

26. Biel *Exp.* Lect. 59 (O–R); Aquinas *S.T.* I–II q. 114 a. 2 *corp.*, ad 1, 2, 3, a. 3 *s.c.*, *corp.*

27. Biel *Exp.* Lect. 59 (O), trans. mine.

28. Aquinas *S.T.* I–II q. 114 a. 2 ad 1.

29. For a fuller analysis of the scholastic distinction between *meritum de condigno* and *meritum de congruo,* see Oberman, *The Harvest of Medieval Theology,* pp. 169–74.

30. Cf. Aquinas *S.T.* q. 114 a. 2 *corp.*, a. 5 *corp.*

31. Ibid., a. 3 *corp.*: "Si consideretur secundum substantiam operis, et secundum quod procedit ex libero arbitrio, sic non potest ibi esse condignitas propter maximam inaequalitatem; sed est ibi congruitas propter quamdam aequalitatem proportionis. Videtur enim congruum ut homini operanti secundum suam virtutem Deus recompenset secundum excellentiam suae virtutis."

32. Ibid., a. 5 *corp.*: "donum gratiae considerari potest dupliciter; uno modo secundum rationem gratuiti doni; et sic manifestum est quod omne meritum repugnat gratiae, ut Apostolos dicit, *si autem gratia, jam non operibus.* Alio modo potest considerari secundum naturam ipsius rei quae donatur; et sic etiam non potest cadere sub merito non habentis gratiam; tum quia excedit proportionem naturae, tum etiam quia ante gratiam in statu peccati homo habet impedimentum promerendi gratiam, scilicet ipsum peccatum."

33. Ibid., a. 1 *corp.*, ad 1.

34. Cf. Harry J. McSorley, *Luther: Right or Wrong? An Ecumenical-Theological Study of Luther's Major Work, 'The Bondage of the Will'* (New York-Minneapolis: Newman-Augsburg, 1969), p. 208. McSorley notes Biel's error but does not acknowledge the degree to which it is part of a larger pattern.

35. Biel *Exp.* Lect. 59 (Q).

36. Biel *Exp.* Lect. 59 (R).

37. Ibid.: "Ex parte dei promittentis est iusticia in reddendo. Iustum enim est ut servetur promissum. Hinc dicitur mercennario: 'Tolle quod tuum est.' Non reddere autem suum iniustum esset. Hec autem iusticia non est ex natura actus, sed ex liberalissima dei promissione, qui volens se debitorem constituit, et sua voluntate se obligavit tali operi tantum reddere premium, et ita surgit ibi condignitas ex veri-

tate pollicentis, quia stante illa domini pollicitatione, iustum est reddere et iniustum non reddere, licet illa iusticia ex sola liberalissima voluntate dei pendeat, tanta premia pollicentis."

38. Biel III *Sent.* d. 35 q. un. a. 1 n. 2 (B): "iste timor etsi non sit bonus meritorie, quia non procedit ex amore boni aeterni, sed ex amore sui, est tamen bonus et utilis . . ." Cf. Aquinas III *Sent.* d. 34 q. 2 a. 2 qla. 1 ad 3.

39. Biel I *Sent.* d. 17 q. 3 a. 2 c. 1 (B); Aquinas *S.T.* I–II q. 114 a. 2 *s.c.*, *corp.* St. Thomas's proof-texts (I Cor. 2.9, Rom. 6.23) are faithfully cited by Biel.

40. Biel II *Sent.* d. 27 q. un. a. 3 dub. 3 (N); Aquinas *S.T.* I–II q. 114 a. 7 arg. 1, *corp.*, ad 1.

41. Biel II *Sent.* d. 27 q. un. a. 3 dub. 3 (N): "Ergo nihil debetur cadenti pro bonis operibus quae fecit stans in gratia; moriuntur etiam omnia merita sua per peccatum mortale." Again Biel makes use of Thomas's proof-text (Ezek. 18.24).

42. Ibid.: "Sed videtur quod ratio non sufficit quantum ad meritum congrui, cum etiam quis per opera mortua extra gratiam facta disponendo se ad gratiam meretur de congruo; ergo multo magis per opera in caritate facta et postea mortificata." Biel's dissent at this point confirms our earlier claim that in I *Sent.* d. 17 q. 3 a. 2 c. 1 (B) Biel's agreement with Thomas's position must be understood as extending only to the question of condign merit.

43. Ibid.

44. Biel *Exp.* Lect. 58 (I); Aquinas IV *Sent.* d. 45 q. 2 a. 1 qla. 4 *sol.*

45. Biel *Exp.* Lect. 62 (K); Aquinas *S.T.* I–II q. 100 a. 10 *corp.*

46. In *Exp.* Lect. 58 (I), Biel expounds a distinction between a *meritum premii essentialis* (which merits some degree of eternal blessedness) and a *meritum premii accidentalis* (which merits some temporal or eternal good other than the beatific vision). He claims—rightly, I believe—that his distinction is the fruit of St. Thomas's tree, corresponding to Aquinas's distinction between an "opus suffragii . . . ut est meritorium vitae aeternae" and an "opus suffragii . . . ut est expiativum poenae," or to the distinction between a work of satisfaction and a work of positive merit. It is true that "implicitly" is not the standard translation of *sententaliter.* R. E. Latham, however, in his *Revised Medieval Word List* (London: Oxford University Press, 1965), p. 433, reports such a use of the term, in British and Irish documents, around 1340 and 1365. The present *locus* in Biel is one of several in which he seems to use the term in this sense.

47. Biel *Exp.* Lect. 62 (K): "non ideo peccat mortaliter servans divina mandata, si in eorum observatione non impletur intentio dei principientis et finis, qui est ut serventur ex charitate et finaliter propter deum. Alioquin honorans parentes ex naturali pietate peccaret, et non existens in gratia non occidendo peccaret, et similiter non furando, non concupiscendo rem alienam. Hec est intentio sancti Thomae, prima secunde, quest. c, art. x . . ."

48. Cf. Aquinas *S.T.* I–II q. 100 a. 10 *s.c.*, *corp.*

49. Biel III *Sent.* d. 18 q. un. a. 1 n. 6 (F–G); Aquinas III *Sent.* d. 18 q. 1 a. 3 *resp.*

50. Biel III *Sent.* d. 18 q. un. a. 1 n. 6 (G): "Haec satis sunt de mente Scoti, Occam, beati Thomae, et aliorum."

51. Biel III *Sent.* d. 18 q. un. a. 1 n. 6 (F); cf. Aquinas *S.T.* I–II q. 110 a. 3 *s.c.*

52. Biel *Exp.* Lect. 56 (L): "Sed opus quandoque est meritorium alicui, non ex dispositione quam iam habet, sed quantum ad aliquod consequens dispositionem vel statum eius, ut dicit Thomas." Cf. Aquinas IV *Sent.* d. 45 q. 2 a. 1 qla. 1 *resp.* It should be noted that the distinction between condign and congruous merit does not enter Aquinas's discussion in the text that Biel seems to be following. *Meritum de congruo* could be described in the language that Biel attributes to Aquinas, but the context gives no indication that this is what either of them has in mind.

53. Biel III *Sent.* d. 25 q. un. a. 2 c. 3 (L); Aquinas III *Sent.* d. 25 q. 2 a. 1 qla. 1 ad 1.

54. Ibid.

55. Biel's "moral heroism"—his emphasis on the importance of moral exertion on the part of the sinner in disposing himself for grace by doing his very best (*faciendo quod in se est*)—leads him to stress each person's responsibility for himself or herself. Consequently he has to be concerned about the case of one who lacks access to knowledge of the things that must be believed as a condition of salvation (*credenda*). How can such a person be responsible for himself? It is in this context that Biel introduces the *facere quod in se est* in II *Sent.* d. 22 q. 2 a. 3 dub. 1 (N). Although Biel does not acknowledge it in II *Sent.* d. 22, Aquinas's language in the text cited is at least compatible with Biel's understanding of the *facere quod in se est* in relation to the hypothetical case of a child of Christian parents who is kidnapped as an infant and raised in a non-Christian culture. Aquinas III *Sent.* d. 25 q. 2 a. 1 qla. 1 ad 2: "si talis faceret quod in se est de quaerendo salutem, Deus illi aliquo dictorum modorum provideret de salute sua."

56. Biel III *Sent.* d. 25 q. un. a. 2 c. 5 (O) 41–46; Aquinas III *Sent.* d. 25 q. 2 a. 2 qla. 3 *sol.*

57. Biel III *Sent.* d. 25 q. un. a. 2 c. 5 (O) 41–46: "De hoc etiam beatus Thomas in tertio Scripto distinctione praesenti q. 4 art. 3 dicit: 'Fides explicita ad hoc necessaria est, quod in finem ultimum intentionem dirigat. Et quia per peccatum homo ab illo fine abductus fuerat, non poterat reduci nisi per mediatorem Dei et hominum, Dominum Iesum Christum. Ideo post peccatum oportuit habere cognitionem explicitam de redemptore, et praecipue quantum ad ea, quibus nos in finem reduxit, victo hoste, quo captivi tenebamur.' Ad hoc autem, quod nos in finem reduceret, quattuor requirebantur. Primum, quod propugnator noster institueretur; quod factum est in nativitate. Secundum, quod propugnaret; quod factum est in passione. Tertium, quod vinceret; quod factum est in resurrectione, quando aeternitatis aditum devicta morte reseravit. Quartum, quod victoriae suae omnes suos participes faceret; quod erit in iudicio, quando bonis bona et malis mala reddet."

58. Cf. Biel III *Sent.* d. 25 q. un a. 2 c. 5 (O) 19–24; Aquinas *S.T.* II–II q. 2 a. 8 *corp.*

59. Ibid. Biel, like Aquinas, qualifies this conclusion by noting that explicit faith in the incarnation and the doctrine of the Trinity became necessary only after the full manifestation of grace, i.e., in the incarnate Christ.

60. Biel III *Sent.* d. 25 q. un. a. 2 c. 5 (N); Aquinas III *Sent.* d. 25 q. 2 a. 1 qla. 3 *sol.*

61. Biel III *Sent.* d. 25. q. un. a. 3 dub. 4 (T); Aquinas *S.T.* II–II q. 2 a. 10 *corp.*

62. Biel III *Sent.* d. 24 q. un. a. 1 n. 1 (A); Aquinas *S.T.* I q. 1 a. 2 *s.c.*, *corp.*, II–II q. 1 a. 5 *corp.*, ad 2.

63. Ibid.

64. Biel's claim is that "non potest ei theologia esse scientia," and he buttresses his argument with an appeal to the authority of Aquinas ("ut opinatur Thomas").

65. Cf. Biel III *Sent.* d. 27 q. un. a. 3 dub. 2 (Q–R). Oberman (*Harvest of Medieval Theology*, pp. 48–49) claims that Biel's talk about *ex puris naturalibus* amounts to no more than an abstraction that makes it possible for him to address the purely hypothetical situation of one who stands between *gratia* and *culpa*. It is a purely hypothetical situation because everyone, in fact, is either *in gratia* or *in culpa*. It is important to note, however, that Biel's category is that of the *viator*. He asks what the *homo errans* can do *ex suis naturalibus*. Clearly such language involves something more than a logical construct: in this life, *everyone* is a *viator*. In any case, Oberman is aware of Biel's teaching that the *viator* is naturally capable of loving God *super omnia* without this possibility first being created through a special enablement by grace. See *Harvest*, pp. 49, 153.

66. Biel IV *Sent.* d. 14 q. 2 a. 1 n. 2 (H): "Aut ergo requiritur detestatio peccatorum sufficiens ad infusionem gratiae et ut ultima dispositio, et tunc statim infunditur gratia . . ."

67. McGrath, "The Anti-Pelagian Structure of 'Nominalist' Doctrines of Justification," in *Ephemerides Theologicae Lovaniensis* 57 (1981), pp. 107–119; idem, *Iustitia Dei: A History of the Christian Doctrine of Justification. I: From the Beginnings to 1500*, pp. 89ff., 138–39, 170–71.

68. McGrath, *Iustitia Dei*, p. 89.

69. Ibid.

70. Ibid.

71. Ibid., pp. 170–71: "The distinction between the *intrinsic* and *imposed* value of moral acts is of decisive importance, as it permits the axiom *facienti quod in se est Deus non denegat gratiam* . . . to be interpreted in a sense which allows a man to play a positive role in his own justification, without elevating that role to Pelagian proportions. In this way the theologians of the *via moderna* were able to maintain the teaching of both the early and later Franciscan schools concerning man's meritorious disposition towards justification, while establishing a conceptual

framework within which this teaching could be safeguarded from the charge of Pelagianism."

72. Ibid., p. 139. Cf. McGrath, "The Anti-Pelagian Structure of 'Nominalist' Doctrines of Justification," especially pp. 109–11.

73. Ibid., pp. 138–39: "Oberman's analysis of Biel's doctrine of predestination is confused by his use of the categories of predestination *post praevisa merita* and *ante praevisa merita*. . . . Biel, naturally, does not use either phrase, nor the conceptual framework within which Protestant Orthodoxy discussed the doctrine of justification. Biel, it must be emphasized, is entitled to be interpreted by the standards of, and within the context of his own conceptural framework, rather than an alien framework imposed upon him."

74. Ibid., pp. 175–76. McGrath's reference is to Biel's use, in *Exp.* Lect. 59 (L), of materials from pseudo-Augustine, as discussed in Oberman's *The Harvest of Medieval Theology*, pp. 160–65.

75. Oberman, *The Harvest of Medieval Theology*, p. 177.

76. Cf. Janz, *Luther and Late Medieval Thomism: A Study in Theological Anthropology*, esp. pp. 156–57, where Janz concludes that there was "a shift in the Thomas-interpretation of the late medieval Thomist school in a non-Augustinian direction on vital questions of theological anthropology. And this shift, coming as it did on the eve of, and during the Reformation movement, must be seen as highly significant, for it was on these issues above all that Luther felt himself to be in disagreement with Thomas. On these issues the fully Augustinian teaching of Thomas was not adequately represented by Luther's Thomist contemporaries."

ESCHATOLOGY

1. Biel III *Sent.* d. 22 q. un. a. 3 dub. 3 (I); Aquinas III *Sent.* d. 22 q. 2 a. 1 qla. 2 *sol.*

2. Biel *Exp.* Lect. 67 (K); Aquinas IV *Sent.* d. 45 q. 1 a. 1 qla. 2 *sol.* Biel *Exp.* Lect. 56 (L); Aquinas IV *Sent.* d. 45 q. 2 a. 1 qla. 2 ad 2; Biel *Exp.* Lect. 57 (T); Aquinas IV *Sent.* d. 45 q. 2 a. 4 qla. 1 *sol.*, a. 1 qla. 3 *sol.*; Biel *Exp.* Lect. 58 (A); Aquinas IV *Sent.* d. 45 q. 2 a. 2 qla. 2 ad 4; Biel *Exp.* Lect. 57 (H); Aquinas IV *Sent.* d. 45 q. 2 a. 1 qla. 1 *sol.*, ad 2, a. 2 qla. 2 *sol.*

3. Biel *Exp.* Lect. 67 (K): "Et addit Thomas exemplum: Sicut in corporibus est gravitas et levitas que feruntur in locum suum, qui est finis motus eorum; ita etiam est in animabus meritum vel demeritum, quibus perveniunt anime ad premium vel ad penam, que sunt fines actionum ipsarum; unde sicut corpus per levitatem vel gravitatem statim fertur ad locum suum nisi prohibeatur; ita animae statim, soluto

vinculo carnis, per quod in statu vie detinebantur, premium consequuntur vel penam nisi aliquid impediat." Cf. Aquinas IV *Sent.* d. 45. q. 1 a. 1 qla. 2 *sol.*

4. Ibid.

5. Ibid. Cf. Biel *Exp.* Lect. 68 (P); Aquinas IV *Sent.* d. 45 q. 1 a. 1 qla. 2 *sol.*

6. Biel *Exp.* Lect. 57 (H); Aquinas IV *Sent.* d. 45 q. 2 a. 1 qla. 1 *sol.*, ad 2; a. 2 qla. 2 *sol.*

7. Biel *Exp.* Lect. 57 (H): "Non enim est aliqua ratio, ait Thomas, quare ecclesia possit transferre merita communia quibus indulgentie innituntur ad vivos et non ad mortuos."

8. Biel claims only that St. Thomas mentions (*adducit*) this argument. In fact, Aquinas lists it as the second *argumentum* in IV *Sent.* d. 45 q. 2 a. 3 qla. 2. It is noteworthy that Aquinas, departing from his customary procedure, does not offer a refutation of this *argumentum.* Biel is correct in suggesting that this *ratio* is supportive of Aquinas's conclusion. Aquinas's only caveat is that such indulgences may benefit the dead *secundario* but not *principaliter:* IV *Sent.* d. 45 q. 2 a. 3 qla. 2 *sol.*

9. Biel *Exp.* Lect. 57 (A); Aquinas IV *Sent.* d. 45 q. 2 a. 3 qla. 1 *sol.*, ad 2.

10. Biel *Exp.* Lect. 56 (R–S); Aquinas IV *Sent.* d. 45 q. 2 a. 2 qla. 1. Cf. Biel *Exp.* Lect. 56 (U); Aquinas IV *Sent.* d. 45 q. 2 a. 2 qla. 1 ad 1. Cf. also Biel *Exp.* Lect. 56 (Y); Aquinas IV *Sent.* d. 45 q. 2 qla. 1 *sol.*

11. Biel *Exp.* Lect. 57 (A); Aquinas IV *Sent.* d. 45 q. 2 a. 3 qla. 1 *sol.*, ad 2.

12. Ibid.

13. Biel *Exp.* Lect. 57 (A): "Ex parte vero intentionis in mortuos directe percipue valet oratio, quia secundum suam rationem non solum dicit respectum ad orantem sicut cetera opera, sed directius ad eum pro quo oratur."

14. Biel *Exp.* Lect. 27 (I); Aquinas IV *Sent.* d. 45 q. 2 a. 1 qla. 1 *sol.*, qla. 2 *sol.*, qla. 4 *sol.* Cf. Biel *Exp.* Lect. 57 (B); Aquinas IV *Sent.* d. 45 q. 2 qla. 2 ad 4.

15. Biel *Exp.* Lect. 57 (T); Aquinas IV *Sent.* d. 45 q. 2 a. 4 qla. 1 *sol.*

16. Biel *Exp.* Lect. 56 (L); Aquinas IV *Sent.* d. 45 q. 2 a. 1 qla. 2 ad 2.

17. Biel *Exp.* Lect. 57 (S); Aquinas IV *Sent.* d. 45 q. 2 a. 1 qla. 1 *sol.*

18. Biel *Exp.* Lect. 57 (S): "Rationem assignat beatus Thomas . . . 'Quia sors glorie redditur secundum mensuram accipientis,' hoc est dispositionis dignitatis eius ad premium. 'Unusquisque autem ex suo actus disponitur, non ex actu alterius,' actu, inquam voluntario." In this citation, Biel's interpolations—associating *mensuram* with *dispositio dignitatis* and emphasizing the voluntariness of the self-disposing act—are entirely consonant with St. Thomas's intention. Indeed, Biel's language (*mensuram, dispositio dignitatis*) is not, strictly speaking, an interpolation at all, since these terms are borrowed directly from the text cited.

19. Biel *Exp.* Lect. 57 (B); Aquinas IV *Sent.* d. 45 q. 2 a. 2 qla. 2 ad 4 (on the benefit of the Church's prayers *ex opere operato*). Biel *Exp.* Lect. 58 (A); Aquinas IV *Sent.* d. 45 q. 2 a. 2 qla. 2 ad 4 (on the benefit of the Church's prayers *ex opere operantis*).

20. Biel *Exp.* Lect. 57 (T); Aquinas IV *Sent.* d. 45 q. 2 a. 1 qla. 3 *sol.* Note that for Aquinas's "existans in peccato," Biel speaks of an "auctor principalis" who "non fuerit in charitate dum mandat vel ordinat." When Aquinas speaks of one who "non sit in statu merendi," Beil takes the liberty of reformulating the matter in terms of a lack of charity. Since Aquinas makes charity the immediate basis of personal merit (*S.T.* I–II q. 114 a. 4 *corp.*), Biel can hardly be accused of putting strange words in St. Thomas's mouth.

21. Biel *Exp.* Lect. 58 (D): "Quantum vero ad eternam retributionem, nullus frauderi potest, nisi per propriam culpam." Cf. Aquinas IV *Sent.* d. 45 q. 2 a. 2 qla. 2 ad 4.

22. Biel *Exp.* Lect. 56 (R–S): "Et additur tertia ratio secundum sanctum Thomam . . . Nam damnati sunt totaliter in termino quantum ad animam et extra viam, recipientes ultimam pro meritis retributis retributionem, sicut et sancti qui sunt in patria . . . et ideo non potest pena eorum diminui, sicut nec premium sanctorum augeri quantum ad gloriam essentialem." Cf. Aquinas IV *Sent.* d. 45 q. 2 a. 2 qla. 1. The critical edition of the *Expositio* includes here a puzzling reference to the *misericordia damnatorum*, substituting *misericordia* for Aquinas's *miseria.* A comparison with the Reutlingen edition of 1488 makes it clear that the error is the editor's, not Biel's.

23. Biel *Exp.* Lect. 56 (Y); Aquinas IV *Sent.* d. 45 q. 2 a. 2 qla. 1 *resp.*

24. Biel *Exp.* Lect. 56 (Y), trans. mine.

25. Biel *Exp.* Lect. 56 (U); Aquinas IV *Sent.* d. 45 q. 2 a. 2 qla. 1 ad 1.

26. Biel *Exp.* Lect. 56 (U): "Ad illud de machabeis dicendum, secundum Thomam, vel quod illa donaria inventa sub tunicis mortuorum non fuerunt accepta in reverentiam idolorum, sed iure belli eis debebantur, tamen per aliqualem avariciam venialiter peccaverunt; ideo non fuerunt in inferno, et ita suffragia eis poterant valere.

"Vel probabilius quod in ipsa pugna videntes sibi imminere periculum, peccatum suum cognoverunt et penituerunt . . . et ita peccatum reemissum fuit per penitentiam, et per consequens non fuerunt in inferno, sed purgaturio."

27. Biel III *Sent.* d. 29 q. un. a. 3 dub. 1 (I); Aquinas *S.T.* II–II q. 26 a. 13 *corp.*

28. For both Biel and Aquinas, this "proximity" is moral rather than ontological, as the context makes clear. The one who is "nearer" to God is not *divinius* but *melior* or *beatior.*

29. Biel III *Sent.* d. 31 q. un. a. 3 dub. 3 (I); Aquinas III *Sent.* d. 31 q. 2 a. 4 *resp.* Cf. Aquinas *S.T.* I–II q. 67 a. 2 *corp.*, ad 1.

30. Ibid. Here Biel cites Aquinas's use of Aristotle's dictum that "nihil est in intellectu quod no fuerit in sensu."

31. Aquinas III *Sent.* d. 31 q. 2 a. 4 *resp.*: "Dicere enim, quod habitus remaneat, et actus nullo modo, videtur absurdum: quia habitus nihil est aliud quam habilitas ad actum."

32. Aquinas III *Sent.* d. 31 q. 2 aa. 1, 2.

33. Cf. Calvin *Inst.* III.25.vi.

34. Luther's position on the status of the soul immediately following the moment of death is ambiguous. In the handful of texts in which he addresses the question, Luther's favorite metaphor is that of sleep. Cf. *WA* 17-II, 235; *WA* 37, 151; *WA, Br* 5, 240; *WA, Br* 5, 213. Here Luther suggests that the interval between death and resurrection is passed in an unconscious state. In other contexts, however, Luther implies that the dead in Christ are conscious and cognizant. Cf. *WA* 53, 400. Still the dominant tendency in Luther's reflections on death and the afterlife is toward a soul-sleep theory which envisions a postponement of reward or punishment until the final judgment.

35. Obviously, we do not know precisely the elements of Tetzel's preaching to which Luther was exposed (and against which he reacted with such fury). Two errors for which Tetzel was criticized by his fellow Dominican, Cajetan, were his claims that the benefit of an indulgence is independent of the purchaser's contrition and that the application of the indulgence's benefit to a soul in purgatory is at the purchaser's discretion. Cf. Aherne, "Tetzel, Johann," p. 1025. On both counts Tetzel places himself outside the pale of Thomistic doctrine, as Biel's summaries of St. Thomas's writings on the subject make clear.

POST THOMAM

1. As Grabmann observes, in "Johannes Capreolus O. P., der 'Princeps Thomistarum' († 1444), und seine Stellung in der Geschichte der Thomistenschule," *Mittelalterliches Geistesleben* 3 (Munich: Max Hueber, 1956), pp. 370, 372, Durandus de S. Porciano was a critic and Petrus de Palude a defender of St. Thomas's theology. According to Wilhelm Ernst, in *Gott und Mensch am Vorabend der Reformation* (Leipzig: St. Benno, 1972), p. 93, Biel alludes to Petrus three times as frequently as to Durandus. In itself such a statistical observation proves nothing conclusively, but it is at least another indication of Biel's openness to Thomistic insights.

2. Carl Feckes, "Gabriel Biel, der erste grosse Dogmatiker der Universität Tübingen in seiner wissenschaftlichen Bedeutung," *Theologische Quartalschrift* 108 (1927), p. 62: "Denn es ist ein schon mehrfach beobachtete Tatsache, dass Biel gerade in seinen Predigten sich hutet vor den extravaganten Meinungen seiner Schule und seinen Horen eine gesundere Kost anbietet." Cf. William M. Landeen, "Gabriel Biel and the Brethren of the Common Life in Germany," *Church History* 20 (1951), p. 35: "His popularity lay no doubt in the facts that his was a mild, calm temperament, void of extremes and partisan debate, and that his style was clear, consise, smooth, and inspirational."

3. Feckes, "Gabriel Biel, der erste grosse Dogmatiker der Universität Tübingen," pp. 55, 75.

4. Oberman, *Harvest of Medieval Theology,* op. cit., p. 141.

5. Ibid., p. 145. Denis R. Janz has shown that Cajetan's interpretation of St. Thomas's doctrine of justification suffered from a tendency quite similar to the pattern of distortions that we have noted in Biel. Cf. *Luther and Late Medieval Thomism: A Study in Theological Anthropology* (Waterloo, Ontario: Wilfrid Laurier University Press, 1983), pp. 123–53, 156–57.

6. Otto Scheel, *Martin Luther: Vom Katholizismus zur Reformation,* II (Tübingen: J. C. B. Mohr, 1917), p. 356.

7. Johannes Capreolus, for instance, makes it clear that on Thomistic principles one cannot affirm (with Durandus de S. Porciano) that "licet ad consecutionem gratiae requiratur specialis motio Dei gratiam infundentis . . . tamen ad eam potest se homo disponere pure, ut videtur, per liberum arbitrium absque tali motione speciali." Capreolus, II *Sent.* d. 28 q. 1 a. 2 arg. Durandi contra quintam con., in *Defensiones theologiae divi Thomae Aquinatis* 4, pp. 296–97 (Tours: Alfred Cattier, 1900–1907; reprint, Frankfurt/Main: Minerva, 1967). Capreolus criticizes the position of Durandus as follows: "Cum enim dicitur quod bonum morale est sufficiens praeparatio ad gratiam, falsum est, si intelligatur de bono morali quod nihil habet de gratuito nec tendit in aliquid supernaturale." Ad arg. contra quintam con., ad secundum. *Defensiones,* 4, p. 316.

8. John P. Donnelley, in his article on "Calvinist Thomism," *Viator* 7 (1976), pp. 441–55, focuses on the continuation of Thomistic themes in the Protestantism of Peter Martyr Vermigli and Jerome Zanchi. The scholastic background of Protestant Orthodoxy involves at several points a significant appropriation of Thomistic perspectives, as is made clear in Richard A. Muller's forthcoming *Post-Reformation Reformed Dogmatics* vol. 1; cf. Muller's *Christ and the Decree* (Durham, N.C.: Labyrinth, 1986), especially on Zanchi, pp. 110–25. On Bucer's relation to St. Thomas, cf. Robert Stupperich, ed., *Martin Bucers Deutsche Schriften, 6, 2: Zum Ius Reformationis. Obrigkeitsschriften aus dem Jahre 1535: Dokumente zur 2. Strassburger Synode von 1539* (Gütersloh: Gerd Mohn, 1984), p. 44: "Die 'Dialogi' sind die erste Zusammenfassung der Gedanken Bucers über das Problem von Obrigkeit und Kirche, wie sie sich schon in seinen früheren Schriften hier und da finden. Als ehemaliger Dominikaner ist er von Thomas von Aquino, als Humanist von der Antike beeinflusst." On p. 19 of his essay, "Martin Bucer: Ecumenical Theologian," which serves as an introduction to David F. Wright, trans. and ed., *Common Places of Martin Bucer* (Appleford/Abingdon/Berkshire: Sutton Courtenay, 1972), pp. 17–41, David F. Wright notes Bucer's ambivalence toward Aquinas and suggests that "Thomas came back into greater favor the further Bucer moved away from his Dominican days."

BIBLIOGRAPHY

PRIMARY SOURCES

Ailly, Pierre d'. *Quaestiones super libros sententiarum cum quibusdam in fine adjunctis.* Strassburg: 1490 (reprinted, Frankfurt/Main: Minerva, 1968).

Alexander of Hales. *Glossa in quatuor libros Sententiarum Petri Lombardi,* I–IV. Quaracchi, Florence: Collegium Bonaventurae, 1951–57.

———. *Summa theologica.* Quaracchi, Florence: Collegium Bonaventurae, 1924–48.

Aquinas, Thomas. *Opera omnia,* I–XXV. Parma: Petrus Fiaccadorus, 1852–73.

Biel, Gabriel. *Canonis misse expositio,* I–V. Edited by Heiko Oberman and William J. Courtenay. Wiesbaden: Franz Steiner, 1963–76.

Biel, Gabriel. *Collectorium circa quatuor libros Sententiarum,* I, II, III, IV-1, IV-2. Edited by Wilfredus Werbeck and Udo Hofmann. Tübingen: J. C. B. Mohr (Paul Siebeck), 1973–84.

Biel, Gabriel. *Epithome et collectorium ex Occamo circa quatuor sententiarum Libros.* Tübingen: 1501 (reprinted, Frankfurt/Main: Minerva, 1965).

Capreolus, Johannes. *Defensiones theologiae divi Thomae Aquinatis.* Edited by C. Paban and T. Pègues. Tours: Alfred Cattier, 1900–1907. Reprint, Frankfurt/Main: Minerva, 1967.

Gigon, Olaf, ed. *Aristotelis opera ex recensione Immanuelis Bekkeri.* Berlolini: W. de Gruyter, 1960–61.

Luther, Martin. *D. Martin Luthers Werke: Kritische Gesamtausgabe.* Edited by J. K. F. Knaake, G. Kamerau, E. Thiel, et al. Weimar: H. Böhlau, 1883–.

Melanchthon, Philip. *Philippi Melanchthonis Opera quae supersunt Omnia. Corpus Reformatorum,* VI. Edited by Carolus Gottlieb Bretschneider. Halis Saxonum: C. A. Schwetschke et Filius, 1839.

Occam, Guilliemus de. *Opera Plurima.* Lyon: 1494–96. Reprint, London: Gregg Press, 1962.

Scotus, Johannes Duns. *Opera Omnia.* Lugduni: Laurentius Durand, 1639. Reprint, Hildesheim: Georg Olms, 1968.

SECONDARY SOURCES

Aherne, C. M. "Tetzel, Johann." *New Catholic Encyclopedia* 13. New York: McGraw-Hill, 1967, p. 1025.

Althaus, Paul. *Die Theologie Martin Luthers.* Gütersloh: Gerd Mohn, 1962.

Bailey, Sydney D. *Prohibitions and Restraints in War.* London: Oxford University Press, 1972.

Bainton, Roland H. *Christian Attitudes toward War and Peace: A Historical Survey and Critical Re-evaluation. Nashville: Abingdon Press, 1960.*

Barbaglio, Giuseppe. *Fede acquisita e fede infusa secundo Duns Scoto, Occam, e Biel.* Brescia: Morcelliana, 1968.

Benery, Friedrich. *Zur Geschichte der Stadt und der Universität Erfurt am Ausgang des Mittelalters,* III. Gotha: Friedrich Andres Perthes A.-G., 1919.

Biechler, James E. "Gabriel Biel on '*liberum arbitrium*': Prelude to Luther's *De servo arbitrio.*" *The Thomist* 34 (1970), pp. 114–27.

Boehmer, Philotheus. *Medieval Logic.* Chicago: University of Chicago Press, 1952.

Bornkamm, Heinrich. "Iustitia Dei in der Scholastik und bei Luther." *Archiv für Reformationsgeschichte* 39 (1942), pp. 1–46.

Bouillard, Henri. *Conversion et grâce chez S. Thomas d'Aquin.* Paris: Montaigne, 1944.

Bourke, Vernon J. *Ethics.* New York: Macmillan, 1951.

———. *History of Ethics.* Garden City, N.Y.: Doubleday, 1968.

Brennan, Robert Edward. *Thomistic Psychology: A Philosophical Analysis of the Nature of Man.* New York: Macmillan, 1941.

Brière, Yves de la. *Le droit de juste guerre.* Paris: Pedone, 1933.

Burkard, Franz Joseph. *Philosophische Lehrgehalte in Gabriel Biels Sentenzenkommentar unter besonderer Berücksichtigung seiner Erkenntnislehre.* Meisenheim am Glan: Anton Hain, 1974.

Busa, Roberto. "De voce *Spiritus* in operibus S. Thomae." *Spiritus* IV. Rome: Edizioni dell'Ateneo, 1984, pp. 191–222.

Cappuyns, M. "Biel, Gabriel." *Dictionnaire d'histoire et de géographie ecclésiastique* 8, cols. 1429–35. Paris: Librairie Letouzey et Ané, 1935.

Carreteri, Manuel Useros. "*Statuta ecclesiae*" *y* "*sacramenta ecclesiae*" *en la eclesiología de st. Thomas de Aquino.* Rome: Università Gregoriana Editrice, 1962.

Catão, Bernard. *Salut et rédemption chez s. Thomas d'Aquin.* Paris: Aubier, 1965.

Chavannes, Henry. *L'Analogie entre Dieu et le monde selon saint Thomas et selon Karl Barth.* Paris: Les Éditions du Cerf, 1969.

Clark, Francis. "A New Appraisal of Late Medieval Theology." *Gregorianum* 46 (1965), pp. 733–65.

Copleston, F. C. *Aquinas.* Baltimore: Penguin Books, 1955.

Courtenay, William J. "Nominalism and Late Medieval Thought: A Bibliographical Essay." *Theological Studies* 33 (1972), pp. 716–34.

Crehan, J. H. "Biel and the Mass." *Clergy Review* 43 (1958), pp. 606–17.

Damerau, Rudolph. *Die Abendmahlslehre des Nominalismus insbesondere die des Gabriel Biel.* Giessen: Wilhelm Schmitz, 1963.

———. *Das Herrengebet.* Giessen: Wilhelm Schmitz, 1964.

Delius, Walter. *Geshichte der Marienverehrung.* Munich: Ernst Reinhardt, 1963.

Dempsey, Bernard W. *Interest and Usury.* Washington, D.C.: American Council on Public Affairs, 1943.

Denifle, Heinrich. *Luther und Luthertum in der ersten Entwickelung* I, 1–2. Mainz: F. Kirchheim, 1904–6.

Dettloff, Werner. *Die Entwicklung der Akzeptations- und Verdienstlsehre von Duns Skotus bis Luther mit besonderer Berücksichtigung der Franziskanertheologen.* Münster: Aschendorff, 1964.

Donnelley, John P. "Calvinist Thomism." *Viator* 7 (1976), pp. 441–55.

Dublanchy, E. "Marie." *Dictionnaire de théologie catholique* 9, II. Paris: Létouzey et Ané, 1927. Cols. 2339–2474.

Elders, L. and Hedwig, K., eds. *The Ethics of Thomas Aquinas.* Vatican City: Libreria Editrice Vaticana, 1984.

Elze, M. "Handschriften von Werken Gabriel Biels aus seinem Nachlass in der Geissener Universitäts-bibliothek." *Zeitschrift für Kirchengeschichte* 81 (1970), no. 1, pp. 70–91.

Ernst, Wilhelm. *Gott und Mensch am Vorabend der Reformation.* Leipzig: St. Benno Verlag, 1972.

Farthing, John L. "The Problem of Divine Exemplarity in St. Thomas." *The Thomist* 49 (April 1985), no. 2, pp. 183–222.

Feckes, Carl. "Gabriel Biel, der erste grosse Dogmatiker der Universität Tübingen in seiner wissenschaftlichen Bedeutung." *Theologische Quartalschrift* 108 (1927), pp. 50–76.

———. *Die Rechtfertigungslehre des Gabriel Biel und ihre Stellung innerhalb der nominalistischen Schule.* Münster: Aschendorff, 1925.

———. "Die Stellung der nominalistischen Schule zur aktuellen Gnade." *Römische Quartalschrift* 32 (1924), pp. 157–65.

Forster, Karl. *Die Verteidigung der Lehre des heiligen Thomas von der Gotteschau durch Johannes Capreolus.* Munich: Karl Zink, 1955.

Friedberger, Walter. *Der Reichtumserwerb in Urteil des Hl. Thomas von Aquin und der Theologen im Zeitalter des Frühkapitalismus.* Passau: Passavia, 1967.

Geiger, L. B. "Les idées divines dans l'oeuvre de S. Thomas." In Maurer, Armand A., et al., eds., *St. Thomas Aquinas, 1274–1974: Commemorative Studies.* Toronto: Pontifical Institute of Medieval Studies, 1974, pp. 175–209.

Gilby, Thomas. *The Political Thought of Thomas Aquinas.* Chicago: University of Chicago Press, 1958.

———. *Principality and Polity: Aquinas and the Rise of State Theory in the West.* New York: Longman, Green, & Co., 1958.

Gilson, Etienne. *The Christian Philosophy of St. Thomas Aquinas.* New York: Random House, 1956.

———. *History of Christian Philosophy in the Middle Ages.* Translated by C. K. Shook. New York: Random House, 1955.

———. *Moral Values and the Moral Life: The System of St. Thomas Aquinas.* Translated by Leo Richard Ward. St. Louis: Herder, 1931.

———. *The Spirit of Thomism.* New York: P. J. Kennedy & Sons, 1964.

Gornall, Thomas. *A Philosophy of God: The Elements of Thomist Natural Theology.* New York: Sheed & Ward, 1963.

Gossman, Maria Elizabeth. *Die Verkündigung an Maria im dogmatischen Verständnis des Mittelalters.* Munich: Max Hueber, 1957.

Grabmann, Martin. "Johannes Capreolus O. P., der 'Princeps Thomistarum' († 1444), und seine Stellung in der Geschichte der Thomistenschule." *Mittelalterliches Geisteslseben: Abhandlungen zur Geschichte der Scholastik und Mystik.* Munich: Max Hueber, 1956, pp. 370–410.

———. *Die Lehre des heiligen Thomas von Aquin von der Kirche als Gotteswerk: Ihre Stellung in der thomistischen System und in der Geschichte des mittelalterlichen Theologie.* Regensburg: G. J. Manz, 1903.

Graef. Hilda. *Mary: A History of Doctrine and Devotion. I: From the Beginnings to the Eve of the Reformation.* New York: Sheed & Ward, 1963.

Grane, Leif. *Contra Gabrielem: Luthers Auseinandersetzung mit Gabriel Biel in der Disputatio Contra Scholasticam Theologiam, 1515.* Gyldendal: Aarhuus, 1962.

———. "Gabriel Biels Lehre von der Allmacht Gottes." *Zeitschrift für Theologie und Kirche* 53 (1956), pp. 53–75.

Habbel, J. *Die Analogie zwischen Gott und Welt nach Thomas von Aquin.* Regensburg: J. Habbel, 1928.

Hägglund, Bengt. *Theologie und Philosophie bei Luther und in der occamistischen Tradition.* Lund: C. W. K. Gleerup, 1955.

———. "Was Luther a Nominalist?" *Theology* 59 (1959), pp. 226–34.

Hamm, Berndt. *Promissio, Pactum, Ordinatio.* Tübingen: J. C. B. Mohr, 1977.

Hartigan, Richard Shelly. "Noncombattant Immunity: Reflections on its Origins and Present Status." *Review of Politics* 29 (1966), pp. 204–20.

Hehir, J. Bryan. "The Just-War Ethic and Catholic Theology." In Shannon, Thomas A., ed., *War or Peace: The Search for New Answers.* Maryknoll: Orbis, 1980, pp. 15–39.

Hennig, Gerhard. *Cajetan und Luther.* Stuttgart: Calwer, 1966.

Hermelink, Heinrich. *Geschichte der theologischen Fakultät in Tübingen vor der Reformation, 1477–1534.* Tübingen: J. C. B. Mohr (Paul Siebeck), 1906.

Heynck, V. "Biel, Gabriel." *New Catholic Encyclopedia* 2. New York: McGraw-Hill, 1967, p. 552.

Hislop, Ian. *The Anthropology of St. Thomas.* Oxford: Blackfriars, 1950.

Iserloh, Irwin. *Gnade und Eucharistie in der philosophischen Theologie des Wilhelm von Ockham: Ihre Bedeutung für die Ursachen der Reformation.* Wiesbaden: Franz Steiner, 1956.

Janz, Denis R. *Luther and Late Medieval Thomism: A Study in Theological Anthropology.* Waterloo, Ont.: Wilfrid Laurier University Press, 1983.

———. "A Reinterpretation of Gabriel Biel on Nature and Grace." *Sixteenth Century Journal* 8 (1977), pp. 104–8.

Johnson, James T. *Ideology, Reason, and the Limitation of War.* Princeton, N.J.: Princeton University Press, 1975.

———. *Just War Tradition and the Restraint of War: A Moral and Historical Inquiry.* Princeton, N.J.: Princeton University Press, 1981.

Johnston, Herbert. "On the Meaning of 'Consumed in Use' in the Problem of Usury." *The Modern Schoolman* 30 (1953), pp. 93–108.

Jordan, Mark D. "The Intelligibility of the World and the Divine Ideas in Aquinas." *Review of Metaphysics* 38 (September 1984), pp. 17–32.

Kasten, Horst. *Taufe und Rechtfertigung bei Thomas von Aquin und Martin Luther.* Munich: Chr. Kaiser, 1970.

Klubertanz, George P. *St. Thomas Aquinas on Analogy: A Textual Analysis and Systematic Synthesis.* Chicago: Loyola University Press, 1960.

Landeen, William M. "Gabriel Biel and the Brethren of the Common Life in Germany." *Church History* 20 (1951), pp. 23–36.

Lang, A. "Nominalismus." *Lexikon für Theologie und Kirche,* cols. 610–12. Freiburg im Breisgau: Herder, 1935.

Lecuyer, J. "Aux origines de la théologie thomiste de l'épiscopat." *Gregorianum* 35 (1954), pp. 56–89.

Leff, Gordon. *The Dissolution of the Medieval Outlook.* New York: University Press, 1976.

Linsenmann, F. X. "Gabriel Biel, der letzte Scholastiker, und der Nominalismus." *Theologische Quartalschrift* 47 (1865), pp. 449–81, 601–76.

———. "Gabriel Biel und die Anfänge der Universität zu Tübingen." *Theologische Quartalschrift* 47 (1865), pp. 195–226.

Lonergan, Bernard J. *Grace and Freedom: Operative Grace in the Thought of St. Thomas Aquinas.* New York: Herder & Herder, 1970.

———. "St. Thomas' Thought on 'Gratia operans.'" *Theological Studies* 2 (1941), pp. 234–89, 3 (1942), pp. 69–88, 375–402, 532–78.

Lortz, Joseph. *Die Reformation in Deutschland.* 2 vols. 3rd ed. Freiburg: Herder, 1948.

———. *Wie kam es zur Reformation?* Einsiedeln: Johannes, 1950.

Lortz, Joseph and Iserloh, Erwin. *Kleine Reformationsgeschichte.* Freiburg im Breisgau: Herder, 1969.

Luyten, N. A., ed. *L'Anthropologie de saint Thomas.* Fribourg: Éditions Universitaires, 1974.

Lynn, William D. *Christ's Redemptive Merit: The Nature of its Causality according to St. Thomas.* Rome: Gregorian University, 1962.

Lyttkins, Hampus. *The Analogy between God and the World: An Investigation of its Background and an Interpretation of its Use by Thomas of Aquino.* Uppsala: Almqvist & Wiksells, 1952.

McGrath, A. E. "The Anti-Pelagian Structure of 'Nominalist' Doctrines of Justification." *Ephemerides Theologicae Lovaniensis* 57 (1981), pp. 107–19.

———. *Iustitia Dei: A History of the Christian Doctrine of Justification. I: From the Beginnings to 1500.* Cambridge: Cambridge University Press, 1986.

McInerny, Ralph. *Ethica Thomistica: The Moral Philosophy of Thomas Aquinas.* Washington, D.C.: Catholic University Press, 1982.

McSorley, Harry J. *Luther: Right or Wrong? An Ecumenical-Theological Study of Luther's Major Work, 'The Bondage of the Will.'* New York-Minneapolis: Newman-Augsburg, 1969.

———. "Was Gabriel Biel a Semipelagian?" In L. Scheffczyk et al., eds., *Wahrheit und Verkündigung. Michael Schmaus zum 70. Geburtstag* 2. Munich: Ferdinand Schöningh, 1967, pp. 1109–1120.

Manser, Gallus M. *Das Wesen des Thomismus.* 3rd ed. *Thomistische Studien* V. Fribourg: Paulusverlag, 1949.

Manzanedo, Marcos F. "La anthropologia filosófica en el commentario tomista al libro de Job." *Angelicum* 62 (1985), pp. 419–71.

Marinelli, Francesco. *Segno e realtà: studi di sacramentaria tomista.* Lateranum, n.s., 43, no. 2, 1977.

Meissinger, Karl August. *Der katholische Luther.* Munich: Leo Lehnen, 1952.

Morgott, Franz. *Die Mariologie des heiligen Thomas von Aquin.* Freiburg: Herder, 1878.

Mtega, Norbert W. *Analogy and Theological Language in the Summa Contra Gentiles: A Textual Survey of the Concept of Analogy and its Theological Application by St. Thomas Aquinas.* New York: Lang, 1984.

Müller, A. V. *Luthers theologische Quellen. Seine Verteidigung gegen Denifle und Grisar.* Giessen: Alfred Töpelmann, 1912.

Muller, Richard A. *Christ and the Decree: Christology and Predestination in Reformed Theology from Calvin to Perkins.* Durham, N.C.: Labyrinth, 1986.

Noonan, J. T. *The Scholastic Analysis of Usury.* Cambridge, Mass.: Harvard University Press, 1957.

Oberman, Heiko A. "Gabriel Biel and Late Medieval Mysticism." *Church History* 30 (1961), pp. 259–87.

———. *The Harvest of Medieval Theology: Gabriel Biel and Late Medieval Nominalism.* 3rd ed. Durham, N.C.: Labyrinth, 1983.

———. "Headwaters of the Reformation: Initia Lutheri—Initia Reformationis." *Luther and the Dawn of the Modern Era.* Edited by Heiko A. Oberman. Leiden: E. J. Brill, 1974, pp. 40–116.

———. "The Shape of Late Medieval Thought: The Birthpangs of the Modern Era." *Archiv für Reformationsgeschichte* 64 (1973), pp. 13–33.

———. "Some Notes on the Theology of Nominalism with Attention to its Relation to the Renaissance." *Harvard Theological Review* 53 (1960), pp. 47–76.

———. "Theologie des späten Mittelalters: Stand und Aufgaben der Forschung." *Theologische Literaturzeitung* 91 (1961), cols. 401–16.

———. *Werden und Wertung der Reformation: Vom Wegestreit zum Glaubenskampf.* Tübingen: J. C. B. Mohr (Paul Siebeck), 1977.

Omoregbe, J. I. "The Moral Philosophy of S. Thomas Aquinas: A Critical Look." *Nigerian Journal of Philosophy* 2 (1982), pp. 20–28.

Ott, Georg. "Recht und Gesetz bei Gabriel Biel: Ein Beitrag zur Spätmittelalterlichen Rechtslehre." *Zeitschrift der Savigny-Stiftung für Rechtsgeschichte* 69 (1952), pp. 251–96.

Ozment, Steve E., ed. *The Reformation in Medieval Perspective.* Chicago: Quadrangle, 1971.

Patfoort, A. *L'Unité d'être dans le Christ d'après s. Thomas: À la croisée de l'ontologie et de la christologie.* Paris: Desclée, 1964.

Pegis, A. C. *At the Origin of the Thomistic Notion of Man.* New York: Macmillan, 1963.

Pesch, Otto H. "Existential and Sapiential Theology: The Theological Confrontation between Luther and Thomas Aquinas." In Jared Wicks, ed., *Catholic Scholars Dialogue with Luther.* Chicago: Loyola University Press, 1970, pp. 61–81.

———. *The God Question in Thomas Aquinas and Martin Luther.* Translated by Gottfried G. Krodel. Philadelphia: Fortress Press, 1972.

———. *Theologie der Rechtfertigung bei Martin Luther und Thomas von Aquin: Versuch eines systematisch-theologischen Dialogs.* Mainz: Matthias-Grünewald, 1967.

Pfürtner, Stephanus. *Luther und Thomas im Gespräch: Unser Heil zwischen Gewissheit und Gefährdung.* Heidelberg: F. H. Kerle, 1961.

Phelan, Gerald B. *St. Thomas and Analogy.* Milwaukee: Marquette University Press, 1941.

Potvin, Thomas R. *The Theology of the Primacy of Christ according to St. Thomas and its Scriptural Foundations.* Fribourg: University Press, 1973.

Rahner, Karl. *Geist in Welt: Zur Metaphysik der endlichen Erkenntnis bei Thomas von Aquin.* 3rd ed. Munich: Kösel-Verlag, 1964.

Ramos, Guido Soaje. "Ensayo de una interpretación de la doctrina moral tomista en terminos de participación." *Ethos* 10–11 (1982–83), pp. 271–94.

Ramsey, Paul. *The Just War: Force and Political Responsibility.* New York: Charles Scribner's Sons, 1968.

Regan, Richard J. "Aquinas on Political Obedience and Disobedience." *Thought* 56 (1981), no. 220, pp. 77–88.

Regout, Robert. *La doctrine de la guerre juste de saint Augustin à nos jours d'après les théologiens et les juristes canoniques.* Paris: Pedone, 1935.

Ritter, Gerhard. "Romantische und revolutionäre Elemente in der deutschen Theologie am Vorabend der Reformation." *Deutsche Vierteljahrschrift für Literaturwissenschaft und Geistesgeschichte* 5 (1927), pp. 342–80.

Rivière, J. "Justification." *Dictionnaire de Théologie Catholique* 8-2, cols. 2042–2227.

Roensch, Friederick J. *Early Thomistic School.* Dubuque, Iowa: Priory, 1964.

Rommen, Heinrich A. *The State in Catholic Thought.* St. Louis: Herder, 1945.

Roover, Raymond de. "The Concept of the Just Price: Theory and Economic Policy." *Journal of Economic History* 18 (1958), pp. 418–34.

———. "The Scholastic Attitude toward Trade and Entrepreneurship." *Business, Banking, and Economic Thought in Late Medieval and Early Modern Europe: Selected Studies of Raymond de Roover.* Edited by J. Kirshner. Chicago: University of Chicago Press, 1974, pp. 336–45.

Roschini, Gabriele M. *La Mariologia di San Tomasso.* Rome: Angelo Belardetti Editore, 1950.

Ruch, C. "Biel, Gabriel." *Dictionnaire de Théologie Catholique* 2, cols. 814–25.

Saint-Blancat, Louis. "Recherches sur les sources de la théologie lutheriènne primitive (1509–1510)." *Verbum Caro* 8 (1954), pp. 81–91.

———. "La théologie de Luther et un nouveau plagiat de Pierre d'Ailly." *Positions Lutheriennes* 4 (1956), pp. 61–77.

Scheel, Otto. *Martin Luther: Vom Katholizismus zur Reformation,* vol. 2. Tübingen: J. C. B. Mohr, 1917.

Schilling, Otto. *Die Staats- und Soziallehre des heiligen Thomas von Aquin.* Munich: Max Hueber 1930.

Schumpeter, Joseph Alois. *History of Economic Analysis.* New York: Oxford University Press, 1954.

Schweizer, Othmar. *Person un hypostatische Union bei Thomas von Aquin.* Freiburg: Universitätsverlag Freiburg Schweiz, 1957.

Scola Angelo. *La fondazione teologica della legge naturale nello Scriptum super Sententiis di San Tommaso d'Aquino.* Freiburg/Schweiz: Universitätsverlag, 1982.

Sertillanges, A. D. *La philosophie morale de St. Thomas d'Aquin.* Paris: Aubier, 1942.

Stegmüller, Friedrich. "Literargeschichtliches zu Gabriel Biel." *Theologie in Geschichte und Gegenwart: Michael Schmaus zum Sechzigsten Geburtstag.* Edited by Johann Auer and Hermann Volk. Munich: Karl Zink, 1957, pp. 309–16.

Steinmetz, David C. *Luther and Staupitz: An Essay in the Intellectual Origins of the Protestant Reformation.* Durham: N.C.: Duke University Press, 1980.

———. *Luther in Context.* Bloomington, Ind.: Indiana University Press, 1986.

———. *Misericordia Dei: The Theology of Johannes von Staupitz in Its Late Medieval Setting.* Leiden: E. J. Brill, 1968.

Stufler, Johann. *Divi Thomae Aquinatis doctrina de Deo operante in omni operatione naturae creatae praesertim liberi arbitrii.* Innsbruck: Buchdruckerie Tyrolia, 1923.

Trinkhaus, Charles and Oberman, Heiko A., eds. *The Pursuit of Holiness in Late Medieval and Renaissance Religion.* Leiden: E. J. Brill, 1974.

Tschackert, P. "Biel, Gabriel." *Realencyklopädie für protestantische Theologie und Kirche,* vol. 3. 3rd ed. Edited by J. J. Herzog. Leipzig: J. C. Hindricks'sche Buchhandlung, 1897.

Vanderpol, Alfred. *La doctrine scholastique du droit de guerre.* Paris: Pedone, 1919.

Van Roo, William A. *Grace and Original Justice according to St. Thomas.* Rome: Gregorian University, 1955.

Varangot, O. A. "El analogado principal." *Ciencia y Fe* 14 (1958), pp. 237–53.

———. "Analogía de atribución intrínseca en Santo Tomás." *Ciencia y Fe* 13 (1957), pp. 293–319.

———. "Analogía de atribución intrínseca y analogía del ente según Santo Tomas." *Ciencia y Fe* 13 (1957), pp. 467–85.

Veysset, Philippe. *Situation de la politique dans la pensée de S. Thomas d'Aquin.* Paris: Le Cèdre, 1981.

Vignaux, Paul. "Luther: Lecteur de Gabriel Biel." *Église et Théologie* 22 (1959), pp. 33–52.

———. "Nominalisme." *Dictionnaire de Théologie Catholique* 11-1, cols. 717–84.

———. *La pensée au moyen age.* Paris: Librairie Armand Colin, 1948.

Vorster, Hans. *Das Freiheitsverständnis bei Thomas von Aquin und Martin Luther.* Göttingen: Vandenhoeck und Ruprecht, 1965.

Watson, Phillip. "Erasmus, Luther and Aquinas." *Concordia Theological Monthly* 40 (1969), pp. 747–58.

Weiler, Anton G. "Antiqui/Moderni (via moderna/via antiqua)." *Historisches Wörterbuch der Philosophie* 1, cols. 407–10. Edited by Joachim Ritter. Basel: Schwabe, 1971.

Wittman, Michael. *Die Ethik des hl. Thomas von Aquin in ihrem systematischen Aufbau dargestellt und in ihren geschichtlichen, besonders in dem antiken Quellen erforscht.* Munich: Max Hueber, 1933.

INDEX

ABOUT THE AUTHOR

John Farthing is Associate Professor of Religion and Classical Languages at Hendrix College, Conway, Arkansas.